THE COMPLETE EDDA

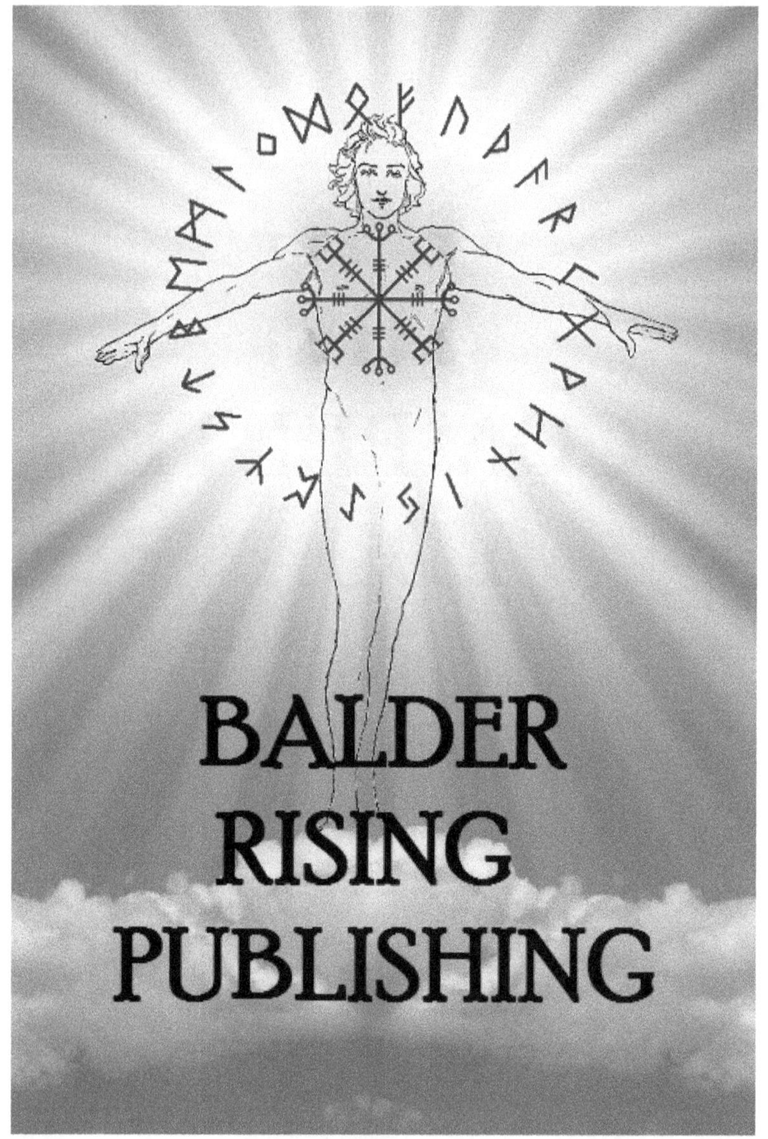
BALDER
RISING
PUBLISHING

THE COMPLETE EDDA

Compiled
by
Robert Blumetti

SNORRI'S EDDA, OR THE PROSE EDDA OR THE FOOLING OF GYLFE, AND THE YOUNGER EDDA OR SAEMUND'S POETIC EDDA AND POEMS BY JULIA CLINTON JONES, MATTHEW ARNOLD, HENRY WADSWORTH LONGFELLOW, AND ROBERT SOUTHEY.

Published by Balder Rising Publishing

ISBN: 978-1-79485-578-6

TABLES OF CONTENTS

PROSE EDDA

POETIC EDDA

MODERN DAY POEMS ABOUT THE GODS

INTRODUCTION

I realized that there is no signal volume containing both the Prose Edda and the Poetic Edda. If there is any books published with both Eddas I have no been able to find it, at least published in the English language. There I set out to publish a book with Snorri's *Fooling of Gylfi* from the Prose Edda and the Poetic Edda poems dealing with the Gods. I decided on Benjamin Thorpe's 1866 translation. He was a scholar of Anglo-Saxon studies in Great Britain (born 1782, died 1870). I also included the 1879 translation of the Prose Edda by the Rasmus Bjorn Anderson (born 1846, died 1936), an American of Scandianian descent, a diplomat, businessman and professor. I hope heathen readers of *The Complete Edda* can use this volume in their studies of the Norse Myths. Wherever possible I tried to retain the original spelling an grammer. You will find that the spelling of words were different from today. One just example is the word "judgment," which is spelled "judgement." Both spellings are correct according to modern-day dictionaries.

I also included in this volume poems by 19th century and early 20th century poets who composed some of the most wonderful poems about the Norse Gods that I think modern-day Heathen should be familiar with.

Robert Blumetti, Master Erulian of the Folk Faith of Balder Rising, 2020

THE PROSE EDDA TRANSLATED (1879)
BY
RASMUS BJORN ANDERSON

CHAPTER ONE: GEFJUN'S PLOWING.

1. King Gylfe ruled the lands that are now called Svithjod (Sweden). Of him it is said that he gave to a wayfaring woman, as a reward for the entertainment she had afforded him by her story-telling, a plow-land in his realm, as large as four oxen could plow it in a day and a night But this woman was of the asa-race; her name was Gefjun. She took from the north, from Jotunheim, four oxen, which were the sons of a giant and her, and set them before the plow. Then went the plow so hard and deep that it tore up the land, and the oxen drew it westward into the sea, until it stood still in a sound. There Gefjun set the land, gave it a name and called it Seeland. And where the land had been taken away became afterward a sea, which in Sweden is now called Logrinn (the Lake, the Malar Lake in Sweden). And in the Malar Lake the bays correspond 50to the capes in Seeland. Thus Brage, the old skald:

Gefjun glad
Drew from Gylfe
The excellent land,
Denmark's increase,
So that it reeked
From the running beasts.
Four heads and eight eyes
Bore the oxen
As they went before the wide
Robbed land of the grassy isle.

CHAPTER TWO: GYLFE'S JOURNEY TO ASGARD.

2. King Gylfe was a wise man and skilled in the black art. He wondered much that the asa-folk was so mighty in knowledge, that all things went after their will. He thought to himself whether this could come from their own nature, or whether the cause must be sought for among the gods whom they worshiped. He therefore undertook a journey to Asgard. He went secretly, having assumed the likeness of an old man, and striving thus to disguise himself. But the asas were wiser, for they see into the future, and, foreseeing his journey before he came, they received him with an eye-deceit. So when he came into the burg he saw there a hall so high that he could hardly look over it. Its roof was thatched with golden shields as with shingles. Thus says Thjodolf of Hvin, that Valhal was thatched with shields:

Thinking thatchers
Thatched the roof;
The beams of the burg
Beamed with gold.

In the door of the hall Gylfe saw a man who played with swords so dexterously that seven were in the air at one time. That man asked him what his name was. Gylfe answered that his name was Ganglere; that he had come a long way, and that he sought lodgings for the night. He also asked who owned the burg. The other answered that it belonged to their king: I will go with you to see him and then you may ask him for his name yourself. Then the man turned and led the way into the hall. Ganglere followed, and suddenly the doors closed behind him. There he saw many rooms and a large number of people, of whom some were playing, others were drinking, and some were fighting with weapons. He looked around him, and much of what he saw seemed to him incredible. Then quoth he:

Gates all,
Before in you go,
You must examine well;
For you cannot know
Where enemies sit
In the house before you.

He saw three high-seats, one above the other, and in each sat a man. He asked what the names of these chiefs were. He, who had conducted him in, answered that the one who sat in the lowest high-seat was king, and hight Har; the one next above him, Jafnhar; but the one who sat on the highest throne, Thride. Har asked the comer what more his errand was, and added that food and drink was there at his service, as for all in Har's hall. Ganglere answered that he first would like to ask whether there was any wise man. Answered Har: You will not come out from here hale unless you are wiser.

And stand now forth
While you ask;
He who answers shall sit.

CHAPTER THREE: OF THE HIGHEST GOD

3. Ganglere then made the following question: Who is the highest and oldest of all the gods? Made answer Har: Alfather he is called in our tongue, but in Asgard of old he had twelve names. The first is Alfather, the second is Herran or Herjan, the third Nikar or Hnikar, the fourth Nikuz or Hnikud, the fifth Fjolner, the sixth Oske, the seventh Ome, the eighth Biflide or Biflinde, the ninth Svidar, the tenth Svidrer, the eleventh Vidrer, the twelfth Jalg or Jalk. Ganglere asks again: Where is this god? What can he do? What mighty works has he accomplished? Answered Har: He lives from everlasting to everlasting, rules over all his realm, and governs all things, great and small. Then remarked Jafnhar: He made heaven and earth, the air and all things in them. Thride added: What is most important, he made man and gave him a spirit, which shall live, and never perish, though the body may turn to dust or burn to ashes. All who live a life of virtue shall dwell with him in Gimle or Vingolf. The wicked, on the other hand, go to Hel, and from her to Niflhel, that is, down into the ninth world. Then asked Ganglere: What was he doing before heaven and earth were made? Har gave answer: Then was he with the frost-giants.

CHAPTER FOUR:
THE CREATION OF THE WORLD

4. Said Ganglere: How came the world into existence, or how did it rise? What was before? Made answer to him Har: Thus is it said in the Vala's Prophecy:

It was Time's morning,
When there nothing was;
Nor sand, nor sea,
Nor cooling billows.
Earth there was not,
Nor heaven above.
The Ginungagap was,
But grass nowhere.

Jafnhar remarked: Many ages before the earth was made, Niflheim had existed, in the midst of which is the well called Hvergelmer, whence flow the following streams: Svol, Gunnthro, Form, Fimbul, Thul, Slid and Hrid, Sylg and Ylg, Vid, Leipt and Gjoll, the last of which is nearest the gate of Hel. Then added Thride: Still there was before a world to the south which hight Muspelheim. It is light and hot, and so bright and dazzling that no stranger, who is not a 57native there, can stand it. Surt is the name of him who stands on its border guarding it. He has a flaming sword in his hand, and at the end of the world he will come and harry, conquer all the gods, and burn up the whole world with fire. Thus it is said in the Vala's Prophecy:

Surt from the south fares
With blazing flames;
From the sword shines
The sun of the war-god.

Rocks dash together
And witches collapse,
Men go the way to Hel
And the heavens are cleft.

5. Said Ganglere: What took place before the races came into existence, and men increased and multiplied? Replied Har, explaining, that as soon as the streams, that are called the Elivogs, had come so far from their source that the venomous yeast which flowed with them hardened, as does dross that runs from the fire, then it turned into ice. And when this ice stopped and flowed no more, then gathered over it the drizzling rain that arose from the venom and froze into rime, and one layer of ice was laid upon the other clear into Ginungagap. Then said Jafnhar: All that part of Ginungagap that turns toward the north was filled with thick and heavy ice and rime, and everywhere within were 58drizzling rains and gusts. But the south part of Ginungagap was lighted up by the glowing sparks that flew out of Muspelheim. Added Thride: As cold and all things grim proceeded from Niflheim, so that which bordered on Muspelheim was hot and bright, and Ginungagap was as warm and mild as windless air. And when the heated blasts from Muspelheim met the rime, so that it melted into drops, then, by the might of him who sent the heat, the drops quickened into life and took the likeness of a man, who got the name Ymer. But the Frost giants call him Aurgelmer. Thus it is said in the short Prophecy of the Vala (the Lay of Hyndla):

All the valas are
From Vidolf descended;
All wizards are
Of Vilmeide's race;

All enchanters
Are sons of Svarthofde;
All giants have
Come from Ymer.

And on this point, when Vafthrudner, the giant, was asked by Gangrad:

Whence came Aurgelmer
Originally to the sons
Of the giants?—thou wise giant!

he said

From the Elivogs
Sprang drops of venom,
And grew till a giant was made.
Thence our race
Are all descended,
Therefore are we all so fierce.

Then asked Ganglere: How were the races developed from him? Or what was done so that more men were made? Or do you believe him to be god of whom you now spake? Made answer Har: By no means do we believe him to be god; evil was he and all his offspring, them we call frost-giants. It is said that when he slept he fell into a sweat, and then there grew under his left arm a man and a woman, and one of his feet begat with the other a son. From these come the races that are called frost-giants. The old frost-giant we call Ymer.

6. Then said Ganglere: Where did Ymer dwell, and on what did he live? Answered Har: The next thing was that when

the rime melted into drops, there was made thereof a cow, which hight Audhumbla. Four milk-streams ran from her teats, and she fed Ymer. Thereupon asked Ganglere: On what did the cow subsist? Answered Har: She licked the salt-stones that were covered with rime, and the first day that she licked the stones there came out of them in the evening a man's hair, the second day a man's head, and the third day the whole man was there. This man's name was Bure; he was fair of face, great and mighty, and he begat a son whose name was Bor. This Bor married a woman whose name was Bestla, the daughter of the giant Bolthorn; they had three sons,—the one hight Odin, the other Vile, and the third Ve. And it is my belief that this Odin and his brothers are the rulers of heaven and earth. We think that he must be so called. That is the name of the man whom we know to be the greatest and most famous, and well may men call him by that name.

7. Ganglere asked: How could these keep peace with Ymer, or who was the stronger? Then answered Har: The sons of Bor slew the giant Ymer, but when he fell, there flowed so much blood from his wounds that they drowned therein the whole race of frost giants; excepting one, who escaped with his household. Him the giants call Bergelmer. He and his wife went on board his ark and saved themselves in it. From them are come new races of frost-giants, as is here said:

Countless winters
Ere the earth was made,
Was born Bergelmer.
This first I call to mind
How that crafty giant
Safe in his ark lay.

8. Then said Ganglere: What was done then by the sons of Bor, since you believe that they were gods? Answered Har: About that there is not a little to be said. They took the body of Ymer, carried it into the midst of Ginungagap and made of him the earth. Of his blood they made the seas and lakes; of his flesh the earth was made, but of his bones the rocks; of his teeth and jaws, and of the bones that were broken, they made stones and pebbles. Jafnhar remarked: Of the blood that flowed from the wounds, and was free, they made the ocean; they fastened the earth together and around it they laid this ocean in a ring without, and it must seem to most men impossible to cross it. Thride added: They took his skull and made thereof the sky, and raised it over the earth with four sides. Under each corner they set a dwarf, and the four dwarfs were called Austre (east), Vestre (West), Nordre (North), Sudre (South). Then they took glowing sparks, that were loose and had been cast out from Muspelheim, and placed them in the midst of the boundless heaven, both above and below, to light up heaven and earth. They gave resting-places to all fires, and set some in heaven; some were made to go free under heaven, but they gave them a place and shaped their course. In old songs it is said that from that time days and years were reckoned. Thus in the Prophecy of the Vala:

The sun knew not
Where her hall she had;
The moon knew not
What might he had;
The stars knew not
Their resting-places.

Thus it was before these things were made. Then said Ganglere: Wonderful tidings are these I now hear; a wondrous great building is this, and deftly constructed. How was the earth fashioned? Made answer Har: The earth is round, and without it round about lies the deep ocean, and along the outer strand of that sea they gave lands for the giant races to dwell in; and against the attack of restless giants they built a burg within the sea and around the earth. For this purpose they used the giant Ymer's eyebrows, and they called the burg Midgard. They also took his brains and cast them into the air, and made therefrom the clouds, as is here said:

Of Ymer's flesh
The earth was made,
And of his sweat the seas;
Rocks of his bones,
Trees of his hair,
And the sky of his skull;
But of his eyebrows
The blithe powers
Made Midgard for the sons of men.
Of his brains
All the melancholy
Clouds were made.

CHAPTER FIVE
THE CREATION—(CONTINUED.)

9. Then said Ganglere: Much had been done, it seemed to me, when heaven and earth were made, when sun and moon were set in their places, and when days were marked out; but whence came the people who inhabit the world? Har answered as follows: As Bor's sons went along the sea-strand, they found two trees. These trees they took up and made men of them. The first gave them spirit and life; the second endowed them with reason and power of motion; and the third gave them form, speech, hearing and eyesight. They gave them clothes and names; the man they called Ask, and the woman Embla. From them all mankind is descended, and a dwelling-place was given them under Midgard. In the next place, the sons of Bor made for themselves in the middle of the world a burg, which is called Asgard, and which we call Troy. There dwelt the gods and their race, and thence were wrought many tidings and adventures, both on earth and in the sky. In Asgard is a place called Hlidskjalf, and when Odin seated himself there in the high-seat, he saw over the whole world, and what every man was doing, and he knew all things that he saw. His wife hight Frigg, and she was the daughter of Fjorgvin, and from their offspring are descended the race that we call asas, who inhabited Asgard the old and the realms that lie about it, and all that race are known to be gods. And for this reason Odin is called Alfather, that he is the father of all gods and men, and of all things that were made by him and by his might. Jord (earth) was his daughter and his wife; with her he begat his first son, and that is Asa-Thor. To him was given force and strength, whereby he conquers all things quick.

10. Norfe, or Narfe, hight a giant, who dwelt in Jotunheim. He had a daughter by name Night. She was swarthy and dark like the race she belonged to. She was first married to a man who hight Naglfare. Their son was Aud. Afterward she was married to Annar. Jord hight their daughter. Her last husband was Delling (Daybreak), who was of asa-race. Their son was Day, who was light and fair after his father. Then took Alfather Night and her son Day, gave them two horses and two cars, and set them up in heaven to drive around the earth, each in twelve hours by turns. Night rides first on the horse which is called Hrimfaxe, and every morning he bedews the earth with the foam from his bit. The horse on which Day rides is called Skinfaxe, and with his mane he lights up all the sky and the earth.

11. Then said Ganglere: How does he steer the course of the sun and the moon? Answered Har: Mundilfare hight the man who had two children. They were so fair and beautiful that he called his son Moon, and his daughter, whom he gave in marriage to a man by name Glener, he called Sun. But the gods became wroth at this arrogance, took both the brother and the sister, set them up in heaven, and made Sun drive the horses that draw the car of the sun, which the gods had made to light up the world from sparks that flew out of Muspelheim. These horses hight Arvak and Alsvid. Under their withers the gods placed two wind-bags to cool them, but in some songs it is called ironcold (ísarnkol). Moon guides the course of the moon, and rules its waxing and waning. He took from the earth two children, who hight Bil and Hjuke, as they were going from the well called Byrger, and were carrying on their shoulders the bucket called Sager and the pole Simul. Their father's name is Vidfin. These children always accompany Moon, as can be seen from the earth.

12. Then said Ganglere: Swift fares Sun, almost as if she were afraid, and she could make no more haste in her course if she feared her destroyer. Then answered Har: Nor is it wonderful that she speeds with all her might. Near is he who pursues her, and there is no escape for her but to run before him. Then asked Ganglere: Who causes her this toil? Answered Har: It is two wolves. The one hight Skol, he runs after her; she fears him and he will one day overtake her. The other hight Hate, Hrodvitner's son; he bounds before her and wants to catch the moon, and so he will at last. Then asked Ganglere: Whose offspring are these wolves? Said Har; A hag dwells east of Midgard, in the forest called Jarnved (Ironwood), where reside the witches called Jarnvidjes. The old hag gives birth to many giant sons, and all in wolf's likeness. Thence come these two wolves. It is said that of this wolf-race one is the mightiest, and is called Moongarm. He is filled with the life-blood of all dead men. He will devour the moon, and stain the heavens and all the sky with blood. Thereby the sun will be darkened, the winds will grow wild, and roar hither and thither, as it is said in the Prophecy of the Vala:

In the east dwells the old hag,
In the Jarnved forest;
And brings forth there
Fenrer's offspring.
There comes of them all
One the worst,
The moon's devourer
In a troll's disguise.

He is filled with the life-blood
Of men doomed to die;

The seats of the gods
He stains with red gore;
Sunshine grows black
The summer thereafter,
All weather gets fickle.
Know you yet or not?

13. Then asked Ganglere: What is the path from earth to heaven? Har answered, laughing: Foolishly do you now ask. Have you not been told that the gods made a bridge from earth to heaven, which is called Bifrost? You must have seen it. It may be that you call it the rainbow. It has three colors, is very strong, and is made with more craft and skill than other structures. Still, however strong it is, it will break when the sons of Muspel come to ride over it, and then they will have to swim their horses over great rivers in order to get on. Then said Ganglere: The gods did not, it seems to me, build that bridge honestly, if it shall be able to break to pieces, since they could have done so, had they desired. Then made answer Har: The gods are worthy of no blame for this structure. Bifrost is indeed a good bridge, but there is no thing in the world that is able to stand when the sons of Muspel come to the fight.

CHAPTER SIX
THE FIRST WORKS OF THE ASAS. THE GOLDEN AGE.

14. Then said Ganglere: What did Alfather do when Asgard had been built? Said Har: In the beginning he appointed rulers in a place in the middle of the burg which is called Idavold, who were to judge with him the disputes of men and decide the affairs of the burg. Their first work was to erect a court, where there were seats for all the twelve, and, besides, a high-seat for Alfather. That is the best and largest house ever built on earth, and is within and without like solid gold. This place is called Gladsheim. Then they built another hall as a home for the goddesses, which also is a very beautiful mansion, and is called Vingolf. Thereupon they built a forge; made hammer, tongs, anvil, and with these all other tools. Afterward they worked in iron, stone and wood, and especially in that metal which is called gold. All their household wares were of gold. That age was called the golden age, until it was lost by the coming of those women from Jotunheim. Then the gods set themselves in their high-seats and held counsel. They remembered how the dwarfs had quickened in the mould of the earth like maggots in flesh. The dwarfs had first been created and had quickened in Ymer's flesh, and were then maggots; but now, by the decision of the gods, they got the understanding and likeness of men, but still had to dwell in the earth and in rocks. Modsogner was one dwarf and Durin another. So it is said in the Vala's Prophecy:

Then went all the gods,
The all-holy gods,
On their judgment seats,
And thereon took counsel

Who should the race
Of dwarfs create
From the bloody sea
And from Blain's bones.
In the likeness of men
Made they many
Dwarfs in the earth,
As Durin said.

And these, says the Vala, are the names of the dwarfs:

Nye, Nide,
Nordre, Sudre,
Austre, Vestre,
Althjof, Dvalin,
Na, Nain,
Niping, Dain,
Bifur, Bafur,
Bombor, Nore,
Ore, Onar,
Oin, Mjodvitner,
Vig, Gandalf,
Vindalf, Thorin,
File, Kile,
Fundin, Vale,
Thro, Throin,
Thek, Lit, Vit,
Ny, Nyrad,
Rek, Radsvid.

But the following are also dwarfs and dwell in the rocks, while the above-named dwell in the mould:

Draupner, Dolgthvare,

Hor, Hugstare,
Hledjolf, Gloin,
Dore, Ore,
Duf, Andvare,
Hepte, File,
Har, Siar.

But the following come from Svarin's How to Aurvang on Joruvold, and from them is sprung Lovar. Their names are:

Skirfer, Virfir,
Skafid, Ae,
Alf, Inge,
Eikinslgalde,
Fal, Froste,
Fid, Ginnar.

CHAPTER SEVEN
ON THE WONDERFUL THINGS IN HEAVEN

15. Then said Ganglere: Where is the chief or most holy place of the gods? Har answered: That is by the ash Ygdrasil. There the gods meet in council every day. Said Ganglere: What is said about this place? Answered Jafnhar: This ash is the best and greatest of all trees; its branches spread over all the world, and reach up above heaven. Three roots sustain the tree and stand wide apart; one root is with the asas and another with the frost-giants, where Ginungagap formerly was; the third reaches into Niflheim; under it is Hvergelmer, where Nidhug gnaws the root from below. But under the second root, which extends to the frost-giants, is the well of Mimer, wherein knowledge and wisdom are concealed. The owner of the well hight Mimer. He is full of wisdom, for he drinks from the well with the Gjallar-horn. Alfather once came there and asked for a drink from the well, but he did not get it before he left one of his eyes as a pledge. So it is said in the Vala's Prophecy:

Well know I, Odin,
Where you hid your eye:
In the crystal-clear
Well of Mimer.
Mead drinks Mimer
Every morning
From Valfather's pledge.
Know you yet or not?

The third root of the ash is in heaven, and beneath it is the most sacred fountain of Urd. Here the gods have their doomstead. The asas ride hither every day over Bifrost, which is also called Asa-bridge. The following are the names of the horses of the gods: Sleipner is the best one; he belongs to Odin, and he has eight feet. The second is Glad, the third Gyller, the fourth Gler, the fifth Skeidbrimer, the sixth Silfertop, the seventh Siner, the eighth Gisl, the ninth Falhofner, the tenth Gulltop, the eleventh Letfet. Balder's horse was burned with him. Thor goes on foot to the doomstead, and wades the following rivers:

Kormt and Ormt
And the two Kerlaugs;
These shall Thor wade
Every day
When he goes to judge
Near the Ygdrasil ash;
For the Asa-bridge
Burns all ablaze,—
The holy waters roar.

Then asked Ganglere: Does fire burn over Bifrost? Har answered: The red which you see in the rainbow is burning fire. The frost-giants and the mountain-giants would go up to heaven if Bifrost were passable for all who desired to go there. Many fair places there are in heaven, and they are all protected by a divine defense. There stands a beautiful hall near the fountain beneath the ash. Out of it come three maids, whose names are Urd, Verdande and Skuld. These maids shape the lives of men, and we call them norns. There are yet more norns, namely those who come to every man when he is born, to shape his life, and these are known to be of the race of gods; others, on the other hand, are of the race of elves, and yet others are of the race of dwarfs. As is here said:

Far asunder, I think,

The norns are born,
They are not of the same race.
Some are of the asas,
Some are of the elves,
Some are daughters of Dvalin.

Then said Ganglere: If the norns rule the fortunes of men, then they deal them out exceedingly unevenly. Some live a good life and are rich; some get neither wealth nor praise. Some have a long, others a short life. Har answered: Good norns and of good descent shape good lives, and when some men are weighed down with misfortune, the evil norns are the cause of it.

16. Then said Ganglere: What other remarkable things are there to be said about the ash? Har answered: Much is to be said about it. On one of the boughs of the ash sits an eagle, who knows many things. Between his eyes sits a hawk that is called Vedfolner. A squirrel, by name Ratatosk, springs up and down the tree, and carries words of envy between the eagle and Nidhug. Four stags leap about in the branches of the ash and bite the leaves. Their names are: Dain, Dvalin, Duney and Durathro. In Hvergelmer with Nidhug are more serpents than tongue can tell. As is here said:

The ash Ygdrasil
Bears distress
Greater than men know.
Stags bite it above,
At the side it rots,
Nidhug gnaws it below.

And so again it is said:

More serpents lie
'Neath the Ygdrasil ash
Than is thought of
By every foolish ape.
Goin and Moin
(They are sons of Grafvitner),
Grabak and Grafvollud,
Ofner and Svafner
Must for aye, methinks,
Gnaw the roots of that tree.

Again, it is said that the norns, that dwell in the fountain of Urd, every day take water from the fountain and take the clay that lies around the fountain and sprinkle therewith the ash, in order that its branches may not wither or decay. This water is so holy that all things that are put into the fountain become as white as the film of an egg-shell As is here said:

An ash I know
Hight Ygdrasil;
A high, holy tree
With white clay sprinkled.
Thence come the dews
That fall in the dales.
Green forever it stands
Over Urd's fountain.

The dew which falls on the earth from this tree men call honey-fall, and it is the food of bees. Two birds are fed in Urd's fountain; they are called swans, and they are the parents of the race of swans.

17. Then said Ganglere: Great tidings you are able to tell of the heavens. Are there other remarkable places than the one

by Urd's fountain? Answered Har: There are many magnificent dwellings. One is there called Alfheim. There dwell the folk that are called light-elves; but the dark-elves dwell down in the earth, and they are unlike the light-elves in appearance, but much more so in deeds. The light-elves are fairer than the sun to look upon, but the dark-elves are blacker than pitch. Another place is called Breidablik, and no place is fairer. There is also a mansion called Glitner, of which the walls and pillars and posts are of red gold, and the roof is of silver. Furthermore, there is a dwelling, by name Himinbjorg, which stands at the end of heaven, where the Bifrost-bridge is united with heaven. And there is a great dwelling called Valaskjalf, which belongs to Odin. The gods made it and thatched it with, sheer silver. In this hall is the high-seat, which is called Hlidskjalf, and when Alfather sits in this seat, he sees over all the world. In the southern end of the world is the palace, which is the fairest of all, and brighter than the sun; its name is Gimle. It shall stand when both heaven and earth shall have passed away. In this hall the good and the righteous shall dwell through all ages. Thus says the Prophecy of the Vala:

A hall I know, standing
Than the sun fairer,
Than gold better,
Gimle by name.
There shall good
People dwell,
And forever
Delights enjoy.

Then said Ganglere: Who guards this palace when Surt's fire burns up heaven and earth? Har answered: It is said that to the south and above this heaven is another heaven, which is called Andlang. But there is a third, which is above these, and is called Vidblain, and in this heaven we believe this mansion (Gimle) to be situated; but we deem that the light-elves alone dwell in it now.

CHAPTER EIGHT
THE ASAS

18. Then said Ganglere: Whence comes the wind? It is so strong that it moves great seas, and fans fires to flame, and yet, strong as it is, it cannot be seen. Therefore it is wonderfully made. Then answered Har: That I can tell you well. At the northern end of heaven sits a giant, who hight Hrasvelg. He is clad in eagles' plumes, and when he spreads his wings for flight, the winds arise from under them. Thus is it here said:

Hrasvelg hight he
Who sits at the end of heaven,
A giant in eagle's disguise.
From his wings, they say,
The wind does come
Over all mankind.

19. Then said Ganglere: How comes it that summer is so hot, but the winter so cold? Har answered: A wise man would not ask such a question, for all are able to tell this; but if you alone have become so stupid that you have not heard of it, then I would rather forgive you for asking unwisely once than that you should go any longer in ignorance of what you ought to know. Svasud is the name of him who is father of summer, and he lives such a life of enjoyment, that everything that is mild is from him called sweet (svasligt). But the father of winter has two names, Vindlone and Vindsval. He is the son of Vasad, and all that race are grim and of icy breath, and winter is like them.

20. Then asked Ganglere: Which are the asas, in whom men are bound to believe? Har answered him: Twelve are

the divine asas. Jafnhar said: No less holy are the asynjes (goddesses), nor is their power less. Then added Thride: Odin is the highest and oldest of the asas. He rules all things, but the other gods, each according to his might, serve him as children a father. Frigg is his wife, and she knows the fate of men, although she tells not thereof, as it is related that Odin himself said to Asa-Loke:

Mad are you, Loke!
And out of your senses;
Why do you not stop?
Fortunes all,
Methinks, Frigg knows,
Though she tells them not herself.

Odin is called Alfather, for he is the father of all the gods; he is also called Valfather, for all who fall in fight are his chosen sons. For them he prepares Valhal and Vingolf, where they are called einherjes (heroes). He is also called Hangagod, Haptagod, Farmagod; and he gave himself still more names when he came to King Geirrod:

Grim is my name,
And Ganglare,
Herjan, Hjalmbore,
Thek, Thride,
Thud, Ud,
Helblinde, Har,
Sad, Svipal,
Sangetal,
Herteit, Hnikar,
Bileyg, Baleyg,
Bolverk, Fjolner,
Grimner, Glapsvid, Fjolsvid,

Sidhot, Sidskeg,
Sigfather, Hnikud,
Alfather, Atrid, Farmatyr,
Oske, Ome,
Jafnhar, Biflinde,
Gondler, Harbard,
Svidur, Svidrir,
Jalk, Kjalar, Vidur,
Thro, Yg, Thund,
Vak, Skilfing,
Vafud, Hroptatyr,
Gaut, Veratyr.

Then said Ganglere: A very great number of names you have given him; and this I know, forsooth, that he must be a very wise man who is able to understand and decide what chances are the causes of all these names. Har answered: Much knowledge is needed to explain it all rightly, but still it is shortest to tell you that most of these names have been given him for the reason that, as there are many tongues in the world, so all peoples thought they ought to turn his name into their tongue, in order that they might be able to worship him and pray to him each in its own language. Other causes of these names must be sought in his journeys, which are told of in old sagas; and you can lay no claim to being called a wise man if you are not able to tell of these wonderful adventures.

21. Then said Ganglere: What are the names of the other asas? What is their occupation, and what works have they wrought? Har answered: Thor is the foremost of them. He is called Asa-Thor, or Oku-Thor. He is the strongest of all gods and men, and rules over the realm which is called Thrudvang. His hall is called Bilskirner. Therein are five

hundred and forty floors, and it is the largest house that men have made. Thus it is said in Grimner's Lay:

Five hundred floors
And forty more,
Methinks, has bowed Bilskirner.
Of houses all
That I know roofed
I know my son's is the largest.

Thor has two goats, by name Tangnjost and Tangrisner, and a chariot, wherein he drives. The goats draw the chariot; wherefore he is called Oku-Thor. He possesses three valuable treasures. One of them is the hammer Mjolner, which the frost-giants and mountain-giants well know when it is raised; and this is not to be wondered at, for with it he has split many a skull of their fathers or friends. The second treasure he possesses is Megingjarder (belt of strength); when he girds himself with it his strength is doubled. His third treasure that is of so great value is his iron gloves; these he cannot do without when he lays hold of the hammer's haft. No one is so wise that he can tell all his great works; but I can tell you so many tidings of him that it will grow late before all is told that I know.

22. Thereupon said Ganglere: I wish to ask tidings of more of the asas. Har gave him answer: Odin's second son is Balder, and of him good things are to be told. He is the best, and all praise him. He is so fair of face and so bright that rays of light issue from him; and there is a plant so white that it is likened unto Balder's brow, and it is the whitest of all plants. From this you can judge of the beauty both of his hair and of his body. He is the wisest, mildest and 84most eloquent of all the asas; and such is his nature

that none can alter the judgment he has pronounced. He inhabits the place in heaven called Breidablik, and there nothing unclean can enter. As is here said:

Breidablik it is called,
Where Balder has
Built for himself a hall
In the land
Where I know is found
The least of evil.

23. The third asa is he who is called Njord. He dwells in Noatun, which is in heaven. He rules the course of the wind and checks the fury of the sea and of fire. He is invoked by seafarers and by fishermen. He is so rich and wealthy that he can give broad lands and abundance to those who call on him for them. He was fostered in Vanaheim, but the vans gave him as a hostage to the gods, and received in his stead as an asa-hostage the god whose name is Honer. He established peace between the gods and vans. Njord took to wife Skade, a daughter of the giant Thjasse. She wished to live where her father had dwelt, that is, on the mountains in Thrymheim; Njord, on the other hand, preferred to be near the sea. They therefore agreed to pass nine nights in Thrymheim and three in Noatun. But when Njord came back from the mountains to Noatun he sang this:

Weary am I of the mountains,
Not long was I there,
Only nine nights.
The howl of the wolves
Methought sounded ill
To the song of the swans.

Skade then sang this:

Sleep I could not
On my sea-strand couch,
For the scream of the sea-fowl.
There wakes me,
As he comes from the sea,
Every morning the mew.

Then went Skade up on the mountain, and dwelt in Thrymheim. She often goes on skees (snow-shoes), with her bow, and shoots wild beasts. She is called skee-goddess or skee-dis. Thus it is said:

Thrymheim it is called
Where Thjasse dwelt,
That mightiest giant.
But now dwells Skade,
Pure bride of the gods,
In her father's old homestead.

24. Njord, in Noatun, afterward begat two children: a son, by name Frey, and a daughter, by name Freyja. They were fair of face, and mighty. Frey is the most famous of the asas. He rules over rain and sunshine, and over the fruits of the earth. It is good to call on him for harvests and peace. He also sways the wealth of men. Freyja is the most famous of the goddesses. She has in heaven a dwelling which is called Folkvang, and when she rides to the battle, one half of the slain belong to her, and the other half to Odin. As is here said:

Folkvang it is called,
And there rules Freyja.

For the seats in the hall
Half of the slain
She chooses each day;
The other half is Odin's.

Her hall is Sesrynmer, and it is large and beautiful. When she goes abroad, she drives in a car drawn by two cats. She lends a favorable ear to men who call upon her, and it is from her name the title has come that women of birth and wealth are called frur.40 She is fond of love ditties, and it is good to call on her in love affairs.

25. Then said Ganglere: Of great importance these asas seem to me to be, and it is not wonderful that you have great power, since you have such excellent knowledge of the gods, and know to which of them to address your prayers on each occasion. But what other gods are there? Har answered: There is yet an asa, whose name is Tyr. He is very daring and stout-hearted. He sways victory in war, wherefore warriors should call on him. There is a saw, that he who surpasses others in bravery, and never yields, is Tyr-strong. He is also so wise, that it is said of anyone who is specially intelligent, that he is Tyr-learned. A proof of his daring is, that when the asas induced the wolf Fenrer to let himself be bound with the chain Gleipner, he would not believe that they would loose him again until Tyr put his hand in his mouth as a pledge. But when the asas would not loose the Fenris-wolf, he bit Tyr's hand off at the place of the wolf's joint (the wrist; Icel. úlfliðr41). From that time Tyr is one-handed, and he is now called a peacemaker among men.

26. Brage is the name of another of the asas. He is famous for his wisdom, eloquence and flowing speech. He is a

master-skald, and from him song-craft is called brag (poetry), and such men or women as distinguish themselves by their eloquence are called brag-men and brag-women. His wife is Idun. She keeps in a box those 88apples of which the gods eat when they grow old, and then they become young again, and so it will be until Ragnarok (the twilight of the gods). Then said Ganglere: Of great importance to the gods it must be, it seems to me, that Idun preserves these apples with care and honesty. Har answered, and laughed: They ran a great risk on one occasion, whereof I might tell you more, but you shall first hear the names of more asas.

27. Heimdal is the name of one. He is also called the white-asa. He is great and holy; born of nine maidens, all of whom were sisters. He hight also Hallinskide and Gullintanne, for his teeth were of gold. His horse hight Gulltop (Gold-top). He dwells in a place called Himinbjorg, near Bifrost. He is the ward of the gods, and sits at the end of heaven, guarding the bridge against the mountain-giants. He needs less sleep than a bird; sees an hundred miles around him, and as well by night as by day. He hears the grass grow and the wool on the backs of the sheep, and of course all things that sound louder than these. He has a trumpet called the Gjallarhorn, and when he blows it it can be heard in all the worlds. The head is called Heimdal's sword. Thus it is here said:

Himinbjorg it is called,
Where Heimdal rules
Over his holy halls;
There drinks the ward of the gods
In his delightful dwelling
Glad the good mead.

And again, in Heimdal's Song, he says himself:

Son I am of maidens nine,
Born I am of sisters nine.

28. Hoder hight one of the asas, who is blind, but exceedingly strong; and the gods would wish that this asa never needed to be named, for the work of his hand will long be kept in memory both by gods and men.

29. Vidar is the name of the silent asa. He has a very thick shoe, and he is the strongest next after Thor. From him the gods have much help in all hard tasks.

30. Ale, or Vale, is the son of Odin and Rind. He is daring in combat, and a good shot.

31. Uller is the name of one, who is a son of Sif, and a step-son of Thor. He is so good an archer, and so fast on his skees, that no one can contend with him. He is fair of face, and possesses every quality of a warrior. Men should invoke him in single combat.

32. Forsete is a son of Balder and Nanna, Nep's daughter. He has in heaven the hall which hight Glitner. All who come to him with disputes go away perfectly reconciled. No better tribunal is to be found among gods and men. Thus it is here said:

Glitner hight the hall,
On gold pillars standing,
And roofed with silver.
There dwells Forsete

Throughout all time,
And settles all disputes.

CHAPTER NINE
LOKE AND HIS OFFSPRING

33. There is yet one who is numbered among the asas, but whom some call the backbiter of the asas. He is the originator of deceit, and the disgrace of all gods and men. His name is Loke, or Lopt. His father is the giant Farbaute, but his mother's name is Laufey, or Nal. His brothers are Byleist and Helblinde. Loke is fair and beautiful of face, but evil in disposition, and very fickle-minded. He surpasses other men in the craft called cunning, and cheats in all things. He has often brought the asas into great trouble, and often helped them out again, with his cunning contrivances. His wife hight Sygin, and their son, Nare, or Narfe.

34. Loke had yet more children. A giantess in Jotunheim, hight Angerboda. With her he begat three children. The first was the Fenris-wolf; the second, Jormungand, that is, the Midgard-serpent, and the third, Hel. When the gods knew that these three children were being fostered in Jotunheim, and were aware of the prophecies that much woe and misfortune would thence come to them, and considering that much evil might be looked for from them on their mother's side, and still more on their father's, Alfather sent some of the gods to take the children and bring them to him. When they came to him he threw the serpent into the deep sea which surrounds all lands. There waxed the serpent so that he lies in the midst of the ocean, surrounds all the earth, and bites his own tail. Hel he cast into Niflheim, and gave her power over nine worlds, that she should appoint abodes to them that are sent to her, namely, those who die from sickness or old age. She has there a great mansion, and the walls around it are of strange

height, and the gates are huge. Eljudner is the name of her hall. Her table hight famine; her knife, starvation. Her man-servant's name is Ganglate; her maid-servant's, Ganglot. Her threshold is called stumbling-block; her bed, care; the precious hangings of her bed, gleaming bale. One-half of her is blue, and the other half is of the hue of flesh; hence she is easily known. Her looks are very stern and grim.

35. The wolf was fostered by the asas at home, and Tyr was the only one who had the courage to go to him and give him food. When the gods saw how much he grew every day, and all prophecies declared that he was predestined to become fatal to them, they resolved to make a very strong fetter, which they called Lading. They brought it to the wolf, and bade him try his strength on the fetter. The wolf, who did not think it would be too strong for him, let them do therewith as they pleased. But as soon as he spurned against it the fetter burst asunder, and he was free from Lading. Then the asas made another fetter, by one-half stronger, and this they called Drome. They wanted the wolf to try this also, saying to him that he would become very famous for his strength, if so strong a chain was not able to hold him. The wolf thought that this fetter was indeed very strong, but also that his strength had increased since he broke Lading. He also took into consideration that it was necessary to expose one's self to some danger if he desired to become famous; so he let them put the fetter on him. When the asas said they were ready, the wolf shook himself, spurned against and dashed the fetter on the ground, so that the broken pieces flew a long distance. Thus he broke loose out of Drome. Since then it has been held as a proverb, "to get loose out of Lading" or "to dash out of Drome," whenever anything is extraordinarily hard. The asas now began to fear that they would not get the wolf

bound. So Alfather sent the youth, who is called Skirner, and is Frey's messenger, to some dwarfs in Svartalfaheim, and had them make the fetter which is called Gleipner. It was made of six things: of the footfall of cats, of the beard of woman, of the roots of the mountain, of the sinews of the bear, of the breath of the fish, and of the spittle of the birds. If you have not known this before, you can easily find out that it is true and that there is no lie about it, since you must have observed that a woman has no beard, that a cat's footfall cannot be heard, and that mountains have no roots; and I know, forsooth, that what I have told you is perfectly true, although there are some things that you do not understand. Then said Ganglere: This I must surely understand to be true. I can see these things which you have taken as proof. But how was the fetter smithied? Answered Har: That I can well explain to you. It was smooth and soft as a silken string. How strong and trusty it was you shall now hear. When the fetter was brought to the asas, they thanked the messenger for doing his errand so well. Then they went out into the lake called Amsvartner, to the holm (rocky island) called Lyngve, and called the wolf to go with them. They showed him the silken band and bade him break it, saying that it was somewhat stronger than its thinness would lead one to suppose. Then they handed it from one to the other and tried its strength with their hands, but it did not break. Still they said the wolf would be able to snap it. The wolf answered: It seems to me that I will get no fame though I break asunder so slender a thread as this is. But if it is made with craft and guile, then, little though it may look, that band will never come on my feet. Then said the asas that he would easily be able to break a slim silken band, since he had already burst large iron fetters asunder. But even if you are unable to break this band, you have nothing to fear from the gods, for we will immediately loose you again. The wolf answered: If you get me bound so fast that I am not able to loose myself again, you will skulk away, and it will be long before I get any help from you, wherefore I am loth to let this band be laid on me; but in order that you may not accuse me of cowardice, let some one of you lay his hand in my mouth as a pledge that this is done without deceit. The one asa looked at the other, and thought there now was a choice of two evils, and no one would offer his hand, before Tyr held out his right hand and laid it in the wolf's mouth. But when the wolf now began to spurn against it the band grew stiffer, and the more he strained the tighter it got. They all laughed except Tyr; he lost his hand. When the asas saw that the wolf was sufficiently well bound, they took the chain which was fixed to the fetter, and which was called Gelgja, and drew it through a large rock which is called Gjol, and fastened this rock deep down in the earth. Then they took a large stone, which is called Tvite, and drove it still deeper into the ground, and used this stone for a fastening-pin. The wolf opened his mouth terribly wide, raged and twisted himself with all his might, and wanted to bite them; but they put a sword in his mouth, in such a manner that the hilt stood in his lower jaw and the point in the upper, that is his gag. He howls terribly, and the saliva which runs from his mouth forms a river called Von. There he will lie until Ragnarok. Then said Ganglere: Very bad are these children of Loke, but they are strong and mighty. But why did not the asas kill the wolf when they have evil to expect from him? Har answered: So great respect have the gods for their holiness and peace-stead, that they would not stain them with the blood of the wolf, though prophecies foretell that he must become the bane of Odin.

CHAPTER TEN
THE GODDESSES (ASYNJES)

36. Ganglere asked: Which are the goddesses? Har answered: Frigg is the first; she possesses the right lordly dwelling which is called Fensaler. The second is Saga, who dwells in Sokvabek, and this is a large dwelling. The third is Eir, who is the best leech. The fourth is Gefjun, who is a may, and those who die maids become her hand-maidens. The fifth is Fulla, who is also a may, she wears her hair flowing and has a golden ribbon about her head; she carries Frigg's chest, takes care of her shoes and knows her secrets. The sixth is Freyja, who is ranked with Frigg. She is wedded to the man whose name is Oder; their daughter's name is Hnos, and she is so fair that all things fair and precious are called, from her name, Hnos. Oder went far away. Freyja weeps for him, but her tears are red gold. Freyja has many names, and the reason therefor is that she changed her name among the various nations to which she came in search of Oder. She is called Mardol, Horn, Gefn, and Syr. She has the necklace Brising, and she is called Vanadis. The seventh is Sjofn, who is fond of turning men's and women's hearts to love, and it is from her name that love is called Sjafne. The eighth is Lofn, who is kind and good to those who call upon her, and she has permission from Alfather or Frigg to bring together men and women, no matter what difficulties may stand in the way; therefore "love" is so called from her name, and also that which is much loved by men. The ninth is Var. She hears the oaths and troths that men and women plight to each other. Hence such vows are called vars, and she takes vengeance on those who break their promises. The tenth is Vor, who is so wise and searching that nothing can be concealed from her. It is a saying that a woman becomes

vor (ware) of what she becomes wise. The eleventh is Syn, who guards the door of the hall, and closes it against those who are not to enter. In trials she guards those suits in which anyone tries to make use of falsehood. Hence is the saying that "syn is set against it," when anyone tries to deny ought. The twelfth is Hlin, who guards those men whom Frigg wants to protect from any danger. Hence is the saying that he hlins who is forewarned. The thirteenth is Snotra, who is wise and courtly. After her, men and women who are wise are called Snotras. The fourteenth is Gna, whom Frigg sends on her errands into various worlds. She rides upon a horse called Hofvarpner, that runs through the air and over the sea. Once, when she was riding, some vans saw her faring through the air. Then said one of them:

What flies there?
What fares there?
What glides in the air?

She answered

I fly not,
Though I fare
And glide through the air
On Hofvarpner,
That Hamskerper,
Begat with Gardrofa.

From Gna's name it is said that anything that fares high in the air gnas. Sol and Bil are numbered among the goddesses, but their nature has already been described.

37. There are still others who are to serve in Valhal, bear the drink around, wait upon the table and pass the ale-horns. Thus they are named in Grimner's Lay:

Hrist and Mist
I want my horn to bring to me;
Skeggold and Skogul,
Hild and Thrud,
Hlok and Heifjoter,
Gol and Geirahod,
Randgrid and Radgrid,
And Reginleif;
These bear ale to the einherjes.

These are called valkyries. Odin sends them to all battles, where they choose those who are to be slain, and rule over the victory. Gud and Rosta, and the youngest norn, Skuld, always ride to sway the battle and choose the slain. Jord, the mother of Thor, and Rind, Vale's mother, are numbered among the goddesses.

CHAPTER ELEVEN
THE GIANTESS GERD AND SKIRNER'S JOURNEY

38. Gymer hight a man whose wife was Orboda, of the race of the mountain giants. Their daughter was Gerd, the fairest of all women. One day when Frey had gone into Hlidskjalf, and was looking out upon all the worlds, he saw toward the north a hamlet wherein was a large and beautiful house. To this house went a woman, and when she raised her hands to open the door, both the sky and the sea glistened therefrom, and she made all the world bright. As a punishment for his audacity in seating himself in that holy seat, Frey went away full of grief. When he came home, he neither spake, slept, nor drank, and no one dared speak to him. Then Njord sent for Skirner, Frey's servant, bade him go to Frey and ask him with whom he was so angry, since he would speak to nobody. Skirner said that he would go, though he was loth to do so, as it was probable that he would get evil words in reply. When he came to Frey and asked him why he was so sad that he would not talk, Frey answered that he had seen a beautiful woman, and for her sake he had become so filled with grief, that he could not live any longer if he could not get her. And now you must go, he added, and ask her hand for me and bring her home to me, whether it be with or without the consent of her father. I will reward you well for your trouble. Skirner answered saying that he would go on this errand, but Frey must give him his sword, that was so excellent that it wielded itself in fight. Frey made no objection to this and gave him the sword. Skirner went on his journey, courted Gerd for him, and got the promise of her that she nine nights thereafter should come to Bar-Isle and there have her wedding with Frey. When Skirner came back and gave an account of his journey, Frey said:

Long is one night,
Long are two nights,
How can I hold out three?
Oft to me one month
Seemed less
Than this half night of love.

This is the reason why Frey was unarmed when he fought with Bele, and slew him with a hart's horn. Then said Ganglere: It is a great wonder that such a lord as Frey would give away his sword, when he did not have another as good. A great loss it was to him when he fought with Bele; and this I know, forsooth, that he must have repented of that gift. Har answered: Of no great account was his meeting with Bele. Frey could have slain him with his hand. But the time will come when he will find himself in a worse plight for not having his sword, and that will be when the sons of Muspel sally forth to the fight.

CHAPTER TWELVE
LIFE IN VALHAL

39. Then said Ganglere: You say that all men who since the beginning of the world have fallen in battle have come to Odin in Valhal. What does he have to give them to eat? It seems to me there must be a great throng of people. Har answered: It is true, as you remark, that there is a great throng; many more are yet to come there, and still they will be thought too few when the wolf comes. But however great may be the throng in Valhal, they will get plenty of flesh of the boar Sahrimner. He is boiled every day and is whole again in the evening. But as to the question you just asked, it seems to me there are but few men so wise that they are able to answer it correctly. The cook's name is Andhrimner, and the kettle is called Eldhrimner as is here said:

Andhrimner cooks
In Eldhrimner
Sahrimner.
'Tis the best of flesh.
There are few who know
What the einherjes eat.

Ganglere asked: Does Odin have the same kind of food as the einherjes? Har answered: The food that is placed on his table he gives to his two wolves, which hight Gere and Freke. He needs no food himself. Wine is to him both food and drink, as is here said:

Gere and Freke
Sates the warfaring,
Famous father of hosts;

But on wine alone
Odin in arms renowned
Forever lives.

Two ravens sit on Odin's shoulders, and bring to his ears all that they hear and see. Their names are Hugin and Munin. At dawn he sends them out to fly over the whole world, and they come back at breakfast time. Thus he gets information about many things, and hence he is called Rafnagud (raven-god). As is here said:

Hugin and Munin
Fly every day
Over the great earth.
I fear for Hugin
That he may not return,
Yet more am I anxious for Munin.

40. Then asked Ganglere: What do the einherjes have to drink that is furnished them as bountifully as the food? Or do they drink water? Har answered: That is a wonderful question. Do you suppose that Alfather invites kings, jarls, or other great men, and gives them water to drink? This I know, forsooth, that many a one comes to Valhal who would think he was paying a big price for his water-drink, if there were no better reception to be found there,—persons, namely, who have died from wounds and pain. But I can tell you other tidings. A she-goat, by name Heidrun, stands up in Valhal and bites the leaves off the branches of that famous tree called Lerad. From her teats runs so much mead that she fills every day a vessel in the hall from which the horns are filled, and which is so large that all the einherjes get all the drink they want out of it. Then said Ganglere: That is a most useful goat, and a right excellent

tree that must be that she feeds upon. Then said Har: Still more remarkable is the hart Eikthyrner, which stands over Valhal and bites the branches of the same tree. From his horns fall so many drops down into Hvergelmer, that thence flow the rivers that are called Sid, Vid, Sekin, Ekin, Svol, Gunthro, Fjorm, Fimbulthul, Gipul, Gopul, Gomul and Geirvimul, all of which fall about the abodes of the asas. The following are also named: Thyn, Vin, Thol, Bol, Grad, Gunthrain, Nyt, Not, Non, Hron, Vina, Vegsvin, Thjodnuma.

41. Then said Ganglere: That was a wonderful tiding that you now told me. A mighty house must Valhal be, and a great crowd there must often be at the door. Then answered Har: Why do you not ask how many doors there are in Valhal, and how large they are? When you find that out, you will confess that it would rather be wonderful if everybody could not easily go in and out. It is also a fact that it is no more difficult to find room within than to get in. Of this you may hear what the Lay of Grimner says:

Five hundred doors
And forty more,
I trow, there are in Valhal.
Eight hundred einherjes
Go at a time through one door
When they fare to fight with the wolf.

42. Then said Ganglere: A mighty band of men there is in Valhal, and, forsooth, I know that Odin is a very great chief, since he commands so mighty a host. But what is the pastime of the einherjes when they do not drink? Har answered: Every morning, when they have dressed themselves, they take their weapons and go out into the

court and fight and slay each other. That is their play. Toward breakfast-time they ride home to Valhal and sit down to drink. As is here said:

All the einherjes
In Odin's court
Hew daily each other.
They choose the slain
And ride from the battle-field,
Then sit they in peace together.

But true it is, as you said, that Odin is a great chief. There are many proofs of that. Thus it is said in the very words of the asas themselves:

The Yggdrasil ash
Is the foremost of trees,
But Skidbladner of ships,
Odin of asas,
Sleipner of steeds,
Bifrost of bridges,
Brage of Skalds,
Habrok of hows,
But Garm of dogs.

CHAPTER THIRTEEN
ODIN'S HORSE AND FREY'S SHIP

43. Ganglere asked: Whose is that horse Sleipner, and what is there to say about it? Har answered: You have no knowledge of Sleipner, nor do you know the circumstances attending his birth; but it must seem to you worth the telling. In the beginning, when the town of the gods was building, when the gods had established Midgard and made Valhal, there came a certain builder and offered to make them a burg, in three half years, so excellent that it should be perfectly safe against the mountain-giants and frost-giants, even though they should get within Midgard. But he demanded as his reward, that he should have Freyja, and he wanted the sun and moon besides. Then the asas came together and held counsel, and the bargain was made with the builder that he should get what he demanded if he could get the burg done in one winter; but if on the first day of summer any part of the burg was unfinished, then the contract should be void. It was also agreed that no man should help him with the work. When they told him these terms, he requested that they should allow him to have the help of his horse, called Svadilfare, and at the suggestion of Loke this was granted him.

On the first day of winter he began to build the burg, but by night he hauled stone for it with his horse. But it seemed a great wonder to the asas what great rocks that horse drew, and the horse did one half more of the mighty task than the builder. The bargain was firmly established with witnesses and oaths, for the giant did not deem it safe to be among the asas without truce if Thor should come home, who now was on a journey to the east fighting trolls. Toward the end of winter the burg was far built, and it was so high and strong that it could in nowise be taken. When there were three days left before summer, the work was all completed excepting the burg gate. Then went the gods to their judgment-seats and held counsel, and asked each other who could have advised to give Freyja in marriage in Jotunheim, or to plunge the air and the heavens in darkness by taking away the sun and the moon and giving them to the giant; and all agreed that this must have been advised by him who gives the most bad counsels, namely, Loke, son of Laufey, and they threatened him with a cruel death if he could not contrive some way of preventing the builder from fulfilling his part of the bargain, and they proceeded to lay hands on Loke. He in his fright then promised with an oath that he should so manage that the builder should lose his wages, let it cost him what it would. And the same evening, when the builder drove out after stone with his horse Svadilfare, a mare suddenly ran out of the woods to the horse and began to neigh at him. The steed, knowing what sort of horse this was, grew excited, burst the reins asunder and ran after the mare, but she ran from him into the woods. The builder hurried after them with all his might, and wanted to catch the steed, but these horses kept running all night, and thus the time was lost, and at dawn the work had not made the usual progress. When the builder saw that his work was not going to be completed, he resumed his giant form. When the asas thus became sure that it was really a mountain-giant that had come among them, they did not heed their oaths, but called on Thor. He came straightway, swung his hammer, Mjolner, and paid the workman his wages,—not with the sun and moon, but rather by preventing him from dwelling in Jotunheim; and this was easily done with the first blow of the hammer, which broke his skull into small pieces and sent him down to Niflhel. But Loke had run such a race with Svadilfare that he some time after bore a foal. It was gray, and had eight feet, and this is the best horse among gods and men. Thus it is said in the Vala's Prophecy:

Then went the gods.
The most holy gods,
Onto their judgment-seats,
And counseled together
Who all the air
With guile had blended
Or to the giant race
Oder's may had given.
Broken were oaths,
And words and promises,—
All mighty speech
That had passed between them.
Thor alone did this,
Swollen with anger.
Seldom sits he still
When such things he hears.

44. Then asked Ganglere: What is there to be said of Skidbladner, which you say is the best of ships? Is there no ship equally good, or equally great? Made answer Har: Skidbladner is the best of ships, and is made with the finest workmanship; but Naglfare, which is in Muspel, is the largest. Some dwarfs, the sons of Ivalde, made Skidbladner and gave it to Frey. It is so large that all the asas, with their weapons and war-gear, can find room on board it, and as soon as the sails are hoisted it has fair wind, no matter whither it is going. When it is not wanted for a voyage, it is made of so many pieces and with so much skill, that Frey can fold it together like a napkin and carry it in his pocket.

CHAPTER FOURTEEN
THOR'S ADVENTURES

Then said Ganglere: A good ship is Skidbladner, but much black art must have been resorted to ere it was so fashioned. Has Thor never come where he has found anything so strong and mighty that it has been superior to him either in strength or in the black art? Har answered: Few men, I know, are able to tell thereof, but still he has often been in difficult straits. But though there have been things so mighty and strong that Thor has not been able to gain the victory, they are such as ought not to be spoken of; for there are many proofs which all must accept that Thor is the mightiest. Then said Ganglere: It seems to me that I have now asked about something that no one can answer. Said Jafnhar: We have heard tell of adventures that seem to us incredible, but here sits one near who is able to tell true tidings thereof, and you may believe that he will not lie for the first time now, who never told a lie before. Then said Ganglere: I will stand here and listen, to see if any answer is to be had to this question. But if you cannot answer my question I declare you to be defeated. Then answered Thride: It is evident that he now is bound to know, though it does not seem proper for us to speak thereof. The beginning of this adventure is that Oku-Thor went on a journey with his goats and chariot, and with him went the asa who is called Loke. In the evening they came to a bonde and got there lodgings for the night. In the evening Thor took his goats and killed them both, whereupon he had them flayed and borne into a kettle. When the flesh was boiled, Thor and his companion sat down to supper. Thor invited the bonde, his wife and their children, a son by name Thjalfe, and a daughter by name Roskva, to eat with them. Then Thor laid the goat-skins away from the fireplace, and requested the bonde and his household to cast the bones onto the skins. Thjalfe, the bonde's son, had the thigh of one of the goats, which he broke asunder with his knife, in order to get at the marrow, Thor remained there over night. In the morning, just before daybreak, he arose, dressed himself, took the hammer Mjolner, lifted it and hallowed the goat-skins. Then the goats arose, but one of them limped on one of its hind legs. When Thor saw this he said that either the bonde or one of his folk had not dealt skillfully with the goat's bones, for he noticed that the thigh was broken. It is not necessary to dwell on this part of the story. All can understand how frightened the bonde became when he saw that Thor let his brows sink down over his eyes. When he saw his eyes he thought he must fall down at the sight of them alone. Thor took hold of the handle of his hammer so hard that his knuckles grew white. As might be expected, the bonde and all his household cried aloud and sued for peace, offering him as an atonement all that they possessed. When he saw their fear, his wrath left him. He was appeased, and took as a ransom the bonders children, Thjalfe and Roskva. They became his servants, and have always accompanied him since that time.

46. He left his goats there and went on his way east into Jotunheim, clear to the sea, and then he went on across the deep ocean, and went ashore on the other side, together with Loke and Thjalfe and Roskva. When they had proceeded a short distance, there stood before them a great wood, through which they kept going the whole day until dark. Thjalfe, who was of all men the fleetest of foot, bore Thor's bag, but the wood was no good place for provisions. When it had become dark, they sought a place for their night lodging, and found a very large hall. At the end of it was a door as wide as the hall. Here they remained through

the night. About midnight there was a great earthquake; the ground trembled beneath them, and the house shook. Then Thor stood up and called his companions. They looked about them and found an adjoining room to the right, in the midst of the hall, and there they went in. Thor seated himself in the door; the others went farther in and were very much frightened. Thor held his hammer by the handle, ready to defend himself. Then they heard a great groaning and roaring. When it began to dawn, Thor went out and saw a man lying not far from him in the wood. He was very large, lay sleeping, and snored loudly. Then Thor thought he had found out what noise it was that they had heard in the night. He girded himself with his Megingjarder, whereby his Asa-might increased. Meanwhile the man woke, and immediately arose. It is said that Thor this once forbore to strike him with the hammer, and asked him for his name. He called himself Skrymer; but, said he, I do not need to ask you what your name is,—I know that you are Asa-Thor. But what have you done with my glove? He stretched out his hand and picked up his glove. Then Thor saw that the glove was the hall in which he had spent the night, and that the adjoining room was the thumb of the glove. Skrymer asked whether they would accept of his company. Thor said yes. Skrymer took and loosed his provision-sack and began to eat his breakfast; but Thor and his fellows did the same in another place. Skrymer proposed that they should lay their store of provisions together, to which Thor consented. Then Skrymer bound all their provisions into one bag, laid it on his back, and led the way all the day, taking gigantic strides. Late in the evening he sought out a place for their night quarters under a large oak. Then Skrymer said to Thor that he wanted to lie down to sleep; they might take the provision-sack and make ready their supper. Then Skrymer fell asleep and snored tremendously. When Thor took the provision-sack and was to open it, then happened what seems incredible, but still it must be told,—that he could not get one knot loosened, nor could he stir a single end of the strings so that it was looser than before. When he saw that all his efforts were in vain he became wroth, seized his hammer Mjolner with both his hands, stepped with one foot forward to where Skrymer was lying and dashed the hammer at his head. Skrymer awoke and asked whether some leaf had fallen upon his head; whether they had taken their supper, and were ready to go to sleep. Thor answered that they were just going to sleep. Then they went under another oak. But the 118truth must be told, that there was no fearless sleeping. About midnight Thor heard that Skrymer was snoring and sleeping so fast that it thundered in the wood. He arose and went over to him, clutched the hammer tight and hard, and gave him a blow in the middle of the crown, so that he knew that the head of the hammer sank deep into his head. But just then Skrymer awoke and asked: What is that? Did an acorn fall onto my head? How is it with you, Thor? Thor hastened back, answered that he had just waked up, and said that it was midnight and still time to sleep. Then Thor made up his mind that if he could get a chance to give him the third blow, he should never see him again, and he now lay watching for Skrymer to sleep fast. Shortly before daybreak he heard that Skrymer had fallen asleep. So he arose and ran over to him. He clutched the hammer with all his might and dashed it at his temples, which he saw uppermost. The hammer sank up to the handle. Skrymer sat up, stroked his temples, and said: Are there any birds sitting in the tree above me? Methought, as I awoke, that some moss from the branches fell on my head. What! are you awake, Thor? It is now time to get up and dress; but you have not far left to the burg that is called Utgard. I have heard that you have been whispering among yourselves that I am not small of stature, but you will see greater men when you come to Utgard. Now I will give you wholesome advice. Do not brag too much of yourselves, for Utgard-Loke's thanes will not brook the boasting of such insignificant little fellows as you are; otherwise turn back, and that is, in fact, the best thing for you to do. But if you are bound to continue your journey, then keep straight on eastward; my way lies to the north, to those mountains that you there see. Skrymer then took the provision-sack and threw it on his back, and, leaving them, turned into the wood, and it has not been learned whether the asas wished to meet him again in health.

47. Thor and his companions went their way and continued their journey until noon. Then they saw a burg standing on a plain, and it was so high that they had to bend their necks clear back before they could look over it. They drew nearer and came to the burg-gate, which was closed. Thor finding himself unable to open it, and being anxious to get within the burg, they crept between the bars and so came in. They discovered a large hall and went to it. Finding the door open they entered, and saw there many men, the most of whom were immensely large, sitting on two benches. Thereupon they approached the king, Utgard-Loke, and greeted him. He scarcely deigned to look at them, smiled scornfully and showed his teeth, saying: It is late to ask for tidings of a long journey, but if I am not mistaken this stripling is Oku-Thor, is it not? It may be, however, that you are really bigger than you look For what feats are you and your companions prepared? No one can stay with us here, unless he is skilled in some craft or accomplishment beyond the most of men. Then answered he who came in last, namely Loke: I know the feat of which I am prepared

to give proof, that there is no one present who can eat his food faster than I. Then said Utgard-Loke: That is a feat, indeed, if you can keep your word, and you shall try it immediately. He then summoned from the bench a man by name Loge, and requested him to come out on the floor and try his strength against Loke. They took a trough full of meat and set it on the floor, whereupon Loke seated himself at one end and Loge at the other. Both ate as fast as they could, and met at the middle of the trough. Loke had eaten all the flesh off from the bones, but Loge had consumed both the flesh and the bones, and the trough too. All agreed that Loke had lost the wager. Then Utgard-Loke asked what game that young man knew? Thjalfe answered that he would try to run a race with anyone that Utgard-Loke might designate. Utgard-Loke said this was a good feat, and added that it was to be hoped that he excelled in swiftness if he expected to win in this game, but he would soon have the matter decided. He arose and went out. There was an excellent race-course along the flat plain. Utgard-Loke then summoned a young man, whose name was Huge, and bade him run a race with Thjalfe. Then they took the first heat, and Huge was so much ahead that when he turned at the goal he met Thjalfe. Said Utgard-Loke: You must lay yourself more forward, Thjalfe, if you want to win the race; but this I confess, that there has never before come anyone hither who was swifter of foot than you. Then they took a second heat, and when Huge came to the goal and turned, there was a long bolt-shot to Thjalfe. Then said Utgard-Loke: Thjalfe seems to me to run well; still I scarcely think he will win the race, but this will be proven when they run the third heat. Then they took one more heat. Huge ran to the goal and turned back, but Thjalfe had not yet gotten to the middle of the course. Then all said that this game had been tried sufficiently. Utgard-Loke now asked Thor what feats there were that he would be willing to exhibit before them, corresponding to the tales that men tell of his great works. Thor replied that he preferred to compete with someone in drinking. Utgard-Loke said there would be no objection to this. He went into the hall, called his cup-bearer, and requested him to take the sconce-horn that his thanes were wont to drink from. The cup-bearer immediately brought forward the horn and handed it to Thor. Said Utgard-Loke: From this horn it is thought to be well drunk if it is emptied in one draught, some men empty it in two draughts, but there is no drinker so wretched that he cannot exhaust it in three. Thor looked at the horn and did not think it was very large, though it seemed pretty long, but he was very thirsty. He put it to his lips and swallowed with all his might, thinking that he should not have to bend over the horn a second time. But when his breath gave out, and he looked into the horn to see how it had gone with his drinking, it seemed to him difficult to determine whether there was less in it than before. Then said Utgard-Loke: That is well drunk, still it is not very much. I could never have believed it, if anyone had told me, that Asa-Thor could not drink more, but I know you will be able to empty it in a second draught. Thor did not answer, but set the horn to his lips, thinking that he would now take a larger draught. He drank as long as he could and drank deep, as he was wont, but still he could not make the tip of the horn come up as much as he would like. And when he set the horn away and looked into it, it seemed to him that he had drunk less than the first time; but the horn could now be borne without spilling. Then said Utgard-Loke: How now, Thor! Are you not leaving more for the third draught than befits your skill? It seems to me that if you are to empty the horn with the third draught, then this will be the greatest. You will not be deemed so great a man here among us as the asas call you, if you do not distinguish yourself more in other feats than you seem to me to have done in this. Then Thor became wroth, set the horn to his mouth and drank with all his might and kept on as long as he could, and when he looked into it its contents had indeed visibly diminished, but he gave back the horn and would not drink any more. Said Utgard-Loke: It is clear that your might is not so great as we thought. Would you like to try other games? It is evident that you gained nothing by the first. Answered Thor: I should like to try other games, but I should be surprised if such a drink at home among the asas would be called small. What game will you now offer me? Answered Utgard-Loke: Young lads here think it nothing but play to lift my cat up from the ground, and I should never have dared to offer such a thing to Asa-Thor had I not already seen that you are much less of a man than I thought. Then there sprang forth on the floor a gray cat, and it was rather large. Thor went over to it, put his hand under the middle of its body and tried to lift it up, but the cat bent its back in the same degree as Thor raised his hands; and when he had stretched them up as far as he was able the cat lifted one foot, and Thor did not carry the game any further. Then said Utgard-Loke: This game ended as I expected. The cat is rather large, and Thor is small, and little compared with the great men that are here with us. Said Thor: Little as you call me, let anyone who likes come hither and wrestle with me, for now I am wroth. Answered Utgard-Loke, looking about him on the benches: I do not see anyone here who would not think it a trifle to wrestle with you. And again he said: Let me see first! Call hither that old woman, Elle, my foster-mother, and let Thor wrestle with her if he wants to. She has thrown to the ground men who have seemed to me no less strong than Thor. Then there came into the hall an old woman.

Utgard-Loke bade her take a wrestle with Asa-Thor. The tale is not long. The result of the grapple was, that the more Thor tightened his grasp, the firmer she stood. Then the woman began to bestir herself, and Thor lost his footing. They had some very hard tussles, and before long Thor was brought down on one knee. Then Utgard-Loke stepped forward, bade them cease the wrestling, and added that Thor did not need to challenge anybody else to wrestle with him in his hall, besides it was now getting late. He showed Thor and his companions to seats, and they spent the night there enjoying the best of hospitality.

48. At daybreak the next day Thor and his companions arose, dressed themselves and were ready to depart. Then came Utgard-Loke and had the table spread for them, and there was no lack of feasting both in food and in drink. When they had breakfasted, they immediately departed from the burg. Utgard-Loke went with them out of the burg, but at parting he spoke to Thor and asked him how he thought his journey had turned out, or whether he had ever met a mightier man than himself. Thor answered that he could not deny that he had been greatly disgraced in this meeting; and this I know, he added, that you will call me a man of little account, whereat I am much mortified. Then said Utgard-Loke: Now I will tell you the truth, since you have come out of the burg, that if I live, and may have my way, you shall never enter it again; and this I know, forsooth, that you should never have come into it had I before known that you were so strong, and that you had come so near bringing us into great misfortune. Know, then, that I have deceived you with illusions. When I first found you in the woods I came to meet you, and when you were to loose the provision-sack I had bound it with iron threads, but you did not find where it was to be untied. In

the next place, you struck me three times with the hammer. The first blow was the least, and still it was so severe that it would have been my death if it had hit me. You saw near my burg a mountain cloven at the top into three square dales, of which one was the deepest,—these were the dints made by your hammer. The mountain I brought before the blows without your seeing it. In like manner I deceived you in your contests with my courtiers. In regard to the first, in which Loke took part, the facts were as follows: He was very hungry and ate fast; but he whose name was Loge was wildfire, and he burned the trough no less rapidly than the meat. When Thjalfe ran a race with him whose name was Huge, that was my thought, and it was impossible for him to keep pace with its swiftness. When you drank from the horn, and thought that it diminished so little, then, by my troth, it was a great wonder, which I never could have deemed possible.. One end of the horn stood in the sea, but that you did not see. When you come to the sea-shore you will discover how much the sea has sunk by your drinking; that is now called the ebb. Furthermore he said: Nor did it seem less wonderful to me that you lifted up the cat; and, to tell you the truth, all who saw it were frightened when they saw that you raised one of its feet from the ground, for it was not such a cat as you thought. It was in reality the Midgard-serpent, which surrounds all lands. It was scarcely long enough to touch the earth with its tail and head, and you raised it so high that your hand nearly reached to heaven. It was also a most astonishing feat when you wrestled with Elle, for none has ever been, and none shall ever be, that Elle (eld, old age) will not get the better of him, though he gets to be old enough to abide her coming. And now the truth is that we must part; and it will be better for us both that you do not visit me again. I will again defend my burg with similar or other delusions, so that you will get no power over me. When Thor heard this tale he seized his hammer and lifted it into the air, but when he was about to strike he saw Utgard-Loke nowhere; and when he turned back to the burg and was going to dash that to pieces, he saw a beautiful and large plain, but no burg. So he turned and went his way back to Thrudvang. But it is truthfully asserted that he then resolved in his own mind to seek that meeting with the Midgard-serpent, which afterward took place. And now I think that no one can tell you truer tidings of this journey of Thor.

49. Then said Ganglere: A most powerful 128man is Utgard-Loke, though he deals much with delusions and sorcery. His power is also proven by the fact that he had thanes who were so mighty. But has not Thor avenged himself for this? Made answer Har: It is not unknown, though no wise men tell thereof, how Thor made amends for the journey that has now been spoken of. He did not remain long at home, before he busked himself so suddenly for a new journey, that he took neither chariot, nor goats nor any companions with him. He went out of Midgard in the guise of a young man, and came in the evening to a giant by name Hymer. Thor tarried there as a guest through the night. In the morning Hymer arose, dressed himself, and busked himself to row out upon the sea to fish. Thor also sprang up, got ready in a hurry and asked Hymer whether he might row out with him. Hymer answered that he would get but little help from Thor, as he was so small and young; and he added, you will get cold if I row as far out and remain as long as I am wont. Thor said that he might row as far from shore as he pleased, for all that, and it was yet to be seen who would be the first to ask to row back to land. And Thor grew so wroth at the giant that he came near letting the hammer ring on his head straightway,

but he restrained himself, for he intended to try his strength elsewhere. He asked Hymer what they were to have for bait, but Hymer replied that he would have to find his own bait. Then Thor turned away to where he saw a herd of oxen, that belonged to Hymer. He took the largest ox, which was called Himinbrjot, twisted his head off and brought it down to the sea-strand. Hymer had then shoved the boat off. Thor went on board and seated himself in the stern; he took two oars and rowed so that Hymer had to confess that the boat sped fast from his rowing. Hymer plied the oars in the bow, and thus the rowing soon ended. Then said Hymer that they had come to the place where he was wont to sit and catch flat-fish, but Thor said he would like to row much farther out, and so they made another swift pull. Then said Hymer that they had come so far out that it was dangerous to stay there, for the Midgard-serpent. Thor said he wished to row a while longer, and so he did; but Hymer was by no means in a happy mood. Thor took in the oars, got ready a very strong line, and the hook was neither less nor weaker. When he had put on the ox-head for bait, he cast it overboard and it sank to the bottom. It must be admitted that Thor now beguiled the Midgard-serpent not a whit less than Utgard-Loke 130mocked him when he was to lift the serpent with his hand. The Midgard-serpent took the ox-head into his mouth, whereby the hook entered his palate, but when the serpent perceived this he tugged so hard that both Thor’s hands were dashed against the gunwale. Now Thor became angry, assumed his asa-might and spurned so hard that both his feet went through the boat and he stood on the bottom of the sea. He pulled the serpent up to the gunwale; and in truth no one has ever seen a more terrible sight than when Thor whet his eyes on the serpent, and the latter stared at him and spouted venom. It is said that the giant Hymer changed hue and grew pale from fear when he saw the serpent and beheld the water flowing into the boat; but just at the moment when Thor grasped the hammer and lifted it in the air, the giant fumbled for his fishing-knife and cut off Thor's line at the gunwale, whereby the serpent sank back into the sea. Thor threw the hammer after it, and it is even said that he struck off his head at the bottom, but I think the truth is that the Midgard-serpent still lives and lies in the ocean. Thor clenched his fist and gave the giant a box on the ear so that he fell backward into the sea, and he saw his heels last, but Thor waded ashore.

CHAPTER FIFTEEN
THE DEATH OF BALDER

50. Then asked Ganglere: Have there happened any other remarkable things among the asas? A great deed it was, forsooth, that Thor wrought on this journey. Har answered: Yes, indeed, there are tidings to be told that seemed of far greater importance to the asas. The beginning of this tale is, that Balder dreamed dreams great and dangerous to his life. When he told these dreams to the asas they took counsel together, and it was decided that they should seek peace for Balder against all kinds of harm. So Frigg exacted an oath from fire, water, iron and all kinds of metal, stones, earth, trees, sicknesses, beasts, birds and creeping things, that they should not hurt Balder. When this was done and made known, it became the pastime of Balder and the asas that he should stand up at their meetings while some of them should shoot at him, others should hew at him, while others should throw stones at him; but no matter what they did, no harm came to him, and this seemed to all a great honor. When Loke, Laufey's son, saw this, it displeased him very much that Balder was not scathed. So he went to Frigg, in Fensal, having taken on himself the likeness of a woman. Frigg asked this woman whether she knew what the asas were doing at their meeting. She answered that all were shooting at Balder, but that he was not scathed thereby. Then said Frigg: Neither weapon nor tree can hurt Balder, I have taken an oath from them all. Then asked the woman: Have all things taken an oath to spare Balder? Frigg answered: West of Valhal there grows a little shrub that is called the mistletoe, that seemed to me too young to exact an oath from. Then the woman suddenly disappeared. Loke went and pulled up the mistletoe and proceeded to the meeting. Hoder stood far to one side in the ring of men,

because he was blind. Loke addressed himself to him, and asked: Why do you not shoot at Balder? He answered: Because I do not see where he is, and furthermore I have no weapons. Then said Loke: Do like the others and show honor to Balder; I will show you where he stands; shoot at him with this wand. Hoder took the mistletoe and shot at Balder under the guidance of Loke. The dart pierced him and he fell dead to the ground. This is the greatest misfortune that has ever happened to gods and men. When Balder had fallen, the asas were struck speechless with horror, and their hands failed them to lay hold of the corpse. One looked at the other, and all were of one mind toward him who had done the deed, but being assembled in a holy peace-stead, no one could take vengeance. When the asas at length tried to speak, the wailing so choked their voices that one could not describe to the other his sorrow. Odin took this misfortune most to heart, since he best comprehended how great a loss and injury the fall of Balder was to the asas. When the gods came to their senses, Frigg spoke and asked who there might be among the asas who desired to win all her love and good will by riding the way to Hel and trying to find Balder, and offering Hel a ransom if she would allow Balder to return home again to Asgard. But he is called Hermod, the Nimble, Odin's swain, who undertook this journey. Odin's steed, Sleipner, was led forth. Hermod mounted him and galloped away.

51. The asas took the corpse of Balder and brought it to the sea-shore. Hringhorn was the name of Balder's ship, and it was the largest of all ships. The gods wanted to launch it and make Balder's bale-fire thereon, but they could not move it. Then they sent to Jotunheim after the giantess whose name is Hyrrokken. She came riding on a wolf, and had twisted serpents for reins. When she alighted, Odin

appointed four berserks to take care of her steed, but they were unable to hold him except by throwing him down on the ground. Hyrrokken went to the prow and launched the ship with one single push, but the motion was so violent that fire sprang from the underlaid rollers and all the earth shook. Then Thor became wroth, grasped his hammer, and would forthwith have crushed her skull, had not all the gods asked peace for her. Balder's corpse was borne out on the ship; and when his wife, Nanna, daughter of Nep, saw this, her heart was broken with grief and she died. She was borne to the funeral-pile and cast on the fire. Thor stood by and hallowed the pile with Mjolner. Before his feet ran a dwarf, whose name is Lit. Him Thor kicked with his foot and dashed him into the fire, and he, too, was burned. But this funeral-pile was attended by many kinds of folk. First of all came Odin, accompanied by Frigg and the valkyries and his ravens. Frey came riding in his chariot drawn by the boar called Gullinburste or Slidrugtanne. Heimdal rode his steed Gulltop, and Freyja drove her cats. There was a large number of frost-giants and mountain-giants. Odin laid on the funeral-pile his gold ring, Draupner, which had the property of producing, every ninth night, eight gold rings of equal weight. Balder's horse, fully caparisoned, was led to his master's pile.

52. But of Hermod it is to be told that he rode nine nights through deep and dark valleys, and did not see light until he came to the Gjallar-river and rode on the Gjallar-bridge, which is thatched with shining gold. Modgud is the name of the may who guards the bridge. She asked him for his name, and of what kin he was, saying that the day before there rode five fylkes (kingdoms, bands) of dead men over the bridge; but she added, it does not shake less under you alone, and you do not have the hue of dead men. Why do

you ride the way to Hel? He answered: I am to ride to Hel to find Balder. Have you seen him pass this way? She answered that Balder had ridden over the Gjallar-bridge; adding: But downward and northward lies the way to Hel. Then Hermod rode on till he came to Hel's gate. He alighted from his horse, drew the girths tighter, remounted him, clapped the spurs into him, and the horse leaped over the gate with so much force that he never touched it. Thereupon Hermod proceeded to the hall and alighted from his steed. He went in, and saw there sitting on the foremost seat his brother Balder. He tarried there over night. In the morning he asked Hel whether Balder might ride home with him, and told how great weeping there was among the asas. But Hel replied that it should now be tried whether Balder was so much beloved as was said. If all things, said she, both quick and dead, will weep for him, then he shall go back to the asas, but if anything refuses to shed tears, then he shall remain with Hel. Hermod arose, and Balder accompanied him out of the hall. He took the ring Draupner and sent it as a keepsake to Odin. Nanna sent Frigg a kerchief and other gifts, and to Fulla she sent a ring. Thereupon Hermod rode back and came to Asgard, where he reported the tidings he had seen and heard.

53. Then the asas sent messengers over all the world, praying that Balder might be wept out of Hel's power. All things did so,—men and beasts, the earth, stones, trees and all metals, just as you must have seen that these things weep when they come out of frost and into heat. When the messengers returned home and had done their errand well, they found a certain cave wherein sat a giantess (gygr = ogress) whose name was Thok. They requested her to weep Balder from Hel; but she answered:

Thok will weep
With dry tears
For Balder's burial;
Neither in life nor in death
Gave he me gladness.
Let Hel keep what she has!

It is generally believed that this Thok was Loke, Laufey's son, who has wrought most evil among the asas.

54. Then said Ganglere: A very great wrong did Loke perpetrate; first of all in causing Balder's death, and next in standing in the way of his being loosed from Hel. Did he get no punishment for this misdeed? Har answered: Yes, he was repaid for this in a way that he will long remember. The gods became exceedingly wroth, as might be expected. So he ran away and hid himself in a rock. Here he built a house with four doors, so that he might keep an outlook on all sides. Oftentimes in the daytime he took on him the likeness of a salmon and concealed himself in Free Franangen Force. Then he thought to himself what stratagems the asas might have recourse to in order to catch him. Now, as he was sitting in his house, he took flax and yarn and worked them into meshes, in the manner that nets have since been made; but a fire was burning before him. Then he saw that the asas were not far distant. Odin had seen from Hlidskjalf where Loke kept himself. Loke immediately sprang up, cast the net on the fire and leaped into the river. When the asas came to the house, he entered first who was wisest of them all, and whose name was Kvaser; and when he saw in the fire the ashes of the net that had been burned, he understood that this must be a contrivance for catching fish, and this he told to the asas. Thereupon they took flax and made themselves a net after the pattern of that which they

saw in the ashes and which Loke had made. When the net was made, the asas went to the river and cast it into the force. Thor held one end of the net, and all the other asas laid hold on the other, thus jointly drawing it along the stream. Loke went before it and laid himself down between two stones, so that they drew the net over him, although they perceived that some living thing touched the meshes. They went up to the force again and cast out the net a second time. This time they hung a great weight to it, making it so heavy that nothing could possibly pass under it. Loke swam before the net, but when he saw that he was near the sea he sprang over the top of the net and hastened back to the force. When the asas saw whither he went they proceeded up to the force, dividing themselves into two bands, but Thor waded in the middle of the stream, and so they dragged the net along to the sea. Loke saw that he now had only two chances of escape,—either to risk his life and swim out to sea, or to leap again over the net. He chose the latter, and made a tremendous leap over the top line of the net. Thor grasped after him and caught him, but he slipped in his hand so that Thor did not get a firm hold before he got to the tail, and this is the reason why the salmon has so slim a tail. Now Loke was taken without truce and was brought to a cave. The gods took three rocks and set them up on edge, and bored a hole through each rock. Then they took Loke's sons, Vale and Nare or Narfe. Vale they changed into the likeness of a wolf, whereupon he tore his brother Narfe to pieces, with whose intestines the asas bound Loke over the three rocks. One stood under his shoulders, another under his loins, and the third under his hams, and the fetters became iron. Skade took a serpent and fastened up over him, so that the venom should drop from the serpent into his face. But Sigyn, his wife, stands by him, and holds a dish under the venom-drops. Whenever the dish becomes full, she goes and pours away the venom, and meanwhile the venom drops onto Loke's face. Then he twists his body so violently that the whole earth shakes, and this you call earthquakes. There he will lie bound until Ragnarok.

CHAPTER SIXTEEN
RAGNAROK

55. Then said Ganglere: What tidings are to be told of Ragnarok? Of this I have never heard before. Har answered: Great things are to be said thereof. First, there is a winter called the Fimbul-winter, when snow drives from all quarters, the frosts are so severe, the winds so keen and piercing, that there is no joy in the sun. There are three such winters in succession, without any intervening summer. But before these there are three other winters, during which great wars rage over all the world. Brothers slay each other for the sake of gain, and no one spares his father or mother in that manslaughter and adultery. Thus says the Vala's Prophecy:

Brothers will fight together
And become each other's bane;
Sisters' children
Their sib shall spoil.
Hard is the world,
Sensual sins grow huge.
There are ax-ages, sword-ages—
Shields are cleft in twain,—
There are wind-ages, wolf-ages,
Ere the world falls dead.

Then happens what will seem a great miracle, that the wolf64 devours the sun, and this will seem a great loss. The other wolf will devour the moon, and this too will cause great mischief. The stars shall be Hurled from heaven. Then it shall come to pass that the earth and the mountains will shake so violently that trees will be torn up by the roots, the mountains will topple down, and all bonds and fetters will be broken and snapped. The Fenris-wolf gets loose. The sea rushes over the earth, for the Midgard-serpent writhes in giant rage and seeks to gain the land. The ship that is called Naglfar also becomes loose. It is made of the nails of dead men; wherefore it is worth warning that, when a man dies with unpared nails, he supplies a large amount of materials for the building of this ship, which both gods and men wish may be finished as late as possible. But in this flood Naglfar gets afloat. The giant Hrym is its steersman. The Fenris-wolf advances with wide open mouth; the upper jaw reaches to heaven and the lower jaw is on the earth. He would open it still wider had he room. Fire flashes from his eyes and nostrils. The Midgard-serpent vomits forth venom, defiling all the air and the sea; he is very terrible, and places himself by the side of the wolf. In the midst of this clash and din the heavens are rent in twain, and the sons of Muspel come riding through the opening. Surt rides first, and before him and after him flames burning fire. He has a very good sword, which shines brighter than the sun. As they ride over Bifrost it breaks to pieces, as has before been stated. The sons of Muspel direct their course to the plain which is called Vigrid. Thither repair also the Fenris-wolf and the Midgard-serpent. To this place have also come Loke and Hrym, and with him all the frost-giants. In Loke's company are all the friends of Hel. The sons of Muspel have there effulgent bands alone by themselves. The plain Vigrid is one hundred miles (rasts) on each side.

56. While these things are happening, Heimdal stands up, blows with all his might in the Gjallar-horn and awakens all the gods, who thereupon hold counsel. Odin rides to Mimer's well to ask advice of Mimer for himself and his folk. Then quivers the ash Ygdrasil, and all things in

heaven and earth fear and tremble. The asas and the einherjes arm themselves and speed forth to the battle-field. Odin rides first; with his golden helmet, resplendent byrnie, and his spear Gungner, he advances against the Fenris-wolf. Thor stands by his side, but can give him no assistance, for he has his hands full in his struggle with the Midgard-serpent. Frey encounters Surt, and heavy blows are exchanged ere Frey falls. The cause of his death is that he has not that good sword which he gave to Skirner. Even the dog Garm, that was bound before the Gnipa-cave, gets loose. He is the greatest plague. He contends with Tyr, and they kill each other. Thor gets great renown by slaying the Midgard-serpent, but retreats only nine paces when he falls to the earth dead, poisoned by the venom that the serpent blows on him. The wolf swallows Odin, and thus causes his death; but Vidar immediately turns and rushes at the wolf, placing one foot on his nether jaw. On this foot he has the shoe for which materials have been gathering through all ages, namely, the strips of leather which men cut off for the toes and heels of shoes; wherefore he who wishes to render assistance to the asas must cast these strips away. With one hand Vidar seizes the upper jaw of the wolf, and thus rends asunder his mouth. Thus the wolf perishes. Loke fights with Heimdal, and they kill each other. Thereupon Surt flings fire over the earth and burns up all the world. Thus it is said in the Vala's Prophecy:

Loud blows Heimdal
His uplifted horn.
Odin speaks
With Mimer's head.
The straight-standing ash
Ygdrasil quivers,
The old tree groans,

And the giant gets loose.

How fare the asas?
How fare the elves?
All Jotunheim roars.
The asas hold counsel;
Before their stone-doors
Groan the dwarfs,
The guides of the wedge-rock.
Know you now more or not?

From the east drives Hrym,
Bears his shield before him.
Jormungand welters
In giant rage
And smites the waves.
The eagle screams,
And with pale beak tears corpses,
Naglfar gets loose.

A ship comes from the east,
The hosts of Muspel
Come o'er the main,
And Loke is steersman.
All the fell powers
Are with the wolf;
Along with them
Is Byleist's brother.

From the south comes Surt
With blazing fire-brand,—
The sun of the war-god
Shines from his sword.
Mountains dash together,

Giant maids are frightened,
Heroes go the way to Hel,
And heaven is rent in twain.

Then comes to Hlin
Another woe,
When Odin goes
With the wolf to fight,
And Bele's bright slayer
To contend with Surt.
There will fall
Frigg's beloved.

Odin's son goes
To fight with the wolf,
And Vidar goes on his way
To the wild beast.
With his hand he thrusts
His sword to the heart
Of the giant's child,
And avenges his father.

Then goes the famous
Son of Hlodyn
To fight with the serpent.
Though about to die,
He fears not the contest;
All men
Abandon their homesteads
When the warder of Midgard
In wrath slays the serpent.

The sun grows dark,
The earth sinks into the sea,

The bright stars
From heaven vanish;
Fire rages,
Heat blazes,
And high flames play
'Gainst heaven itself.

And again it is said as follows:

Vigrid is the name of the plain
Where in fight shall meet
Surt and the gentle god.
A hundred miles
It is every way.
This field is marked out for them.

CHAPTER SEVENTEEN
REGENERATION

57. Then asked Ganglere: What happens when heaven and earth and all the world are consumed in flames, and when all the gods and all the einherjes and all men are dead? You have already said that all men shall live in some world through all ages. Har answered: There are many good and many bad abodes. Best it is to be in Gimle, in heaven. Plenty is there of good drink for those who deem this a joy in the hall called Brimer. That is also in heaven. There is also an excellent hall which stands on the Nida mountains. It is built of red gold, and is called Sindre. In this hall good and well-minded men shall dwell. Nastrand is a large and terrible hall, and its doors open to the north. It is built of serpents wattled together, and all the heads of the serpents turn into the hall and vomit forth venom that flows in streams along the hall, and in these streams wade perjurers and murderers. So it is here said:

A hall I know standing
Far from the sun
On the strand of dead bodies.
Drops of venom
Fall through the loop-holes.
Of serpents' backs
The hall is made.

There shall wade
Through heavy streams
Perjurers
And murderers.

But in Hvergelmer it is worst.

There tortures Nidhug
The bodies of the dead.

58. Then said Ganglere: Do any gods live then? Is there any earth or heaven? Har answered: The earth rises again from the sea, and is green and fair. The fields unsown produce their harvests. Vidar and Vale live. Neither the sea nor Surfs fire has harmed them, and they dwell on the plains of Ida, where Asgard was before. Thither come also the sons of Thor, Mode and Magne, and they have Mjolner. Then come Balder and Hoder from Hel. They all sit together and talk about the things that happened aforetime,—about the Midgard-serpent and the Fenris-wolf. They find in the grass those golden tables which the asas once had. Thus it is said:

Vidar and Vale
Dwell in the house of the gods,
When quenched is the fire of Surt.
Mode and Magne
Vingner's Mjolner shall have
When the fight is ended.

In a place called Hodmimer's-holt are concealed two persons during Surt's fire, called Lif and Lifthraser. They feed on the morning dew. From these so numerous a race is descended that they fill the whole world with people, as is here said:

Lif and Lifthraser
Will lie hid
In Hodmimer's-holt.
The morning dew
They have for food.

From them are the races descended.

But what will seem wonderful to you is that the sun has brought forth a daughter not less fair than herself, and she rides in the heavenly course of her mother, as is here said:

A daughter
Is born of the sun
Ere Fenrer takes her.
In her mother's course
When the gods are dead
This maid shall ride.

And if you now can ask more questions, said Har to Ganglere, I know not whence that power came to you. I have never heard any one tell further the fate of the world. Make now the best use you can of what has been told you.

59. Then Ganglere heard a terrible noise on all sides, and when he looked about him he stood out-doors on a level plain. He saw neither hall nor burg. He went his way and came back to his kingdom, and told the tidings which he had seen and heard, and ever since those tidings have been handed down from man to man.

THE FIRST COMPLETE ENGLISH TRANSLATION OF THE POETIC EDDA

by

Benjamin Thorpe

with the assistance of Elise C. Otté

(1866)

INTRODUCTION

As introductory to the Völuspa, the following description of a wandering Vala or prophetess may be thought both desirable and interesting: "We find them present at the birth of children, when they seem to represent the Norns. They acquired their knowledge either by means of seid, during the night, which all others in the house were sleeping, and uttered their oracles in the morning; or they received sudden inspirations during the signing of certain songs appropriated to the purpose, without which the sorcery could not perfectly succeed. These seid-women were common over all of the North. When invited by the master of a family, they appeared in a peculiar costume, sometimes with a considerable number of followers, e.g. with fifteen young men and fifteen girls. For their soothsaying they received money, gold rings, and other precious things. Sometimes it was necessary to compel them to prophesy. An old description of such a Vala, who went from guild to guild telling fortunes, will give the best idea of these women and their proceedings: Thorbiörg, nicknamed the little Vala, during the winter attended the guilds, at the invitation of those who desired to know their fate, or the quality of the coming year. Everything was prepared in the most sumptuous manner for her reception. There was an elevated seat, on which lay a cushion stuffed with feathers. A man was sent to meet her. She came in the evening dressed in a blue mantle fastened with thongs and set with stones down to the lap; round her neck she had a necklace of glass beads, on her head a hood of black lambskin lined with white catskin; in her hand a staff, the head of which was mounted with brass and ornamented with stones; round her body she wore a girdle of agaric (knöske), from which hung a bag containing her conjuring apparatus; on her feet were rough calfskin shoes with long ties and tin buttons, on her hands catskin gloves, white and hairy within. All bade her welcome with a reverent salutation; the master himself conducted her by the hand to her seat. She undertook no prophecy on the first day, but would first pass a night there. In the evening of the following day she ascended her elevated seat, caused the women to place themselves round her, and desired them to sing certain songs, which they did in a strong, clear voice. She then prophesied of the coming year, and afterwards, all that would advanced and asked her such questions as they thought proper, to which they received plain answers." Northern Mythology I. p.214, Den Ældre Edda I.

In the following grand and ancient lay, dating most probably from the time of heathenism, are set forth, as the utterances of a Vala, or wandering prophetess, as above described, the story of the creation of the world from chaos, of the origin of the giants, the gods, the dwarfs, and the human race, together with other events relating to the mythology of the North, and ending with the destruction of the gods and the world, and their renewal.

1: Völuspâ: The Valás Prophecy

1. For silence I pray all
sacred children,
great and small, sons of
Heimdall[1]
they will that I Valfatheŕs
deeds recount,
meńs ancient saws, those
that I best remember.

2. The Jötuns I remember
early born,
those who me of old have
reared.
I nine worlds remember,
nine trees,[2]
the great central tree,[3]
beneath the earth.

3. There was in times of
old, where Ymir dwelt,
nor sand nor sea, nor
gelid waves;
earth existed not, nor
heaven above,
'twas a chaotic chasm,
and grass nowhere.

4. Before Buŕs sons
raised up heaveńs vault,
they who the noble mid-
earth shaped.
The sun shone from the
south over the structurés
rocks: then was the earth
begrown with herbage
green.

5. The sun from the
south, the moońs
companion,
her right hand cast about
the heavenly horses.
The sun knew not where
she[4] a dwelling had,
the moon knew not what
power he possessed,
the stars knew not where
they had a station.

6. Then went the power
all to their judge-ment
seats, the all-holy gods,
and thereon held council:
to night and to the waning
moon gave names;
morn they named, and
mid-day,
afternoon and eve,
whereby to reckon years.

7. The Æsir met on Ida's
plain;

they altar-steads and
temples high constructed;
their strength they
proved, all things tried,
furnaces established,
precious things forged,
formed tongs, and
fabricated tools;

8. at tables played at
home; joyous they were;
to them was naught the
want of gold,
until there came Thurs-
maidens three,
all powerful, from
Jötunheim.

9. Then went all the
powers to their
judgement-seats, the all-
holy gods, and thereon
held council,
who should of the dwarfs
the race create,
from the sea-giant's
blood and livid bones.[5]

10. Then was Mötsognir
created greatest
of all the dwarfs, and
Durin second;
there in man's likeness
they created many
dwarfs from the earth, as
Durin said.

11. Nýi and Nidi, Nordri
and Sudri, Asutri and
Vestri, Althiöf, Dvalin
Nár and Náin, Niping,
Dáin, Bivör, Bavör,
Bömbur, Nori, An and
Anar,
Ai, Miödvitnir,

12. Veig and Gandálf,
Vindálf, Thráin, Thekk
and Thorin, Thror, Vitr,
and Litr, Núr and Nýrád,
Regin and Rádsvid. Now
of the dwarfs I have
rightly told.

13. Fili, Kili, Fundin,
Nali, Hepti, Vili, Hanar,
Svior, Billing, Bruni,
Bild, Búri, Frár,
Hornbori,
Fræg and Lóni, Aurvang,
Iari, Eikinskialdi.

14. Time ́tis of the dwarfs
in Dvaliń s band,
to the sons of men, to
Lofar up to reckon,
those who came forth
from the worlds ́ rock,

earth́s foundation, to Iorás plains.

15. There were Draupnir, and Dólgthrasir, Hár, Haugspori, Hlævang, Glói, Skirvir, Virvir, Skafid, Ai, Alf and Yngvi, Eikinskialdi,

16. Fjalar and Frosti, Finn and Ginnar, Heri, Höggstari, Hliódolf, Móin: that above shall, while mortals live, the progeny of Lofar, accounted be.

17. Until there came three mighty and benevolent Æsir to the world from their assembly.
They found on earth, nearly powerless,
Ask and Embla, void of destiny.

18. Spirit they possessed not, sense they had not, blood nor motive powers, nor goodly colour.
Spirit gave Odin, sense gave Hoenir,
blood gave Lodur, and goodly colour.

19. I know an ash
standing Yggdrasil hight, a lofty tree, laved with limpid water:
thence come the dews
into the dales that fallæ ever stands it green over Urd́s fountain.

20. Thence come maidens, much knowing, three from the hall, which under that tree stands;
Urd hight the one, the second Verdandi, -
on a tablet they graved -
[6] Skuld the third.
Laws they established,
life allotted
to the sons of men;
destinies pronounced.

21. Alone she[7] sat without, when came that ancient dread Æsiŕs prince; and in his eyes she gazed.

22. "Of what wouldst thou ask me? Odin!

I know all, where thou
thine eye didst sink
in the pure well of Mim."
Mim drinks mead each
morn from Valfather's
pledge.[8]
Understand ye yet, or
what?

23. The chief of hosts
gave her rings and
necklace, useful
discourse, and a divining
spirit:
wide and far she saw o'er
every world.

24. She the Valkyriur saw
from afar coming,
ready to ride to the gods'
people:
Skuld held a sheild,
Skögul was second,
then Gunn, Hild, Göndul,
and Geirskögul.
Now are enumerated
Heriańs maidens,
the Valkyriur, ready over
the earth to ride.

25. She that war
remembers, the first on
earth,
when Gullveig[9] they
with lances pierced,
and in the high onés[10]
hall her burnt,
thrice burnt, thrice brough
her forth,
oft not seldom; yet she
still lives.

26. Heidi they called her,
whithersoér she came,
the well-forseeing Vala:
wolves she tamed,
magic arts she knew,
magic arts practised;
ever was she the joy of
evil people.

27. Then went the powers
all to their judgement-
seats, the all-holy gods,
and thereon held council,
whether the Æsir should
avenge the crime,[11]
or all the gods receive
atonement.

28. Broken was the outer
wall of the Æsiŕs burgh.
The Vanir, forseeing
conflict tramp oér the
plains.
Odin cast (his spear), and
mid the people hurled it:

that was the first warfare
in the world.

29. Then went the powers
all to their judgement-
seats, the all-holy gods,
and thereon held council:
who had all the air with
evil mingled?
or to the Jötun race Oďs
maid had given?

30. There alone was Thor
with anger swollen.
He seldom sits, when of
the like he hears.
Oaths are not held sacred;
nor words, nor swearing,
nor binding compacts
reciprocally made.

31. She knows that
Heimdall's horn is hidden
under the heaven-bright
holy tree.
A river she sees flow,
with foamy fall,
from Valfather's pledge.
Understand ye yet, or
what?[12]

32. East sat the crone, in
Iárnvidir,[13]
Fenriŕs progeny: of all
shall be
one especially the moon's
devourer,
in a troll's semblance.[14]

33. He is sated with the
last breath
of dying men; the gods'
seat he
with red gore defiles:
swart is the sunshine then
for summers after; all
weather turns to storm.
Understand ye yet, or
what?

34. There on a height sat,
striking a harp,
the giantess's watch, the
joyous Egdir;
by him crowed, in the
bird-wood,
the bright red cock, which
Fialar hight.

35. Crowed o'er the Æsir
Gullinkambi,
which wakens heroes
with the sire of hosts;
but another crows
beneath the earth,
a soot-red cock, in the
halls of Hel.

36. I saw of Baldr, the
blood-stained god,
Odin's son, the hidden
fate.
There stood grown up,
high on the plain,
slender and passing fair,
the mistletoe.

37. From that shrub was
made, as to me
it seemed, a deadly,
noxious dart.
Hödr shot it forth;[15]
But Frigg bewailed,
in Fensalir, Valhall's
calamity.
Understand ye yet, or
what?

38. Bound she saw lying,
under Hveralund,[16]
a monstrous form, to Loki
like.
There sits Sigyn, for her
consort's sake,
not right glad. Understand
ye yet, or what?

39. Then the Vala knew
the fatal bonds were
twisting, most rigid,
bonds from entrails made.

40. From the east a river
falls, through venom
dales, with mire and
clods,[17] Slid is its
name.

41. On the north there
stood, on Nida-fells,
a hall of gold, for Sindri's
race; and another stood
in Okolnir, the Jötuns
beer-hall which
Brimir[18] hight.

42. She saw a hall
standing, far from the
sun,
in Náströnd; its doors are
northward turned,
venom-drops fall in
through its apertures:
entwined is that hall with
serpent's backs.

43. She there saw wading
the sluggish streams
bloodthirsty men and
perjurers,
and him who the ear
beguiles of another's
wife.
There Nidhögg sucks the
corpses of the dead;

the wolf tears men.
Understand ye yet, or
what?

44. Further forward I see,
much can I say
of Ragnarök and the
godśconflict.

45. Brothers shall fight,
and slay each other;
cousins shall kinship
violate.
The earth resounds, the
giantesses flee;
no man will another
spare.

46. Hard is it in the
world, great whoredom,
an axe age, a sword age,
sheilds will be cloven,
a wind age, a wolf age,
ere the world sinks.

47. Mim's sons dance,
but the central tree takes
fire,[19] at the resounding
Gjallar-horn.
Loud blows Heimdall, his
horn is raised;
Odin speaks with Mim's
head.

48. Trembles Yggdrasil's
ash yet standing;
groans that aged tree, and
the jötun[20] is loosed.
Loud bays Garm before
the Gnupa-cave,
his bonds he rends
asunder; and the wolf
runs.

49. Hrym steers from the
east, the waters rise,
the mundane snake is
coiled in jötun-rage.
The worm beats the
water, and the eagle
screams:
the pale of beak tears
carcases; Naglfar is
loosed.

50. That ship fares from
the east: come will
Muspell's people o'er the
sea, and Loki steers.
The monster's kin goes
all with the wolf;
with them the brother is
of Byleist on their course.

51. Surt from the south
comes with flickering
flame; shines from his
sword the Val-god's sun.

The stony hills are dashed together, the giantesses totter; men tread the path of Hel, and heaven is cloven.

52. How is it with the Æsir? How with the Alfar?
All Jötunheim resounds; the Æsir are in council. The dwarfs groan before their stony doors, the sages of the rocky walls. Understand ye yet, or what?

53. Then arises Hlińs second grief, when Odin goes with the wolf to fight, and the bright slayer of Beli with Surt. Then will Friggś beloved fall.

54. Then comes the great victor-sire's son, Vidar, to fight with the deadly beast.
He with his hands will make his sword pierce to the heart of the giant's son[21]: then avenges he his father.

55. Then comes the mighty son of Hlódyn: (Odin's son goes with the monster to fight); Midgárds Veor in his rage will slay the worm.
Nine feet will go Fiörgyńs son, bowed by the serpent, who feared no foe.
All men will their homes forsake.

56. The sun darkens, earth in ocean sinks, fall from heaven the bright stars, firés breath assails the all-nourishing tree, towering fire plays against heaven itself.

57. She sees arise, a second time, earth from ocean, beauteously green, waterfalls descending; the eagle flying over, which in the fell captures fish.

58. The Æsir meet on Idás plain, and of the mighty earth-encircler speak, and there to

memory call their mighty deeds, and the supreme god's[22] ancient lore.

59. There shall again the wondrous golden tables in the grass be found, which in days of old had possessed the ruler of the gods, and Fjölnir's race.

60. Unsown shall the fields bring forth, all evil be amended; Baldr shall come; Hödr and Baldr, the heavenly gods, Hropt's glorious dwellings shall inhabit. Understand ye yet, or what?

61. Then can Hoenir choose his lot,[23] and the two brother's sons inhabit the spacious Vindheim.
Understand ye yet, or what?

62. She a hall sees standing than the sun brighter,
with gold bedecked, in Gimill: there shall the righteous people dwell, and for evermore happiness enjoy.

64. Then comes the mighty one to the great judgement, the powerful from above, who rules o'er all. He shall dooms pronounce, and strifes allay, holy peace establish, which shall ever be.

65. There comes the dark dragon flying from beneath, the glistening serpent, from Nida-fells. On his wings bears Nidhögg, flying o'er the plain,
a corpse. Now she will descend.

2: Váfþrúðnismál: The Lay of Vafthrúdnir.

Odin visits the Giant (Jötun) Vafthrudnir, for the purpose of proving his knowledge. They propose questions relative to the Cosmogony of the Northern creed, on the condition that the baffled party forfeit his head. The Jötun incurs the penalty.

Odin
1. Counsel thou me now,
Frigg! as I long to go
Vafthrudnir to visit; great
desire, I say,
I have, in ancient lore
with athat all-wise Jötun
to contend.

Frigg
2. At home to bide
Hærfather I would
counsel, in the
godśdwellings; because
no Jötun is, I believe, so
mighty as is Vafthrudnir.

Odin
3. Much have I
journeyed, much
experienced,
mighty ones many
proved; but this I fain
would know, how in
Vafthrudnir's halls it is.

Frigg
4. In safety mayest thou
go, in safety return, in
safety on thy journeyings
be; may thy wit avail
thee, when thou, father of
men! Shalt hold converse
with the Jötun.

5. Then went Odin the
lore to prove of that all-
wise Jötun. To the hall he
came which Irńs father
owned. Ygg went
forthwith in.

Odin
6. Hail to thee,
Vafthrudnir! to thy hall I
am now come, theyself to
see; for I fain would
know,
whether thou art a
cunning and all-wise
Jötun.

Vafthrudnir
7. What man is this, that in my habitation by word addresses me? Out thou goest not from our halls, if thou art not the wiser.

Odin
8. Gagnrad is my name, from my journey I am come thirsty to thy halls, needing hospitality, - for I long have journeyed - and kind reception from thee, Jötun!

Vafthrudnir
9. Why then, Gagnrad! speakest thou from the floor? Take in the hall a seat; then shall be proved which knows most, the guest or the ancient talker.

Gagnrad
10. A poor man should, who to a rich man comes, speak usefully or hold his tongue: over-much talk brings him, I ween, no good, who visits an austere man.

Vafthrudnir
11. Tell me, Gagnrad! since on the floor thou wilt
prove thy proficiency, how the horse is called that draws each day forth over human kind?

Gagnrad
12. Skinfaxi he is named, that the bright day draws forth over human kind. Of coursers he is best accounted among the Reid-goths. Ever sheds light that horse's mane.

Vafthrudnir
13. Tell me now, Gagnrad! since on the floor thou wilt prove thy proficiency, how that steed is called, which from the east draws night o'er the beneficent powers?

Gagnrad
14. Hrimfaxi he is called, that each night draws forth
over the beneficent powers.

He from his bit lets fall
drops every morn,
whence in the dales
comes dew.

Vafthrudnir
15. Tell me, Gagnrad!
since on the floor thou
wilt
prove thy proficiency,
how the stream is called,
which earth divides
between
the Jötuns and the Gods?

Gagnrad
16. Ifing the stream is called which earth divides between the Jötuns and the Gods: open shall it run
throughout all time. On that stream no ice shall be.

Vafthrudnir
17. Tell me, Gagnrad!
since on the floor thou
wilt
prove thy proficiency,
how that plain is called,
where in fight shall meet
Surt and the gentle Gods?

Gagnrad
18. Vigrid the plain is called, where in fight shall meet Surt and the gentle Gods; a hundred rasts it is on every side. That plain is to them decreed.

Vafthrudnir
19. Wise art thou, o guest! Approach the Jötuns bench, and sitting let us together talk: we will our heads in the hall pledge, guest! for wise utterance.

Gagnrad
20. Tell me first, if thy wit suffices, and thou, Vafthrudnir! knowest, whence first came the earth, and the high heaven, thou, sagacious Jötun?

Vafthrudnir
21. From Ymir's flesh the earth was formed, and from his bones the hills, the heaven from the skull of that ice-cold giant, and from his blood the sea.

Gagnrad
22. Tell me secondly, if thy wit suffices, and thou, Vafthrudnir! knowest, whence came the moon, which over mankind passes, and the sun likewise?

Vafthrudnir
23. Mundilfoeri hight he, who the moon's father is, and eke the sun's: round heaven journey each day they must, to count years for men.

Gagnrad
24. Tell me thirdly, since thou art called wise, and if thou, Vafthrudnir! knowest, whence came the day, which over people passes, and night with waning moons?

Vafthrudnir
25. Delling hight he who the day's father is, but night was of Nörvi born; the new and waning moons the beneficent powers created, to count years for men.

Gagnrad
26. Tell me fourthly, since they pronounce thee sage, and if thou, Vafthrudnir! knowest, whence winter came, and warm summer first among the wise gods?

Vafthrudnir
27. Vindsval hight he, who winter's father is, and Svasud summer's; yearly they both shall ever journey, until the powers perish.

Gagnrad
28. Tell me fifthly, since they pronounce thee sage, and if thou, Vafthrudnir! knowest, which of the Æsir earliest, or of Ymir's sons in days of old existed?

Vafthrudnir
29. Countless winters, ere earth was formed, was Bergelmir born;

Thrudgelmir was his sire, his grandsire Arugelmir.

Gagnrad
30. Tell me sixthly, since thou art called wise, and if thou, Vafthrudnir! knowest, whence first came Aurgelmir, amongh the Jötuńs sons, thou sagacious Jötun?

Vafthrudnir
31. From Elivagar sprang venom drops, which grew till they became a Jötun; but sparks flew from the south-world:to the ice the fire gave life.

Gagnrad
32. Tell me seventhly, since thou art called wise, and if thou knowest, Vafthrudnir! how he children begat, the bold Jötun,as he had no giantess's company?

Vafthrudnir
33. Under the armpit grew, 'tis said, of the Hrimthurs, a girl and boy together; foot with foot begat, of that wise Jötun, a six-headed son.

Gagnrad
34. Tell me eighthly, since thou art called wise, and if thou knowest, Vafthrudnir! what thou doest first remember, or earliest knowest? Thou art an all-wise Jötun.

Vafthrudnir
35. Countless winters, ere earth was formed, Bergelmir was born. That I first remember, when that wise Jötun in an ark was laid.

Gagnrad
36. Tell me ninthly, since thou art called wise, and if thou knowest, Vafthrudnir! whence the wind comes, that over ocean passes, itself invisible to man?

Vafthrudnir
37. Hræsvelg he is called, who at the end of heaven sits, a Jötun in an eaglés

plumage: from his wings comes, it is said, the wind,that over all men passes.

Gagnrad
38. Tell me tenthly, since thou all the origin of the gods knowest, Vafthrudnir! whence Niörd came among the Æsir's sons?
O'er fanes and offer-steads he rules by hundreds,
yet was not among the Æsir born.

Vafthrudnir
39. In Vanaheim wise powers him created, and to the gods a hostage gave.
At the world's dissolution he will return to the wise Vanir.

Gagnrad
40. Tell me eleventhly, since all the condition of the gods thou knowest, Vafthrudnir! what the Einherjar do in Hærfather's halls, until the powers perish?

Vafthrudnir
41. All the Einherjar in Odin's halls each day together fight; the fallen they choose, and from the conflict ride; beer with the Æsir drink, of Sæhrimnir eat their fill, then sit in harmony together.

Gagnrad
42. Tell me twelfthly, as thou all the condition of the gods knowest, Vafthrudnir! of the Jötuns' secrets, and of all the gods', say what truest is, thou all-knowing Jötun!

Vafthrudnir
43. Of the secrets of the Jötuns and of all the gods, I can truly tell; for I have over each world travelled; to nine worlds I came, to Niflhel beneath: here die men from Hel.

Gagnrad

44. Much have I journeyed, much experienced, mighty ones many proved. What mortals will live, when the great 'Fimbulwinter' shall from men have passed?

Vafthrudnir
45. Lif and Lifthrasir; but they will be concealed in Hoddmimir's holt. The morning dews they will have for food. From them shall men be born.

Gagnrad
46. Much have I journeyed, much experienced, mighty ones many proved.
Whence will come the sun in that fair heaven, when Fenrir has this devoured?

Vafthrudnir
47. A daughter shall Alfrödull bear,ere Fenrir shall have swallowed her. The maid shall ride, when the powers die, on her mother's course.

Gagnrad
48. Much have I journeyed, (&c.) who are the maidens that o'er the ocean travel, wise of spirit, journey?

Vafthrudnir
49. O'er people's dwellings three descend of Mögthrasir's maidens, the sole Hamingiur who are in the world, although with Jötuns nurtured.

Gagnrad
50. Much have I journeyed, (&c.) Which of the Æsir will rule o'er the gods' possession, when Surt's fire shall be quenched?

Vafthrudnir
51. Vidar and Vali will the gods' holy fanes inhabit, when Surt's fire shall be quenched.
Modi and Magni will Mjöllnir possess, and warfare strive to end.

Gagnrad
52. Much have I journeyed, (&c.) What of Odin will the life's end be, when the powers perish?

Vafthrudnir
53. The wolf will the father of men devour; him Vidar will avenge: he his cold jaws will cleave, in conflict with the wolf.

Gagnrad
54. Much have I journeyed, (&c.) What said Odin in his son's ear, ere he on the pile was laid?

Vaftthrudnir
55. That no one knoweth, what thou in days of old saidst in thy son's ear. With dying mouth my ancient saws I have said, and the gods' destruction. With Odin I have contended in wise utterances: of men thou ever art the wisest!

3: Grimismál: The Lay of Grimnir

King Hraudung had two sons, one named Agnar, the other Geirröd. Agnar was ten, and Geirröd eight winters old. They both rowed out in a boat, with their hooks and lines, to catch small fish; but the wind drove them out to sea. In the darkness of the night they were wrecked on the shore, and went up into the country, where they found a cottager, with whom they stayed through the winter. The cottager's wife brought up Agnar, and the cottager, Geirröd, and gave him good advice. In the spring the man got them a ship; but when he and his wife accompanied them to the strand, the man talked apart with Geirröd. They had a fair wind, and reached their fathers place. Geirröd was at the ship's prow: he sprang on shore, but pushed the ship out, saying, "Go where an evil spirit may get thee." The vessel was driven out to sea, but Geirröd went up to the town, where he was well recieved; but his father was dead. Geirröd was then taken for king, and became a famous man.

Odin and Frigg were sitting in Hlidskialf, looking over all the world. Odin said, 'Seest thou Agnar, thy foster-son, where he is getting children with a giantess in a cave? while Geirröd, my foster-son, is a king residing in his country." Frigg answered, "He is so inhospitable that he tortures his guests, if he thinks too many come." Odin replied that that was the greatest falsehood; and they wagered thereupon. Frigg sent her waiting-maid Fulla to bid Geirröd be on his gaurd, lest the trollmann who was coming should do him harm, and also say that a token whereby he might be known was, that no dog, however fierce, would attack him. But that King Geirröd was not hospitable was mere idle talk. He, nevertheless, caused the man to be secured whom no dog would assail. He was clad in a blue cloak, and was named Grimnir, and would say no more concerning himself, although he was questioned. The king ordered him to be tortured to make him confess, and to be set between two fires; and there he sat for eight nights. King Geirröd had a son ten years old, whom he named Agnar, after his brother. Agnar went to Grimnir and gave him a full horn to drink from, saying that the king did wrong in causing him to be tortured, though innocent. Grimnir drank from it. The fire had then so approached him that his cloak was burnt; whereupon he said: -

1. Fire! thou art hot, and
much too great; flame! let
us separate.
My garment is singed,
although I lift it up, my
cloak is scorched before
it.

2. Eight nights have I sat
between fires here, and to
me no one food has
offered, save only Agnar,
the son of Geirröd, who
alone shall rule over the
land of the Goths.

3. Be thou blessed,
Agnar! as blessed as the
god of men bids thee to
be.
For one draught thou
never shalt get better
recompense.

4. Holy is the land, which
I see lying to Æsir and
Alfar near; but in
Thrundheim Thor shall
dwell until the powers
perish.

5. Ydalir it is called,
where Ullr has himself a
dwelling made.
Alfheim the gods to Frey
gave in days of yore for a
tooth-gift.

6. The third dwelling is,
where the kind powers
have with silver decked
the hall;
Valaskjalf 'tis called,
which for himself
acquired
the As* in days of old.
*Odin, SnE, 17.

7. Sökkvabekk the fourth is named oe'r which the gelid waves resound; Odin and Saga there, joyful each day, from golden beakers quaff.

8. Gladsheim the fifth is named, there the golden-bright Valhall stands spacious, there Hropt selects
each day those men who die by weapons.

9. Easily to be known is, by those who to Odin come, the mansion by its aspect.
Its roof with spears is laid, its hall with shields is decked, with corselets are its benches strewed.

10. Easily to be known is, by those who to Odin come, the mansion by its aspect.
A wolf hangs before the western door, over it an eagle hovers.

11. Thrymheim the sixth is named, where Thiassi dwelt, that all-powerful Jötun; but Skadi now inhabits, the bright bride of the gods, her father's ancient home.

12. Breidablik is the seventh, where Baldr has built for himself a hall, in that land, in which I know exists the fewest crimes.

13. Himinbjörg is the eighth, where Heimdall, it is said, rules o'er the holy fanes: there the gods' watchman,-in his tranquil home, drinks joyful the good mead.

14. Folkvang is the ninth, there Freyja directs the sittings in the hall.
She half the fallen chooses each day, but Odin th' other half.

15. Glitnir is the tenth; it is on gold sustained, and eke with silver decked.
There Forseti dwells

throughout all time, and every strife allays.

16. Noatun is the eleventh, there Niörd has himself a dwelling made, prince of men; guiltless of sin, he rules o'er the high-built fane.

17. O'ergrown with branches and high grass is Vidar's spacious Landvidi: There will the son descend, from the steed's back, bold to avenge his father.

18. Andhrimnir makes, in Eldhrimnir, Sæhrimnir to boil, of meats the best; but few know how many Einherjar it feeds.

19. Geri and Freki the war-wont sates, the triumphant sire of hosts; but on wine only the famed in arms, Odin, ever lives.

20. Hugin and Munin fly each day over the spacious earth. I fear for Hugin, that he come not back, yet more anxious am I for Munin.

21. Thund roars; joyful in Thiodvitnir's water lives the fish; the rapid river seems too great for the battle-steed to ford.

22. Valgrind is the lattice called, in the plain that stands, holy before the holy gates: ancient is that lattice, but few only know how it is closed with lock.

23. Five hundred doors, and forty eke, I think, are in Valhall.
Eight hundred Einherjar will at once from each door go when they issue with the wolf to fight.

24. Five hundred floors, and forty eke, I think, has Bilskirnir with its windings.
Of all the roofed houses that I know, is my son's the greatest.

25. Heidrun the goat is called, that stands o'er Odin's hall, and bits from Lærad's branches.
He a bowl shall fill with the bright mead; that drink shall never fail.

26. Eikthyrnir the hart is called, that stands o'er Odin's hall, and bits from Lærad's branches; from his horns fall drops into Hvergelmir, whence all waters rise:-

27. Sid and Vid, Soekin and Eikin, Svöl and Gunntro, Fiörm and Fimbulthul, Rin and Rennandi, Gipul and Göpul, Gömul and Geirvimul: they round the gods' dwellings wind.
Thyn and Vin, Thöll and Höll, Grad and Gunnthorin.

28. Vina one is called, a second Vegsvin, a third Thiodnuma; Nyt and Nöt, Nön and Hrön, Slid and Hrid, Sylg and Ylg, Vid and Van, Vönd and Strönd, Giöll and Leipt; these (two) fall near to men, but fall hence to Hel,

29. Körmt and Örmt, and the Kerlaugs twain: these Thor must wade each day, when he to council goes at Yggdrasil's ash; for the As-bridge
is all on fire,the holy waters boil.

30. Glad and Gyllir, Gler and Skeidbrimir, Sillfrintopp and Sinir, Gisl and Falhofnir, Gulltopp and Lettfeti; on these steeds the Æsir each day ride, when they to council go, at Yggdrasil's ash.

31. Three roots stand on three ways under Yggdrasil's ash: Hel under one abides, under the second the Hrimthursar, under the third mankind.

32. Ratatösk is the squirrel named, which has

to run in Yggdrasil's ash; he from above the eagle's words must carry, and beneath to Nidhögg repeat.

33. Harts there are also four, which from its summits, arch-necked, gnaw. Dain and Dvalin, Duneyr and Durathror.

34. More serpents lie under Yggdrasil's ash, than any one would think of witless mortals: Goin and Moin -they are Grafvitnir's sons - Grabak and Grafvöllud, Ofnir and Svafnir, will, I ween, the branches of that tree ever lacerate.

35. Yggdrasil's ash hardship suffers greater than men know of; a hart bits it above, and in its side it rots, Nidhögg beneath tears it.

36. Hrist and Mist the horn shall bear me Skeggöld and Skögul, Hlökk and Herfjötur, Hildi and Thrudi, Göll and Geirölul, Randgrid and Radgrid, and Reginleif, these bear been to the Einherjar.

37. Arvakr and Alsvid, theirs ́tis up hence fasting the sun to draw: under their shoulder the gentle powers, the Æsir, have concealed an iron-coolness.

38. Svalin the sheild is called, which stands before the sun,the refulgent deity: rocks and ocean must, I ween, be burnt, fell it from its place.

39. Sköll the wolf is named, that the fair-faced goddess to the ocean chases; another Hati hight, he is Hrodvitnir's son; he the bright maid of heaven shall precede.

40. Of Ymir's flesh was earth created, of his blood the sea, of his bones the hills, of his hair trees and

plants, of his skull the heaven;

41. and of his brows the gentle powers formed Midgard for the sons of men; but of his brain the heavy clouds are all created.

42. Ullr's and all the gods' favour shall have, whoever first shall look to the fire; for open will the dwelling be, to the Æsirś sons, when the kettles are lifted off.

43. Ivald's sons went in days of old Skidbladnir to form, of ships the best, for the bright Frey, Njörds benign son.

44. Yggdrasil's ash is of all trees most excellent, and of all ships, Skidbladnir, of the Æsir, Odin, and of horses, Sleipnir, Bifröst of bridges, and of skalds, Bragi, Habrok of hawks, and of dogs, Garm, (Brimir of swords.)

45. Now I my face have raised to the godś triumphant sons, at that will welcome help awake; from all the Æsir, that shall penetrate, to Aegir's bench, to Aegir's compotation.

46. I am called Grim, I am called Gangleri, Herian and Hjalmberi, Thekk and Thridi, Thund and Ud,
Helblindi and Har,

47. Sad and Svipall, and Sanngetall, Herteit and Hnikar Bileyg, Baleyg, Bölverk, Fjölnir, Grim and Grimnir, Glapsvid and Fjölsvid,

48. Sidhött, Sidskegg Sigfödr, Hnikud, Alfödr, Valfödr, Atrid and Farmatýr; by one name I never have been called, since among men I have gone.

49. Grimnir I am called at Geirröds, and at Asmunds

Jalk and Kialar, when a sledge I drew; Thror at the public meetings, Vidur in battles, Oski and Omi, Jafnhar and Biflindi, Göndlir and Harbard with the gods.

50. Svidur and Svidrir I was at Sökkmimir's called, and beguiled that ancient Jötun, when of Midvitnir's renowned son I was the sole destroyer.

51. Drunken art thou, Geirröd, thou hast drunk too much, thou art greatly by mead beguiled. Much didst thou lose, when thou wast of my help bereft, of all the Einherjar's and Odin's favour.

52. Many things I told thee, but thou hast few remembered: thy friends mislead thee. My friend's sword lying I see, with blood all dripping.

53. The fallen by the sword Ygg shall now have; thy life is now run out: Wroth with thee are the Disir: Odin thou now shalt see: draw near to me if thou canst.

54. Odin I now am named, Ygg I was called before, before that, Thund, Vakr and Skilfing, Vafudr and Hroptatýr, with the gods, Gaut and Jalk, Ofnir and Svafnir, all which I believe to be names of me alone.

King Geirröd was sitting with his sword lying across his knees, half drawn from the scabbard, but on finding that it was Odin, he rose for the purpose of removing him from the fires, when the sword slipt from his hand with the hilt downwards; and the king having stumbled, the sword peirced him through and killed him. Odin then vanished, and Agnar was king for a long time after.

4: Hrafnagaldur Óðins: Odin's Ravens' Song

This very obscure poem has been regarded as a fragment only of a poem, of which the beginning and end are wanting. With regard to the beginning, the want may possibly be more apparent than real; the strophes 2-5 being in fact a sort of introduction, although they do not at first strike us as such, in consequence of the obscurity of the 1st strophe, which seems very slightly connected with the following ones, in which the gods and dwarfs are described as in council, on account of certain warnings and forebodings of their approaching downfall, or Ragnarök. Another point of difficulty is its title, there being nothing in the whole poem to connect it with Odin's ravens, except the mention of Hugr (Hugin) in the 3rd strophe. Erik Halson, a learned Icelander, after having spent or wasted ten years in an attempt to explain this poem, confessed that he understood little or nothing of it. In its mythology, too, we find parts assigned to some of the personages, of which no traces occur in either Sæmunds' or Snorri's Edda; though we are hardly justified in pronouncing it, with more than one scholar of eminence, a fabrication of later times.

1. Alfather works,[1] the Alfar discern,[2] the Vanir know,[3] the Nornir indicate,[4] the Ividia brings forth,[5] men endure,[6] the Thursar await,[7] the Valkyriur long.[8]

2. The forebodings the Æsir suspected to be evil; treacherous Vættar had the runes confounded. Urd was enjoined to guard Odhroerir, powerfully to protect it against the increasing multitude.

3. Hug[9] then goes forth, explores the heavens, the powers fear disaster from

delay. 'Twas Thrain's belief that the dream was ominous; Dain's thought that the dream was dark.

4. Among the dwarfs virtue decays; worlds sink down to Ginnung's abyss. Oft will Asvid strike them down, oft the fallen again collect.

5. Stand no longer shall earth or sun.
The stream of air with corruption laden shall not cease.
Hidden is in Mim's limpid well men's certain knowledge. Understand ye yet, or what?

6. In the dales dwells the prescient Dis, from Yggdrasil's ash sunk down, of alfen race, Idun by name, the youngest of Ivaldi's elder children.

7. She ill brooked her descent, under the hoar tree's trunk confined. She would not happy be with Nörvi's daughter, accustomed to a pleasanter abode at home.

8. The triumphant gods saw Nanna[10] sorrowing in earth's deep sanctuaries; a wolf's skin they gave her, in which herself she clad, changed her feelings, practiced guile, alter'd her aspect.

9. Vidrir selected Bifröst's guardian, of the Giöll-sun's keeper to inquire all that she knew of every world; Bragi and Lopt should witness bear.

10. Magic songs they sung, rode on wolves the god[11] and gods.[12] At the heavenly house, Odin listened, in Hlidskjalf; let them go forth on their long way.

11. The wise god asked the cupbearer of the gods' progeny and their associates, whether of heaven, or Hel, or earth, she knew the origin, duration, or dissolution?

12. She spoke not, she could no words to the anxious gods bring forth, nor a sound uttered; tears flowed from the head's orbs; with pain repressed they flow anew.

13. As from the east, from Elivagar, the thorn is impelled by the ice-cold Thurs, wherewith Dain all people strikes over the fair mid-earth;

14. When every faculty is lulled, the hands sink, totters with drowsiness the bright, sword-girt As;[13] drives away the current the giantess's[14] blandishment of the mind's agitations of all people,[15]

15. So to the gods appeared Jorun to be affected, with sorrows swollen, when they no answer got;
they strove the more the greater the repulse; still less than they had hoped did their words prevail.

16. When the leader of the inquiring travellers, the guardian of Herian's loud-sounding horn took the son of Nal for his companion, Grimnir's skald[16]
at the place kept watch.

17. Vingolf reached Vidur's ministers, both borne
by Forniots kin. They entered, and the Æsir forthwith saluted, at Ygg's convivial meeting.

18. Hangatyr they hailed, of Æsir the most blissful; potent drink in the high seat they wished him to enjoy, and the gods to sit happy at the feast, ever with Yggiung pleasure to share.

19. On benches seated, at Bölverk's bidding, the company of gods were with Sæhrimnir sated. Skögul at the tables, from

Hnikaŕs vessel, measured out mead, in Mimiŕs[17] horns.

20. Of many thing inquired, when the meal was over, the high gods of Heimdall, the goddesses of Loki, - whether the maid had uttered divinations or wise words?- From noon until twilight's advent.

21. Ill they showed it had fallen out, their errand bootless, little to glory in. A lack of counsel seemed likely, how from the maiden they might an answer get.

22. Omi answered; "Night is the time for new counsels; till the morrow let reflect each one competent to give advice helpful to the Æsir."
23. Ran along the ways of mother Rind,[18] the desired repast of Fenrisulf.[19]

Went from the guild, bade the gods farewell Hropt and Frigg, as, before Hrimfaxi,

24. the son of Delling urged on his horse adorned with precious jewels.
Over Mannheim shines the horse's mane, the steed Dvalin's deluder drew in his chariot.

25. In the north boundary of the spacious earth, under the outmost root of the noble tree, went to their couches Gygiar and Thursar, spectres, dwarfs,and Murk Alfs.

26. The powers rose, the Alfs' illuminator northwards towards Niflheim[20] chased the night.
Up Argjöll ran Ulfruńs son, the mighty hornblower, of heaveńs heights.

[1] through all nature.
[2] impending evil
[3] that evil is at hand
[4] evil
[5] her monstrous offspring
[6] calamity
[7] their day of freedom
[8] for conflict
[9] Hugin, Odin's raven?
[10] Here Idun is apparently so called.
[11] Rögnir, Odin [Rydberg identifies Rognir as the elf-smith Thjazi, who becomes Volund the sword-smith]
[12] Rögnir and Regin, Odin and the powers? [Rydberg reads this as Volund and his brothers, who aspire to be gods. They are also called vættr, wights and dokkalfr, dark-elves in this poem according to Rydberg..]
[13] Heimdall
[14] Night
[15] This and the preceding strophe appear to be out of their place, and have by Simrock, not without reason, been inserted after the 21st.
[16] Bragi
[17] Minni's horns, Stockh. Edit. See Grimm D.M. p 52, 53 Petersen, N.M. p. 179. Minni is probably a later gloss.
[18] Earth
[19] All conjectures. Fenri seems confounded with Hati. See N.M.
[20] That the poem lacks the end as well as the beginning appears probable from the circumstance that no further mention is made of Bragi and Idun. Simrock is inclined to think that in the Vegtamskviða we are to look for the ending; but this does not fill up the chasm.

5: Vegtamskvida eða Baldrs Dreams
The Lay of Vegtam, or Baldŕs Dreams.

1. Together were the Æsir all in council, and the Asyniur all in conference, and they consulted, the mighty gods, why Baldr had oppressive dreams.

2. To that god his slumber was most afflicting; his auspicious dreams seemed departed.
They the Jötuns questioned, wise seers of the future, whether this might not forebode calamity?

3. The responses said that to death destined was Ullr's kinsman, of all the dearest: that caused grief to Frigg and Svafnir, and to the other powers —
On a course they resolved:

4. that they would send to every being, assurance to solicit, Baldr not to harm.
All species swore oaths to spare him; Frigg received all their vows and compacts.

5. Valfather fears something defective; he thinks the Hamingiur may have departed; the Æsir he convenes, their counsel craves: at the deliberation
much is devised.

6. Uprose Odin lord of men, and on Sleipnir he the saddle laid; rode thence down to Niflhel.
A dog he met, from Hel coming.

7. It was blood—stained on its breast, on its slaughter—craving throat, and nether jaw.
It bayed and widely gaped at the sire of magic song: — long it howled.

8. Forth rode Odin — the ground rattled — till to Hel's lofty house he came.
Then rode Ygg to the eastern gate, where he knew there was a Vala's grave.

9. To the prophetess he began a magic song to chant, towards the north looked, potent runes applied, a spell pronounced, an answer demanded,
until compelled she rose, and with deathlike voice she said:

Vala
10. "What man is this, to me unknown who has for me increased an irksome course?
I have with snow been decked by rain beaten, and with dew moistened: long have I been dead."

Vegtam
11. "Vegtam is my name, I am Valtam's son.
Tell thou me of Hel: from earth I call on thee.
For whom are those benches strewed o'er with rings, those costly couches o'erlaid with gold?"

Vala
12. "Here stands mead, for Baldr brewed, over the bright potion a shield is laid; but the Æsir race are in despair.
By compulsion I have spokenI will now be silent."

Vegtam
13. "Be thou not silent, Vala!I will question thee, until I know all.
I will yet knowwho will Baldr's slayer be, and Odin's son of life bereave."

Vala
14. "Hödr will hither his glorious brother send, he of Baldr will the slayer be,and Odin's son of life bereave.

By compulsion I have spoken; I will now be silent."

Vegtam
15. "Be not silent, Vala! I will question thee, until I know all.
I will yet know who on Hödr vengeance will inflict or Baldr's slayer raise on the pile."

Vala
16. "Rind a son shall bear, in the western halls: he shall slay Odin's son, when one night old.
He a hand will not wash, nor his head comb, ere he to the pile has borne Baldr's adversary.
By compulsion I have spoken; I will now be silent."

Vegtam
17. "Be not silent, Vala! I will question thee, until I know all.
I will yet know who the maidens are, that weep at will, and heavenward cast their neck—veils?
Tell me but that: till then thou sleepest not."

Vala
18. "Not Vegtam art thou, as I before believed; rather art thou Odin, lord of men!"

Odin
19. "Thou art no Vala, nor wise woman,rather art thou the mother of three Thursar."

Vala
20. "Home ride thou, Odin! and exult.
Thus shall never more man again visit me, until Loki free from his bonds escapes, and Ragnarök all—destroying comes."

6: Hávamál: The High One's[1] Lay

Council to the visitor.

1. All door-ways, before going forward, should be looked to; for difficult it is to know where foes may sit within a dwelling.

2. Givers, hail! A guest is come in: where shall he sit? In much hast is he, who on the ways has to try his luck.

3. Fire is needful to him who is come in, and whose knees are frozen; food and raiment a man requires, who o'er the fell has travelled.

4. Water to him is needful who for refection comes, a towel and hospitable invitation, a good reception; if he can get it, discourse and answer.

5. Wit is needful to him who travels far: at home all is easy. A laughing-stock is he who nothing knows, and with the instructed sits.

6. Of his understanding no one should be proud, but rather in conduct cautious. When the prudent and taciturn come to a dwelling, harm seldom befalls the cautious; for a firmer friend no man ever gets than great sagacity.

7. A way guest,[2] who to refection comes, keeps a cautious silence, with his ears listens, and with his eyes observes: so explores every prudent man.

8. He is happy, who for himself obtains fame and kind words: less sure is that which a man must have in another's breast.

9. He is happy, who in himself possesses fame and wit while living; for bad counsels have oft been received from another's breast.

10. A better burthen no man bears on the way than much good sense; that is thought better than riches in a strange place; such is the recourse of the indigent.

11. A worse provision on the way he cannot carry than too much beer-bibbing; so good is not, as it is said, beer for the sons of men.

12. A worse provision no man can take from table than too much beer-bibbing: for the more he drinks the less control he has of his own mind.

13. Oblivion's heron 'tis called that over potations hovers,[3] he steals the minds of men. With this bird's pinions I was fettered in Gunnlöds dwelling.

14. Drunk I was, I was over-drunk, at that cunning Fjalar's. It's the best drunkenness, when every one after it regains his reason.

15. Taciturn and prudent, and in war daring should a king's children be; joyous and liberal every one should be until the hour of his death.

16. A cowardly man thinks he will ever live, if warfare he avoids; but old age will give him no peace, though spears may spare him.

17. A fool gapes when to a house he comes, to himself mutters or is silent; but all at once, if he gets drink, then is the man's mind displayed.

18. He alone knows who wanders wide, and has

much experienced, by what disposition each man is ruled, who common sense possesses.

19. Let a man hold the cup, yet of the mead drink moderately, speak sensibly or be silent. As of a fault no man will admonish thee, if thou goest betimes to sleep.

20. A greedy man, if he be not moderate, eats to his mortal sorrow. Oftentimes his belly draws laughter on a silly man, who among the prudent comes.

21. Cattle know when to go home, and then from grazing cease; but a foolish man never knows his stomach's measure.

22. A miserable man, and ill-conditioned, sneers at every thing; one thing he knows not, which he ought to know, that he is not free from faults.

23. A foolish man is all night awake, pondering over everything; he than grows tired; and when morning comes, all is lament as before.

24. A foolish man thinks all who on him smile to be his friends; he feels it not, although they speak ill of him, when he sits among the clever.

25. A foolish man thinks all who speak him fair to be his friends; but he will find, if into court he comes, that he has few advocates.

26. A foolish man thinks he know everything if placed in unexpected difficulty; but he knows not
what to answer, if to the test he is put.

27. A foolish man, who among people comes, had best be silent; for no one knows that he knows

nothing, unless he talks to much.
He who previously knew nothing will still know nothing talk he ever so much.

28. He thinks himself wise, who can ask questions
and converse also; conceal his ignorance no one can, because it circulates among men.

29. He utters too many futile words who is never silent; a garrulous tongue, if it be not checked, sings often to its own harm.

30. For a gazing-stock no man shall have another, although he come a stranger to his house.
Many a one thinks himself wise, if he is not questioned, and can sit in a dry habit.

31. Clever thinks himself the guest who jeers a guest, if he takes to flight.
Knows it not certainly he who prates at meat, whether he babbles among foes.

32. Many men are mutually well-disposed, yet at table will torment each other.
That strife will ever be; guest will guest irritate.

33. Early meals a man should often take, unless to a friend's house he goes; else he will sit and mope, will seem half-famished, and can of few things inquire.

34. Long is and indirect the way to a bad friend's, though by the road he dwell; but to a good friend's the paths lie direct, though he be far away.

35. A guest should depart, not always stay in one place.
The welcome becomes unwelcome, if he too long

continues in another's house.

36. One's own house is best, small though it be; at home is every one his own master.
Though he but two goats possess, and a straw-thatched cot, even that is better than begging.

37. One's own house is best, small though it be, at home is every one his own master.
Bleeding at heart is he, who has to ask for food at every meal-tide.

38. Leaving in the field his arms, let no man go a foot's length forward; for it is hard to know when on the way a man may need his weapon.

39. I have never found a man so bountiful, or so hospitable that he refused a present; of his property so liberal that he scorned a recompense.

40. Of the property which he has gained no man should suffer need; for the hated oft is spared what for the dear was destined.
Much goes worse than is expected.

41. With arms and vestments friends should each other gladden, those which are in themselves most sightly.
Givers and requiters are longest friends, if all [else] goes well.[4]

42. To his friend a man should be a friend, and gifts with gifts requite.
Laughter with laughter men should receive, but leasing with lying.

43. To his friend a man should be a friend, to him and to his friend; but of his foe no man shall the friend's friend be.

44. Know, if thou has a friend whom thou fully trustest, and from whom

thou woulds't good derive, thou shouldst blend thy mind with his, and gifts exchange, and often go to see him.

45. If thou hast another, whom thou little trustest, yet wouldst good from him derive, thou shouldst speak him fair, but think craftily, and leasing pay with lying.

46. But of him yet further, whom thou little trustest, and thou suspectest his affection; before him thou shouldst laugh, and contrary to thy thoughts speak: requital should the gift resemble.

47. I was once young, I was journeying alone, and lost my way; rich I thought myself, when I met another. Man is the joy of man.

48. Liberal and brave men live best, they seldom cherish sorrow; but a base-minded man dreads everything; the niggardly is uneasy even at gifts.

49. My garments in a field I gave away to two wooden men: heroes they seemed to be, when they got cloaks: exposed to insult is a naked man.[5]

50. A tree withers that on a hill-top stands; protects it neither bark nor leaves: such is the man whom no one favours: why should he live long?

51. Hotter than fire love for five days burns between false friends; but is quenched when the sixth day comes, and friendship is all impaired.

52. Something great is not [always] to be given, praise is often for a trifle bought. With half a loaf and a tilted vessel I got myself a comrade.

53. Little are the sand-grains, little the wits, little

the minds of [some] men; for all men are not wise alike: men are everywhere by halves.

54. Moderately wise should each one be, but never over-wise: of those men the lives are fairest, who know much well.

55. Moderately wise should each one be, but never over-wise; for a wise man's heart is seldom glad, if he is all-wise who owns it.

56. Moderately wise should each one be, but never over-wise. His destiny let know no man beforehand; his mind will be freest from care.

57. Brand burns from brand until it is burnt out; fire is from fire quickened. Man to man becomes known by speech, but a fool by his bashful silence.

58. He should early rise, who another's property or life desires to have. Seldom a sluggish wolf gets prey, or a sleeping man victory.

59. Early should rise he who has few workers, and go his work to see to; greatly is he retarded who sleeps the morn away. Wealth half depends on energy.

60. Of dry planks and roof-shingles a man knows the measure; of the fire-wood that may suffice, both measure and time.

61. Washed and reflected let a man ride to the Thing,[6] although his garments be not too good; of his shoes and breeches let no one be ashamed, nor of his horse, although he have not a good one.

62. Inquire and impart should every man of sense,

who will be accounted sage. Let one only know, a second may not; if three, all the world knows.

63. Gasps and gapes, when to the sea he comes, the eagles over old ocean; so is a man, who among many comes, and has few advocates.

64. His power should every sagacious man use with discretion; for he will find, when among the bold he comes, that no one alone is the doughtiest.

65. Circumspect and reserved every man should be, and wary in trusting friends. Of the words that a man says to another he often pays the penalty.

66. Much too early I came to many places, but too late to others; the beer was drunk, or not ready: the disliked seldom hits the moment.

67. Here and there I should have been invited, if I a meal had needed; or two hams had hung, at that true friend's, where of one I had eaten.

68. Fire is best among the sons of men, and the sight of the sun, if his health a man can have, with a life free from vice.

69. No man lacks everything, although his health be bad: one in his sons is happy, one in abundant wealth, one in his good works.

70. It is better to live, even to live miserably; a living man can always get a cow. I saw fire consume the rich man's property, and death stood without his door.

71. The halt can ride on horseback, the one-handed drive cattle; the

deaf fight and be useful: to be blind is better than to be burnt:[7] no one gets good from a corpse.

72. A son is better, even if born late, after his father's departure. Gravestones seldom stand by the way-side unless raised by a kinsman to a kinsman.

73. Two are adversaries: the tongue is the bane of the head: under every cloak I expect a hand.

74. At night is joyful he who is sure of travelling enjoyment. [A ship's yards are short.][8] Variable is an autumn night. Many are the weather's changes in five days, but more in a month.

75. He [only] knows not who knows nothing, that many a one apes another. One man is rich, another poor: let him not be thought blameworthy.

76. Cattle die, kindred die, we ourselves also die;
but the fair fame never dies of him who has earned it.

77. Cattle die, kindred die, we ourselves also die; but I know one thing that never dies, - judgment on each one dead.

78. Full storehouses I saw at Dives' sons': now bear they the beggar's staff. Such are riches; as is the twinkling of an eye: of friends they are most fickle.

79. A foolish man, if he acquires wealth or a woman's love, pride grows within him, but wisdom never: he goes on more and more arrogant.

Advice for all men.

80. Then 'tis made manifest, if of runes thou questionest him, those to

the high ones known, which the great powers invented, and the great talker[9] painted, that he had best hold silence.

81. At eve the day is to be praised, a woman after she is burnt, a sword after it is proved, a maid after she is married, ice after it has passed away, beer after it is drunk.

82. In the wind one should hew wood, in a breeze row out to sea, in the dark talk with a lass: many are the eyes of day. In a ship voyages are to be made, but a shield is for protection, a sword for striking, but a damsel for a kiss.

83. By the fire one should drink beer, on the ice slide; but a horse that is lean, a sword that is rusty; feed a horse at home, but a dog at the farm.

84. In a maiden's words no one should place faith, nor in what a woman says; for on a turning wheel
have their hearts been formed, and guile in their breasts been laid;

85. in a creaking bow, a burning flame, a yawning wolf, a chattering crow, a grunting swine, a rootless tree, a waxing wave, a boiling kettle,

86. a flying dart, a falling billow, a one night's ice, a coiled serpent, a woman's bed-talk, or a broken sword, a bear's play, or a royal child,

87. a sick calf, a self-willed thrall, a flattering prophetess, a corpse newly slain, [a serene sky, a laughing lord, a barking dog, and a harlot's grief];

88. an early sown field let no one trust,nor prematurely in a son: weather rules the field,

and wit the son, each of which is doubtful;

89. a brother's murderer, though on the high road met, a half-burnt house, an over-swift horse, (a horse is useless, if a leg be broken, no man is so confiding as to trust any of these.

Lessons for lovers.

90. Such is the love of women, who falsehood meditate, as if one drove not rough-shod, on slippery ice, a spirited two-years old and unbroken horse; or as in a raging storm a helmless ship is beaten; or as if the halt were set to catch a reindeer in the thawing fell.[10]

91. Openly I now speak, because I both sexes know: unstable are men's minds towards women; 'tis then we speak most fair when we most falsely think: that deceives even the cautious.

92. Fair shall speak, and money offer, who would obtain a woman's love. Praise the form of a fair damsel; he gets who courts her.

93. At love should no one ever wonder in another: a beauteous countenance oft captivates the wise, which captivates not the foolish.

94. Let no one wonder at another's folly, it is the lot of many. All-powerful desire makes of the sons of men fools even of the wise.

95. The mind only knows what lies near the heart, that alone is conscious of our affections. No disease is worse to a sensible man than not to be content with himself.

96. That I experienced, when in the reeds I sat, awaiting my delight. Body and soul to me was

that discreet maiden: nevertheless I posses her not.

Odin's love quests

97. Billing's lass[11] on her couch I found, sun-bright, sleeping. A prince's joy to me seemed naught, if not with that form to live.

98. "Yet nearer eve must thou, Odin, come, if thou wilt talk the maiden over; all will be disastrous, unless we alone are privy to such misdeed."

99. I returned, thinking to love, at her wise desire. I thought I should obtain her whole heart and love.

100. When next I came the bold warriors were all awake, with lights burning, and bearing torches: thus was the way to pleasure closed.

101. But at the approach of morn, when again I came, the household all was sleeping; the good damsel's dog alone I found tied to the bed.

102. Many a fair maiden, when rightly known, towards men is fickle: that I experienced, when that discreet maiden I strove to seduce: contumely of every kind that wily girl heaped upon me; nor of that damsel gained I aught.

103. At home let a man be cheerful, and towards a guest liberal; of wise conduct he should be, of good memory and ready speech; if much knowledge he desires, he must often talk on good.

104. Fimbulfambi he is called who little has to say: such is the nature of the simple.

105. The old Jötun I sought; now I am come back: little got I there by silence; in many words I

spoke to my advantage in Suttung's halls.[12]

106. Gunnlöd gave me, on her golden seat, a draught of the precious mead; a bad recompense I afterwards made her, for her whole soul, her fervent love.

107. Rati's mouth I caused to make a space, and to gnaw the rock; over and under me were the Jötun's ways: thus I my head did peril.

108. Of a well-assumed form I made good use: few things fail the wise; for Odhrærir is now come up to men's earthly dwellings.

109. 'Tis to me doubtful that I could have come from the Jötun's courts, had not Gunnlöd aided me, that good damsel, over whom I laid my arm.

110. On the day following came the Hrim-thursar,
to learn something of the High One, in the High One's hall: after Bölverk they inquired, whether he with the gods were come, or Suttung had destroyed him?

111. Odin, I believe, a ring-oath[13] gave. Who in his faith will trust? Suttung defrauded, of his drink bereft, and Gunnlöd made to weep!

Loddfafnismal: counseling the stray-singer

112. Time 'tis to discourse from the preacher's chair. — By the well of Urd I silent sat, I saw and meditated, I listened to men's words.

113. Of runes I heard discourse, and of things divine, nor of graving them were they silent, nor of sage counsels, at the High One's hall. In the

High One's hall. I thus heard say:

114. I counsel thee, Loddfafnir, to take advise: thou wilt profit if thou takest it. Rise not a night, unless to explore, or art compelled to go out.

115. I counsel thee, Loddfafnir, to take advice, thou wilt profit if thou takest it. In an enchantress's embrace thou mayest not sleep, so that in her arms she clasp thee.

116. She will be the cause that thou carest not for Thing or prince's words; food thou wilt shun and human joys; sorrowful wilt thou go to sleep.

117. I counsel thee, etc. Another's wife entice thou never to secret converse.

118. I counsel thee, etc. By fell or firth if thou have to travel, provide thee well with food.

119. I counsel thee, etc. A bad man let thou never know thy misfortunes; for from a bad man thou never wilt obtain a return for thy good will.

120. I saw mortally wound a man a wicked woman's words; a false tongue caused his death, and most unrighteously.

121. I counsel thee, etc. If thou knowest thou has a friend, whom thou well canst trust, go oft to visit him; for with brushwood overgrown, and with high grass, is the way that no one treads.

122. I counsel thee, etc. — A good man attract to thee in pleasant converse; and salutary speech learn while thou livest.

123. I counsel thee, etc. With thy friend be thou never first to quarrel.

Care gnaws the heart, if thou to no one canst thy whole mind disclose.

124. I counsel thee, etc. Words thou never shouldst exchange with a witless fool;

125. for from an ill-conditioned man thou wilt never get a return for good; but a good man will
bring thee favour by his praise.

126. There is a mingling of affection, where one can tell another all his mind. Everything is better than being with the deceitful. He is not another's friend who ever says as he says.

127. I counsel thee, etc. Even in three words quarrel not with a worse man: often the better yields, when the worse strikes.

128. I counsel thee, etc. Be not a shoemaker, nor a shaftmaker, unless for thyself it be; for a shoe if ill made, or a shaft if crooked, will call down evil on thee.

129. I counsel thee, etc. Wherever of injury thou knowest, regard that injury as thy own; and give to thy foes no peace.

130. I counsel thee, etc. Rejoiced at evil be thou never; but let good give thee pleasure.

131. I counsel thee, etc. In a battle look not up, (like swine the sons of men become) that men may not fascinate thee.

132. If thou wilt induce a good woman to pleasant converse, thou must promise fair, and hold to it; no one turns from good if it can be got.

133. I enjoin thee to be wary, but not over wary;

at drinking be thou most wary, and with another's wife; and thirdly, that thieves delude thee not.

134. With insult or derision treat thou never a guest or wayfarer, they often little know, who sit within, or what race they are who come.

135. Vices and virtues the sons of mortals bear in their breasts mingled; no one is so good that no failing attends him, nor so bad as to be good for nothing.

136. At a hoary speaker laugh thou never; often is good that which the aged utter, oft from a shriveled hide discreet words issue; from those whose skin is pendent and decked with scars, and who go tottering among the vile.

137. I counsel thee, etc. Rail not at a guest, nor from thy gate thrust him; treat well the indigent; they will speak well of thee.

138. Strong is the bar that must be raised to admit all. Do thou give a penny, or they will call down on thee every ill in thy limbs.

139. I counsel thee, etc. Wherever thou beer drinkest, invoke to thee the power of earth; for earth is good against drink, fire for distempers, the oak for constipation, a corn-ear for sorcery a hall for domestic strife. In bitter hates invoke the moon; the biter for bite-injuries is good; but runes against calamity; fluid let earth absorb.

Continued in: RunatalsÞáttr Oðins or Odińs Rune-song.

[1] Odin is the 'High One.' The poem is a collection of rules and maxims and stories, of himself, some of them not very consistent with our ideas of a supreme deity.

[2] In the Copenhagen paper Ms. F, this strophe begins with the following three lines—

Wit is needful
To him who travels far:
Harm seldom befalls the wary:

They are printed in the Stockholm edition of the original by Afzelius and Rask, and in the Swedish translation of Afzelius.

[3] I am unable to explain this allusion; but see Grimm, D.M. p. 1086. 2nd edit. It was in an eagle's guise that Odin escaped from Gunnlöd's dwelling. See Northern Mythology I, p. 42

[4] The sense of this line seems doubtful: I have adopted the version of Finn Magnusen.

[5] Akin to this are Danish proverbs: Man kan og klæde en Staver op: Even a stake may be dressed up; Som man er klædt er man hædt: As one is clad so is one honoured, as the toad said springing out of the cream bowl. P. Syv, Danske Ordsprog, p. 70.

[6] The public meeting.

[7] That is dead on a funeral pyre.

[8] This line is evidently an interpolation.

[9] Odin.

[10] From this line it appears that the poem is of Norwegian or Swedish origin, as the reindeer was unknown in Iceland before the middle of the 18th century, when it was introduced by royal command. Note by Finn Magnusen in 4to edit. III. P. 107.

[11] The story of Odin and Billing's daughter is no longer extant; but compare the story of Odin and Rinda in Saxo, p. 126, edit. Müller & Vellschow.

[12] For the story of Suttung and Gunnlöd, see the Prose, or Snorri's Edda in "Northern Antiquities," edit. Bohn. P. 461. North. Mythol. I, p. 42.

[13] In the pagan North oaths were taken on a holy ring or bracelet, as with us on the Gospels, a sacred ring being kept in the temple for the purpose.

7: Hávamál: RunatalsÞáttr Oðins: Odińs Rune-song.

140. I know that I hung, on a wind-rocked tree, nine whole nights, with a spear wounded, and to Odin offered, myself to myself; on that tree, of which no one knows from what root it springs.

141. Bread no one gave me, nor a horn of drink, downward I peered, to runes applied myself, wailing learnt them, then fell down thence.

142. Potent songs nine from the famed son I learned of Bölthorn, Bestla's sire, and a draught obtained of the precious mead, drawn from Odhrærir.

143. Then I began to bear fruit, and to know many things, to grow and well thrive: word by word I sought out words, fact by fact I sought out facts.

144. Runes thou wilt find, and explained characters, very large characters, very potent characters, which the great speaker depicted, and the high powers formed, and the powers' prince graved:

145. Odin among the Æsir,
but among the Alfar, Dáin,
and Dvalin for the dwarfs,
Ásvid for the Jötuns:
some I myself graved.

146. Knowest thou how to grave them?
knowest thou how to expound them?
knowest thou how to depict them?
knowest thou how to prove them?
knowest thou how to pray?
knowest thou how to offer?

knowest thou how to send?[2]
knowest thou how to consume?

147. ‘Tis better not to pray than too much offer; a gift ever looks to a return. ‘Tis better not to send
than too much consume. So Thund graved before the origin of men, where he ascended, to whence he afterwards came.

148. Those songs I know which the king’s wife knows not nor son of man. Help the first is called,
for that will help thee against strifes and cares.

149. For the second I know, what the sons of men require, who will as leeches live.

150. For the third I know,[3] if I have great need
to restrain my foes, the weapons’ edge I deaden: of my adversaries nor arms nor wiles harm aught.

151. For the forth I know, if men place bonds on my limbs, I so sing that I can walk; the fetter starts from my feet, and the manacle from my hands.

152. For the fifth I know, I see a shot from a hostile hand, a shaft flying amid the host, so swift it cannot fly that I cannot arrest it, if only I get sight of it.

153. For the sixth I know, if one wounds me with a green tree’s roots;[4] also if a man declares hatred to me, harm shall consume them sooner than me.

154. For the seventh I know, if a lofty house I see
blaze o’er its inmates, so furiously it shall not burn that I cannot save it. That song I can sing.

155. For the eighth I know, what to all is useful to learn: where hatred grows among the sons of men - that I can quickly assuage.

156. For the ninth I know, if I stand in need my bark on the water to save, I can the wind on the waves allay, and the sea lull.

157. For the tenth I know, if I see troll-wives sporting in air, I can so operate that they will forsake their own forms, and their own minds.

158. For the eleventh I know, if I have to lead my ancient friends to battle, under their shields I sing,
and with power they go safe to the fight, safe from the fight; safe on every side they go.

159. For the twelfth I know, if on a tree I see a corpse swinging from a halter, I can so grave and in runes depict, that the man shall walk, and with me converse.

160. For the thirteenth I know, if on a young man I sprinkle water, he shall not fall, though he into battle come: that man shall not sink before swords.

161. For the fourteenth I know, if in the society of men I have to enumerate the gods, Æsir and Alfar, I know the distinctions of all. This few unskilled can do.

162. For the fifteenth I know what the dwarf Thiodreyrir sang before Delling's doors. Strength he sang to the Æsir, and to the Alfar prosperity, wisdom to Hroptatýr.

163. For the sixteenth I know, if a modest maiden's favour and affection I desire to possess,

the soul I change of the white-armed damsel, and wholly turn her mind.

164. For the seventeenth I know, that that young maiden will reluctantly avoid me. These songs, Loddfafnir! thou wilt long have lacked; yet it may be good if thou understandest them, profitable if thou learnest them.

165. For the eighteenth I know that which I never teach to maid or wife of man, (all is better what one only knows. This is the closing of the songs) save her alone who clasps me in her arms, or is my sister.

166. Now are sung the High-one's songs, in the High-one's hall, to the sons of men all-useful, but useless to the Jötun's sons.
Hail to him who has sung them!
Hail to him who knows them!
May he profit who has learnt them!
Hail to hose who have listened to them!

[1] The first eight strophes of this composition require an explanation which I am incompetent to afford. They have had many interpreters and as many interpretations. The idea of Odin hanging on a tree would seem to have been suggested by what we read of the grove at Upsala, or Sigtuna, in which the victims to that deity were suspended from the trees. In the guise of an unknown wanderer, Odin may be supposed to have been captured and thus offered to himself. It no doubt refers to some lost legend.
[2] Probably, send them (the runes) forth on their several missions.

[3] The miraculous powers here ascribed by Odin to himself bear, in many instances, a remarkable similarity to those attributed to him by Snorri (Yngl. Saga, cc. 6+7).
[4] The ancient inhabitants of the North believed that the roots of trees were particularly fitted for hurtful trolldom, or witchcraft, and that wounds caused thereby were mortal. In India, a similar superstition prevails of the hurtfulness of the roots of trees. F.M.

8: Hymiskviða: The Lay of Hymir.

1. Once the celestial gods had been taking fish, and were in compotation, ere they the truth discovered.[1] Rods[2] they shook, and blood inspected, when they found at Ægir's a lack of kettles.

2. Sat the rock-dweller glad as a child, much like the son of Miskorblindi. In his eyes looked Ygg's son[3] steadfastly. "Thou to the Æsir shalt oft a compotation give."

3. Caused trouble to the Jötun th' unwelcomed-worded As: he forthwith meditated vengeance on the gods. Sif's husband he besought a kettle him to bring. "in which I beer for all of you may brew."

4. The illustrious gods found that impossible, nor could the exalted powers it accomplish, till from trueheartedness, Tý to Hlorridi much friendly counsel gave.

5. "There dwell eastward of Elivagar the all-wise Hýmir, at heaven's end. My sire, fierce of mood, a kettle owns, a capacious caldron, a rast in depth."

Thor
6. "Knowest thou whether we can get the liquor-boiler?" Tý Yes, friend! if we stratagem employ." Rapidly they drove forward that day from Asgard, till to the giant's home they came.

7. Thor stalled his goats, splendid of horn, then turned him to the hall that Hýmir owned. The son his granddam found to him most loathful; heads she had nine hundred.

8. But another came all-golden forth, fair-browed, bearing the beer-cup to her son:

9. "Ye Jötuns' kindred! I will you both, ye daring pair, under the kettles place. My husband is oftentimes niggard toward guests, to ill-humour prone."

10. But the monster, the fierce-souled Hýmir, late returned home from the chase. He the hall entered, the icebergs resounded, as the churl approached; the thicket on his cheeks was frozen.

11. "Hail to thee, Hýmir! be of good cheer: now they son is come to thy hall, whom we expected from his long journey; him accompanies our famed adversary, the friend of man, who Veor hight.

12. See where they sit under the hall's gable, as if to shun thee: the pillar stands before them." In shivers flew the pillar at the Jötun's glance; the beam was first broken in two.

13. Eight kettles fell, but only one of them, a hard-hammered cauldron, whole from the column. The two came forth, but the old Jötun with eyes surveyed his adversary.

14. Augured to him his mind no good, when he saw the giantess's sorrow on the floor coming. Then were three oxen taken, and the Jötun bade them forthwith be boiled.

15. Each one they made by the head shorter, and to the fire afterwards bore them. Sif's consort ate, ere to sleep he went, completely, he alone, two of Hýmir's beeves.

16. Seemed to the hoary friend of Hrúgnir Hlorridi's refection full well large: "We three to-morrow night shall be compelled on what we catch to live."

17. Veor said he would on the sea row, if the bold Jötun him would with baits supply: "To the herd betake thee, (if thou in thy courage trustest, crusher of the rock-dwellers!) for baits to seek.

18. I expect that thou wilt bait from an ox easily obtain." The guest in haste to the forest went, where stood an all-black ox before him.

19. The Thursar's bane wrung from an ox the high fastness of his two horns. "To me thy work seems
worse by far, ruler of keels! than if thou hadst sat quiet."

20. The lord of goats the apes' kinsman besought the horse of plank farther out to move; but the Jötun declared his slight desire farther to row.

21. The mightily Hýmir drew, he alone, two whales up with his hook; but at the stern abaft Veor cunningly made him a line.

22. Fixed on the hook the shield of men, the serpent's slayer, the ox's head. Gaped at the bait the foe of gods, the encircler beneath of every land.[4]

23. Drew up boldly the mighty Thor the worm with venom glistening, up to the side; with his hammer struck, on his foul head's summit, like a rock towering, the wolf's own brother.

24. The icebergs resounded, the caverns howled, the old earth shrank together: at length the fish back into the ocean sank.[5]

25. The Jötun was little glad, as they rowed back, so that the powerful

Hýmir nothing spake, but the oar moved in another course.

26. "Wilt thou do half the work with me, either the whales home to the dwelling bear, or the boat fast bind?"

27. Hlorridi went, grasped the prow, quickly, with its hold-water, lifted the water-steed, together with its oars and scoop; bore to the dwelling the Jötun's ocean-swine, the curved vessel, through the wooded hills.

28. But the Jötun yet ever frowned, to strife accustomed, with Thor disputed, said that no one was strong, however vigorously he might row, unless he his cup could break.

29. But Hlorridi, when to his hands it came, forthwith brake an upright stone in twain; sitting dashed the cup through the pillars: yet they brought it whole to Hýmir back.

30. Until the beauteous woman gave important, friendly counsel, which she only knew: "Strike at the head of Hýmir, the Jötun with food oppressed,
that is harder than any cup."

31. Rose then on his knee the stern lord of goats, clad in all his godlike power. Unhurt remained the old man's helm-block, but the round wine-bearer was in shivers broken.

32. "Much good, I know, has departed from me, now that my cup I see hurled from my knees." Thus the old man spake: I can never say again, beer thou art too hot.

33. Now 'tis to be tried if ye can carry the beer-vessel out of our

dwelling." Tý twice assayed to move the vessel, yet at each time stood the kettle fast.

34. Then Modi's father by the brim grasped it, and trod through the dwelling's floor. Sif's consort lifted the kettle on his head, while about his heels
its rings jingled.

35. They had far journeyed before Odin's son cast one look backward: he from the caverns saw, with Hýmir from the east, a troop of many-headed monsters coming.

36. From his shoulders he lifted the kettle down; Mjöllnir hurled forth towards the savage crew, and slew all the mountain-giants, who with Hýmir
had him pursued.

37. Long they had not journeyed when of Hlorridi's goats one lay down half-dead before the car. It from the pole had sprung across the trace; but the false Loki was of this the cause.

38. Now ye have heard, - for what fabulist can more fully tell - what indemnity he from the giant got: he paid for it with his children both.[6]

39. In his strength exulting he to the gods' counsel came, and had the kettle, which Hýmir had possessed, out of which every god shall beer with Ægir drink at every harvest-tide.

[1] To wit, that they were short of kettles for brewing.
[2] That is divining rods. So Tacitus of the ancient Germans: Sortium consuetudo simplex: virgam, frugiferae arbori decisam, in surculos amputant, eosque, notis

quibusdam discretos, super candidam vestem temere ac fortuito spargunt: mox, si publice consuletur, sacerdos civitatis, sin privatim, ipse paterfamiliae, precatus deos coelumque suspiciens, ter singulos tollit, sublatos secundum impressam ante notam interpretatur, Germania X. ["The use of the lots is simple. A little bough is lopped off a fruit-bearing tree, and cut into small pieces; these are distinguished by certain marks, and thrown carelessly and at random over a white garment. In public questions the priest of the particular state, in private the father of the family, invokes the gods, and, with his eyes towards heaven, takes up each piece three times, and finds in them a meaning according to the mark previously impressed on them."—translated by Alfred John Church and William Jackson Brodribb.]
[3] Thor.
[4] The serpent that encircles the earth.
[5] According to the Prose Edda (p. 445), the giant, overcome with fright, took out his knife and severed Thor's line.
[6] This strophe belongs apparently to another poem.

9: Thrymskviða eðr Hamarsheimt: The Lay of Thrym, or the Hammer recovered.

1. Wroth was Vingthor, when he awoke, and his hammer missed; his beard he shook, his forehead struck, the son of earth felt all around him;

2. and first of all these words he uttered: "Hear now, Loki! what I now say, which no ones knows anywhere on earth, nor in heaven above; the As's hammer is stolen!"

3. They went to the fair Freyja's dwelling, and he these words first of all said: "Wilt thou me, Freyja, thy feather-garment lend, that perchance my hammer I may find?"

Freyja
4. "That I would give thee, although of gold it were, and trust it to thee, though it were of silver."

5. Flew then Loki - the plumage rattled - until he came beyond the Æsiŕs dwellings, and came within the Jötuńs land.

6. On a mound sat Thrym, the Thursar's lord, for his greyhounds plaiting gold bands and his horses'
manes smoothing.

7. "How goes it with the Æsir How goes it with the Alfar, Why art thou come alone to Jötunheim?"

Loki
8. "Ill it goes with the Æsir, Ill it goes with the Alfar. Hast thou Hlorridi's hammer hidden?"

Thrym
9. "I have Hlorridi's hammer hidden eight rasts beneath the earth; it shall no man get again,

unless he bring me Freyja to wife."

10. Flew then Loki - the plumage rattled - until he came beyond the Jötun's dwellings, and came within the Æsir's courts; there he met Thor, in the middle court, who these words first of all uttered.

11. "Hast thou had success as well as labour? Tell me from the air the long tidings. Oft of him who sits are the tales defective, and he who lied down
utters falsehood."

Loki
12. "I have had labour and success: Thrym has thy hammer, the Thursar's lord. It shall no man get again, unless he bring him Freyja to wife."

13. They went the fair Freyja to find; and he those words first of all said: "Bind thee, Freyja, in bridal raiment, we two must drive to Jötunheim."

13. Wroth then was Freyja, and with anger chafed,
all the Æsir's hall beneath her trembled: in shivers flew the famed Brisinga necklace. "Know me to be of women lewdest, if with thee I drive to Jötunheim."[1]

15. Straightway went the Æsir all to counsel, and the Asyniur all to hold converse; and deliberated the mighty gods, how they Hlorridi's hammer might get back.

16. Then said Heimdall, of Æsir brightest - he well foresaw, like other Vanir - "Let us clothe Thor with bridal raiment, let him have the famed Brisinga necklace.

17. "Let by his side keys jingle, and woman's weeds fall round his knees, but on his breast

place precious stones, and a neat coif set on his head."

18. Then said Thor, the mighty As: "Me the Æsir will call womanish, if I let myself be clad in bridal raiment."

19. Then spake Loki, Laufey's son: "Do thou, Thor! Refrain from suchlike words: forthwith the Jötuns will Asgard inhabit, unless thy hammer thou gettest back."

20. Then they clad Thor in bridal raiment, and with the noble Brisinga necklace, let by his side keys jingle, and woman's weeds fall round his knees: and on his breast places precious stones, and a neat coif sat on his head.

21. Then said Loki, Laufey's son: "I will with thee as a servant go: we two will drive to Jötunheim."

22. Straightway were the goats homeward driven, hurried to the traces; they had fast to run. The rocks were shivered, the earth was in a blaze; Odin's son drove to Jötunheim.

23. Then said Thrym, the Thursar's lord: "Rise up, Jötuns! and the benches deck, now they bring me Freyja to wife, Niörd's daughter, from Noatún.

24. "Hither to our court let bring gold-horned cows, all-black oxen, for the Jötuns' joy. Treasures I have many, necklaces many, Freyja alone seemed to me wanting."

25. In the evening they early came, and for the Jötuns beer was brought forth. Thor alone an ox devoured, salmons eight, and all the sweetmeats women should have. Sif's

consort drank three salds of mead.

26. Then said Thrym, the Thursar's prince: "Where hast thou seen brides eat more voraciously? I never saw brides feed more amply, nor a maiden drink more mead."

27. Sat the all-crafty serving-maid close by, who words fitting found against the Jötun's speech: "Freyja has nothing eaten for eight nights, so eager was she for Jötunheim."

28. Under her veil he stooped desirous to salute her, but sprang back along the hall. "Why are so piercing Freyja's looks? Methinks that fire burns from her eyes."

29. Sat the all-crafty serving-maid close by, who words fitting found against the Jötun's speech: "Freyja for eight nights has not slept, so eager was she for Jötunheim."

30. In came the Jötun's luckless sister, for a bride-gift she dared to ask: "Give me from thy hands the ruddy rings, if thou wouldst gain my love, my love and favour all."

31. Then said Thrym, the Thursar's lord: "Bring the hammer in, the bride to consecrate; lay Mjöllnir on the maiden's knee; unite us each with other by the hand of Vör.

32. Laughed Hlorridi's soul in his breast, when the fierce-hearted his hammer recognized. He first slew Thrym, the Thursar's lord, and the Jötun's race all crushed;

33. He slew the Jötuńs aged sister, her who a bride-gift had demanded; she a blow got instead of skillings, a hammer's

stroke for many rings. So got Odin's son his hammer back.

[1] A rather awkward story about Freyja and the Brisinga men is given in "Northern Mythology," I, p. 32 note* from Olaf Triggvason's Saga, reprinted in Snorri's Edda, edit. Rask p. 354. According to an allusion to it in Beowulf, where it is called Brôsinga men, it had come to be possessed by Hermanric.

10: Alvíssmál: The Lay of the Dwarf.

Alvis
1. The benches they are decking, now shall the bride[1] with me bend her way home. That beyond my strength I have hurried will to every one appear: at home naught shall disturb my quiet.

Vingthor
2. What man is this? Why about the nose art thou so pale? Hast thou last night with corpses lain? To me thou seemst to bear resemblances to the Thursar. Thou art not born to carry off a bride.

Alvis
3. Alvis I am named, beneath the earth I dwell, under the rock I own a place. The lord of chariots I am come to visit. A promise once confirmed let no one break.[2]

Vingthor
4. I will break it; for o'er the maid I have, as father, greatest power. I was from home when the promise was given thee. Among the gods I the sole giver am.

Alvis
5. What man is this, lays claim to power over that fair, bright maiden? For far-reaching shafts few will know thee.
Who has decked thee with bracelets?

Vingthor
6. Vingthor I am named, wide I have wandered; I am Sidgrani's son: with my dissent thou shalt not that young maiden have, nor that union obtain.

Alvis
7. Thy consent I fain would obtain. Rather would I possess
than be without that snow-white maiden.

Vingthor
8. The maiden's love shall not, wise guest! be unto thee denied, if thou of every world canst tell all I desire to know.

Alvis
9. Vingthor! thou canst try, as thou art desirous the knowledge of the dwarf to prove. All the nine worlds I have travelled over, and every being known.

Vinthor
10. Tell me, Alvis! - for all men's concerns I presume thee, dwarf, to know- how the earth is called, which lies before the sons of men, in every world.

Alvis
11. Jörd among men 'tis called, but with the Æsir fold; the Vanir call it vega, the Jötuns igroen, the Alfar groandi, the powers supreme aur.

Vingthor
12. Tell me Alvis! etc. how the heaven is called, which is perceptible, in every world.

Alvis
13. Himinn tis called by men; but hlýrnir with the gods; vindofni the Vanir call it, uppheimr the Jötuns, the Alfar fagraræfr, the dwarfs driupansal.

Vingthor
14. Tell me Alvis! etc. how the moon is called, which men see in every world.

Alvis
15. Mani 'tis called by men, but mylinn with the gods, hverfanda hvel in Hel[3] they call it, skyndi the Jötuns, but the dwarfs skin; the Alfar name it artali.

Vingthor
16. Tell me, Alvis! etc. how the sun is called,

which men's sons see in every world.

Alvis
17. Sol among men 'tis called, but with the gods sunna, the dwarfs call it Dvalinn's leika, the Jötuns eyglo, the Alfar fagrahvel, the Æsir's sons alskir.

Vingthor
18. Tell me, Alvis! etc. how the clouds are called, which with showers are mingled in every world.

Alvis
19. Ský they are called by men, but skurvan by the gods; the Vanir call them vindflot, the Jötuns urvan, the Alfar veðrmegin; in Hel they are called hialm huliðs.

Vingthor
20. Tell me, Alvis! etc. how the wind is called, which widely passes over every world.

Alvis
21. Windr 'tis called by men, but vavuðr by the gods, the wide-ruling powers call it gneggiuð, the Jötuns æpir the Alfar dynfari, in Hel they call it hviðuðr.

Vingthor
22. Tell me Alvis! etc. how the calm is called, which has to rest in every world.

Alvis
23. Logn 'tis called by men, but lægi by the gods, the Vanir call it vindslot, the Jötuns ofhlý, the Alfar dagsevi, the Dwarfs call it dags vera.

Vingthor
24. Tell me, Alvis! etc. what the sea is called, which men row over in every world.

Alvis
25. Sær ́tis called by men, but silægia with the gods; the Vanir call it vagr, the Jötuns alheimr, the Alfar

lagastafr, the Dwarfs call it diupan mar.

Vingthor
26. Tell me, Alvis! etc. how the fire is called, which burns before meńs sons in every world.

Alvis
27. Eldr´tis called by men, but by the Æsir funi; the Vanir call it vagr, the Jötuns frekr, but the Dwarfs forbrennir; in Hel they call it hröðuðr.

Vingthor
28. Tell me, Alvis! etc. how the forest it called, which grows for the sons of men in every world.
Alvis
29. Viðr´tis called by men, but vallarfax by gods, Heĺs inmates call it hliðÞangr, the Jötuns eldi, the Alfar fagrlimi; the Vanir call it vöndr.

Vingthor
30. Tell me, Alvis! etc. how the night is called, that Nörvís daughter hight, in every world.

Alvis
31. Nott it is called by men, but by the gods niol; the wide-ruling powers call it grima, the Jötuns olios, the Alfar svefngaman; the Dwarfs call it draumniörunn.

Vingthor
32. Tell me, Alvis! etc. how the seed is called, which the sons of men sow in every world.

Alvis
33. Bygg it is called by men, but by the gods barr, the Vanir call it vaxtr, the Jötuns æti, the Alfar lagastafr; in Hel´tis hnipinn called.

Vingthor
34. Tell me, Alvis! etc. how the beer is called, which the sons of men drink in every world.

Alvis

35. Öl it is called by men, but by the Æsir biorr, the Vanir call it veig, hreinna lögr the Jötuns, but in Hel 'tis called miöðr: Suttung's sons call it sumbl.

Vingthor

36. In one breast I have never found more ancient lore. - By great wiles thou hast, I tell thee, been deluded. Thou art above ground, dwarf! at dawn; already in the hall the sun is shining!

[1] Thrud, Thor's daughter by his wife Sif. Skaldskap. pp. 101, 119.
[2] This appears to allude to a promise made to the dwarf; but of which the story is lost.
[3] When this composition was written, it appears that Hel was no longer regarded as a person, but as a place.

11: Harbarðslióð: The Lay of Harbard.

Thor journeying from the eastern parts came to a strait or sound, on the other side of which was a ferryman with his boat. Thor cried out: -

1. Who is the knave of knaves, that by the sound stands yonder?

Harbard
2. Who is the churl of churls, that cries across the water?

Thor
3. Ferry me across the sound, to-morrow Íll regale thee. I have a basket on my back: there is no better food: at my ease I ate, before I quitted home, herrings and oats, with which I yet feel sated.

Harbard
4. Thou art in haste to praise thy meal: thou surely hast no foreknowledge; for sad will be thy home: thy mother, I believe, is dead.

Thor
5. Thou sayest now what seems to every one most unwelcome to know - that my mother is dead.

Harbard
6. Thou dost not look like one who owns three country dwellings, bare-legged thou standest, and like a beggar clothed; thou hast not even breeches.

Thor
7. Steer hitherward thy boat; I will direct thee where to land. But who owns this skiff, which by the strand thou holdest?

Harbard
8. Hildolf he is named who bade me hold it, a

man in council wise, who dwells in Radsö sound. Robbers he bade me not to ferry, or horse-stealers, but good men only, and those whom I well knew. Tell me then they name, if thou wilt cross the sound.

Thor
9. I my name will tell, (although I am an outlaw) and all my kin: I am Odin's son, Meili's brother, and Magni's sire, the gods' mighty leader: With Thor thou here mayst speak. I will now ask how thou art called.

Harbard
10. I am Harbard called; seldom I my name conceal.

Thor
11. Why shouldst thou thy name conceal, unless thou crime has perpetrated?

Harbard
12. Yet, thou I may crime have perpetrated, I will nathless gaurd my life against such as thou art; unless I death-doomed am.

Thor
13. It seems to me a foul annoyance to wade across the strait to thee, and wet my garments: but I will pay thee, mannikin! for thy sharp speeches, if o'er the sound I come.

Harbard
14. Here will I stand, and here await thee. Thou wilt have found no stouter one since Hrugnir's death.

Thor
15. Thou now remindest me how I with Hrugnir fought, that stout-hearted Jötun, whose head was all of stone; yet I made him fall, and sink before me. What meanwhile didst thou, Harbard?

Harbard

16. I was with Fjölvari five winters through, in the isle which Algrön hight. There we could fight, and slaughter make, many perils prove, indulge in love.

Thor
17. How did your women prove towards you?

Harbard
18. Sprightly women we had, had they but been meek; shrewd ones we had, had they but been kind. Of sand a rope they twisted, and from the deep valley dug the earth: to them all I alone was superior in cunning. I rested with the sisters seven, and their love and pleasures shared. What meanwhile didst thou, Thor?

Thor
19. I slew Thiassi, that stout-hearted Jötun: up I cast the eyes of Allvaldi's son into the heaven serene: they are signs the greatest of my deeds.[2] What meanwhile didst thou, Harbard?

Harbard
20. Great seductive arts I used against the riders of the night,[3] when from their husbands I enticed them. A mighty Jötun I believed Hlebard to be: a magic wand he gave me, but from his wits I charmed him.

Thor
21. With evil mind then thou didst good gifts requite.

Harbard
22. One tree gets that which is from another scraped: each one in such case is for self. What meanwhile didst thou, Thor?

Thor
23. In the east I was, and slew the Jötun brides, crafty in evil, as they to the mountain went. Great would have been the

Jötun race, had they all lived; and not a man left in Midgard. What meanwhile didst thou, Harbard?

Harbard
24. I was in Valland, and followed warfare; princes I excited, but never reconciled. Odin has all the jarls that in conflict fall; but Thor the race of thralls.

Thor
25. Unequally thou wouldst divide the folk among the Æsir, if thou but hadst the power.

Harbard
26. Thor has strength overmuch, but courage none; from cowardice and fear, thou wast crammed into a glove, and hardly thoughtest thou was Thor. Thou durst not then, through thy terror, either sneeze or cough, lest Fjalar it might hear.

Thor
27. Harbard, thou wretch! I would strike thee dead, could I but stretch my arm across the sound.

Harbard
28. Why wouldst thou stretch they arm across the sound, when there is altogether no offence? But what didst thou, Thor?

Thor
29. In the east I was, and a river I defended, when the sons of Svarang me assailed, and with stones pelted me, though in their success they little joyed: they were the first to sue for peace. What meanwhile didst thou, Harbard?

Harbard
30. I was in the east, and with a certain lass held converse; with that fair I dallied, and long meetings had. I that gold-bright one delighted; the game amused her.

Thor
31. Then you had kind damsels there?

Harbard
32. Of thy aid I had need, Thor! in retaining that maiden lily-fair.

Thor
33. I would have given it thee, if I had had the opportunity.

Harbard
34. I would have trusted thee, my confidence if thou hadst not betrayed it.

Thor
35. I am not such a heel-chafer as an old leather shoe in spring.

Harbard
36. What meanwhile didst thou, Thor?

Thor
37. The Berserkers' brides I on Læssö cudgeled; they the worst had perpetrated, the whole people had seduced.

Harbard
38. Dastardly didst thou act, Thor! when thou didst cudgel women.

Thor
39. She-wolves they were, and scarcely women. They crushed my ship, which with props I had secured, with iron clubs threatened me, and drove away Thialfi. What meanwhile didst thou, Harbard?

Harbard
40. I in the army was, which was hither sent, war-banners to raise, lances to redden.

Thor
41. Of that thou now wilt speak, as thou wentest forth us hard terms to offer.

Harbard
42. That shall be indemnified by a hand-

ring, such as arbitrators give, who wish to reconcile us.

Thor
43. Where didst thou learn words than which I never heard
more irritating?

Harbard
44. From men I learned them, from ancient men, whose home is in the woods.

Thor
45. Thou givest certainly a good name to grave-mounds, when thou callest them homes in the woods.

Harbard
46. So speak I of such a subject.

Thor
47. Thy shrewd words will bring thee evil, if I resolve the sound to ford. Louder than a wold thou wilt howl, I trow, if of my hammer thou gettest a touch.

Harbard
48. Sif has a gallant at home; thou wilt anxious be to find him: thou shalt that arduous work perform; it will beseem thee better.

Thor
49. Thou utterest what comes upmost, so that to me it be most annoying, thou dastardly varlet! I believe thou art lying.

Harbard
50. I believe I am telling truth. Thou art travelling slowly; thou wouldst have long since arrived, hadst thou assumed another form.

Thor
51. Harbard! thou wretch! rather is it thou who has detained me.

Harbard
52. I never thought that a

ferryman could the course of Asa-Thor retard.

Thor
53. One advice I now will give thee: row hither with thy boat; let us cease from threats; approach the sire of Magni.

Harbard
54. Go farther from the sound, the passage is refused thee.

Thor
55. Show me then the way, if thou wilt not ferry me across the water.

Harbard
56. That's too little to refuse. 'Tis far to go; 'tis to the stock an hour, and to the stone another; then keep the left hand way, until thou reachest Verland; there will Fjörgyn find her son Thor, and point out to him his kinsmen's ways to Odin's land.

Thor
57. Can I get there to-day?

Harbard
58. With pain and toil thou mayest get there, while the sun is up, which, I believe, is now nigh.

Thor
59. Our talk shall now be short, as thou answerest with scoffing only. For refusing to ferry me I will reward thee, if another time we meet.

Harbard
60. Just go to where all the powers of evil may have thee.

[1] Harbard is Odin disguised as a ferryman. This composition, as also the Ægisdrekka, look very like burlesques on the Odinic religion, written when on its decline.

[2] See the story in Prose Edda, p. 461, and N.M. I. p. 44, where it is told differently.
[3] Giantesses, witches, &c.

12: För Skirnis eðr Skirnismál: The Journey of Lay of Skirnir.

Frey, son of Niörd, had one day seated himself in Hlidskjalf, and was looking over all regions, when turning his eyes to Jötunheim, he there saw a beautiful girl, as she was passing from her fatheŕs dwelling to her bower. Thereupon he became greatly troubled in mind. Freýs attendant was named Skirnir; him Niörd desired to speak with Frey; when Skadi said: -

1. Rise up now, Skirnir!
go and request our son to speak;
and inquire with whom he
so sage may be offended.

Skirnir
2. Harsh words I have
from your son to fear, if I
go and speak with him,
and to inquire with whom
he so sage may be offended.

Skirnir
3. Tell me now, Frey,
prince of gods! for I desire to know,
why alone thou sittest in
the spacious hall the livelong day?

Frey
4. Why shall I tell thee,
thou young man, my
mind's great trouble? for
the Alfs' illuminator
shines every day,yet not
for my pleasure.

Skirnir
5. Thy care cannot, I think,
be so great,
that to me thou canst not tell it;
for in early days
we were young together:
well might we trust each other.

Frey
6. In Gýmir's courts
I saw walking

a maid for whom I long.
Her arms gave forth light
wherewith shone
all air and water.

7. Is more desirable
to me that maid
than to any youth
in early days;
yet will no one,
Æsir or Alfar,
that we together live.

Skirnir
8. Give me but thy steed,
which can bear me
through
the dusk, flickering
flame,
and that sword,
which brandishes itself
against the Jötuns' race.

Frey
9. I will give thee my
steed,
which can bear thee
through
the dusk, flickering
flame,
and that sword,
which will itself brandish,
if he is bold who raises it.

Skirnir speaks to the
horse....

10. Dark it is without,
'tis time, I say, for us to
go
across the misty fells,
over the Thursar's land:
we shall both return,
or the all-potent Jötun
will seize us both.

Skirnir rides to Jötunheim, to Gýmir's mansion, where fierce dogs were chained at the gate of the enclosure that was round Gýmir's hall. He rides on to where a cowherd was sitting on a mound, and says to him:

11. Tell me, cowherd!
as on the mound thou
sittest,
and watchest all the ways,
how I to the speech may
come,
of the young maiden,
for Gýmir's dogs?

12. Either thou art death-
doomed,
or thou art a departed one.

Speech wilt thou
ever lack
with the good maid of
Gýmir.

Skirnir
13. Better choices than to
whine
there are for him
who is prepared to die:
for one day
was my age decreed,
and my whole life
determined.

Gerd
14. What is that sound of
sounds,
which I now sounding
hear
within our dwelling?
The earth is shaken,
and with it all
the house of Gýmir
trembles.

A serving-maid.
15. A man is here
without,
dismounted from his
horse's back:
he lets his steed browse
on the grass.

Gerd
16. Bid him enter
into our hall,
and drink of the bright
mead;
although I fear
it is my brother's slayer
who waits without.

17. Who is this of the
Alfar's,
or of the Æsiŕs sons,
or of the wise Vanir's?
Why art thou come alone,
through the hostile fire,
our halls to visit?

Skirnir
18. I am not of the
Alfar's,
nor of the Æsir's sons,
nor of the wise Vanir's;
yet I am come alone,
through the hostile fire,
your halls to visit.

19. Apples all-golden
I have here eleven:
these I will give thee,
Gerd,
thy love to gain,
that thou mayest say that
Frey
to thee lives dearest.

Gerd
20. The apples eleven
I never will accept
for any mortal's pleasure;
nor will I and Frey,
while our lives last,
live both together.

Skirnir
21. The ring too I will give thee,
which was burnt
with the young son of Odin.
Eight of equal weight
will from it drop,
every ninth night.
Gerd
22. The ring I will not accept,
burnt thou it may have been
with the young son of Odin.
I have no lack of gold
in Gýmir's courts;
for my father's wealth I share.

Skirnir
23. Seest thou this sword,
young maiden!
thin, glittering-bright,
which I have here in hand?
I thy head will sever
from thy neck,
if thou speakest not
favourably to me.

Gerd
24. Suffer compulsion
will I never,
to please any man;
yet this I foresee,
if thou and Gýmir meet,
yet will eagerly engage in fight.

Skirnir
25. Seest thou this sword,
young maiden!
thin, glittering-bright,
which I have here in hand?
Beneath its edge
shall the old Jötun fall:
thy sire is death-doomed.

26. With a taming-wand I smite thee,
and I will tame thee,
maiden! to my will.
Thou shalt go thither,
where the sons of men
shall never more behold thee.

27. On an eagle's mount
thou shalt early sit,
looking and turned
towards Hel.
Food shall to thee more
loathsome be
than is to any one
the glistening serpent
among men.

28. As a prodigy thou
shalt be,
when thou goest forth;
Hrinmir shall at thee
gaze,
all being at thee stare;
more wide-known thou
shalt become
than the watch among the
gods,[1]
if thou from thy gratings
gape.

29. Solitude and disgust,
bonds and impatience,
shall thy tears with grief
augment.
Set thee down,
and I will tell thee of
a whelming flood of care,
and a double grief.

30. Terrors shall bow thee
down
the livelong day,
in the Jötuns' courts.
To the Hrimthursar's
halls,
thou shalt each day
crawl exhausted,
joyless crawl;
wail for pastime
shalt thou have,
and tears and misery.

31. With a three-headed
Thurs
thou shalt be ever bound,
or be without a mate.
Thy mind shall tear thee
from morn to morn:
as the thistle thou shalt be
which has thrust itself
on the house-top.

32. To the wold I have
been,
and to the humid grove,
a magic wand to get.
A magic wand I got.

33. Wroth with thee is
Odin,
wroth with thee is the
Æsir's prince;
Frey shall loathe thee,

even ere thou, wicked
maid!
shalt have felt
the gods' dire vengeance.

34. Hear ye, Jötuns!
hear ye, Hrimtursar!
sons of Suttung!
also ye, Æsir's friends!
how I forbid
how I prohibit
man's joy unto the
damsel,
man's converse to the
damsel.

35. Hrimgrimnir the
Thurs is named,
that shall possess thee,
in the grating of the dead
beneath;
there shall wretched
thralls,
from the tree's roots,
goats' water give thee.
Other drink shalt thou,
maiden! never get,
either for thy pleasure,
or for my pleasure.

36. Þurs[2] I cut for thee,
and three letters more:
ergi, and oenði,
and oÞola.
So will I cut them out,
as I have cut them in,
if there need shall be.

Gerd
37. Hail rather to thee,
youth!
and accept an icy cup,
filled with old mead;
although I thought not
that I ever should
love one of Vanir race.

Skirnir
38. All my errand
will I know,
ere I hence ride home.
When wilt thou converse
hold
with the powerful
son of Niörd?

Gerd
39. Barri the grove is
named,
which we both know,
the grove of tranquil
paths.
Nine nights hence,
there to Niörd's son
Gerd will grant delight.

Skirnir then rode home. Frey was standing without, and spoke to him, asking tidings:

40. Tell me, Skirnir!
ere thou thy steed
unsaddlest,
and a foot hence goest,
what thou hast
accomplished
in Jötunheim,
for my pleasure or thine?

Skirnir
41. Barri the grove is
named,
which we both know,
the grove of tranquil
paths.
Nine nights hence,
there to Niörd's son
Gerd will grant delight.

Frey
42. Long is one night,
yet longer two will be;
how shall I three endure.
Often a month to me
less has seemed
than half a night of
longing.

[1] Heimdall.
[2] Þurs, &c The names of magical runes.

13: Rigsmál: The Lay of Rig.

In ancient Sagas it is related that one of the Æsir named Heimdall, being on a journey to a certain sea-shore, came to a village, where he called himself Rig. In accordance with this Saga is the following:

1. In ancient days, they say,
along the green ways went
the powerful and upright
sagacious As,
the strong and active Rig,
his onward course pursuing.

2. Forward he went
on the mid-way,
and to a dwelling came.
The door stood ajar,
he went in,
fire was on the floor.
There man and wife sat there,
hoary-haired, by the hearth,
Ai and Edda,
in old guise clad.

3. Rig would counsel
give to them both,
and himself seated
in the middle seat,
having on either side
the domestic pair.

4. Then Edda from the ashes
took a loaf,
heavy and thick,
and with bran mixed;
more besides she laid
on the middle of the board;
there in a bowl was broth
on the table set,
there was a calf boiled,
of cates more excellent.

5. Then rose he up,
prepared to sleep:
Rig would counsel
give to them both;
laid him down
in the middle of the bed;
the domestic pair lay
one on either side.

6. There he continued
three nights together,

then departed
on the mid-way.
Nine months then
passed away.

7. Edda a child brought
forth:
they with water sprinkled
its swarthy skin,
and named it Thræl.

8. It grew up,
and well it throve;
of its hands
the skin was shriveled,
the knuckles knotty,
and fingers thick;
a hideous countenance it
had,
a curved back,
and protruding heels.

9. He then began
his strength to prove,
bast to bind,
make of it loads;
then faggots carried
home,
the livelong day.

10. Then to the dwelling
came
a woman walking,
scarred were her foot-
soles,
her arms sunburnt,
her nose compressed,
her name was Thý.

11. In the middle seat
herself she placed;
by her sat
the house's son.
They spoke and
whispered,
prepared a bed,
Thræl and Thý,
and days of care.

12. Children they begat,
and lived content:
Their names, I think,
were
Hrimr and Fjósnir,
Klur and Kleggi,
Kefsir, Fulnir,
Drumb, Digraldi,
Drött and Hösvir,
Lút and Leggialdi.
Fences they erected,
fields manured,
tended swine,
kept goats,
dug turf.

13. The daughters were
Drumba and Kumba,

Ökkvinkalfa,
and Arinnefia,
Ysia and Ambatt,
Eikintiasna,
Tötrughypia,
and Trönubeina,
whence are sprung
the race of thralls.

14. Rig then went on,
in a direct course,
and came to a house;
the door stood ajar:
he went in;
fire was on the floor,
man and wife sat there
engaged at work.

15. The man was planing
wood for a weaver's
beam;
his beard was trimmed,
a lock was on his
forehead,
his shirt close;
he chest stood on the
floor.

16. His wife sat by,
plied her rock,
with outstretched arms,
prepared for clothing.
A hood was on her head,
a loose sark over her
breast,
a kerchief round her neck,
studs on her shoulders.
Afi and Amma
owned the house.

17. Rig would counsel
give to them both;
rose from the table,
prepared to sleep;
laid him down
in the middle of the bed,
the domestic pair lay
one on either side.

18. There he continued
three nights together.
Nine months then
passed away.
Amma a child brought
forth,
they with water sprinkled
it,
and called it Karl.
The mother in linen
swathed
the ruddy redhead:
its eyes twinkled.

19. It grew up,
and well throve;
learned to tame oxen,
make a plough,

houses build,
and barns construct,
make carts,
and the plough drive.

20. Then they home
conveyed
a lass with pendant keys,
and goatskin kirtle;
married her to Karl.
Snör was her name,
under a veil she sat.
The couple dwelt
together,
rings exchanged,
spread couches,
and a household formed.

21. Children they begat,
and lived content.
Hal and Dreng, these
were named,
Held, Thegn, Smith,
Breidrbondi,
Bundinskegg,
Bui and Boddi,
Brattskegg and Segg.

22. But (the daughters)
were thus called,
by other names:
Snot, Brud, Svanni,
Svarri, Sprakki,
Fliod, Sprund, and Vif,
Feima, Ristil;
whence are sprung
the races of churls.

23. Rig then went thence,
in a direct course,
and came to a hall:
the entrance looked
southward,
the door was half closed,
a ring was on the door-
post.

24. He went in;
the floor was strewed,
a couple sat
facing each other,
Fadir and Modir,
with fingers playing.

25. The husband sat,
and twisted string,
bent his bow,
and arrow-shafts
prepared;
but the housewife
looked on her arms,
smoothed her veil,
and her sleeves fastened;

26. her head-gear
adjusted.
A clasp was on her
breast;

ample her robe,
her sark was blue;
brighter was her brow,
her breast fairer,
her neck whiter
than driven snow.

27. Rig would counsel
give to them both,
and himself seated
on the middle seat,
having on either side
the domestic pair.

28. Then took Modir
a figured cloth
of white linen,
and the table decked.
She then took
thin cakes
of snow-white wheat,
and on the table laid.

29. She set forth salvers
full, adorned with silver,
on the table game and
pork,
and roasted birds.
In a can was wine;
the cups were
ornamented.
They drank and talked;
the day was fast
departing,
Rig would counsel
give to them both.

30. Rig then rose,
the bed prepared;
there he then remained
three nights together,
then departed
on the mid-way.
Nine months after that
passed away.

31. Modir then brought
forth a boy;
in silk they wrapped him,
with water sprinkled him,
and named him Jarl.
Light was his hair,
bright his cheeks,
his eyes piercing
as a young serpent's.

32. There at home
Jarl grew up,
learned the shield to
shake,
to fix the string,
the bow to bend,
arrows to shaft,
javelins to hurl,
spears to brandish,
horses to ride,
dogs to let slip,
swords to draw,

swimming to practice.

33. Thither from the
forest came
Rig walking,
Rig walking:
runes he taught him,
and his own son declared
him,
whom he bade possess
his alodial fields,
his alodial fields,
his ancient dwellings.

34. Jarl then rode thence,
through a murky way,
over humid fells,
till to a hall he came.
His spear he brandished,
his shield he shook,
made his horse curvet,
and his falchion drew,
strife began to raise,
the field to redden,
carnage to make;
and conquer lands.

35. Then he ruled alone
over eight vills,
riches distributed,
gave to all
treasures and precious
things;
lank-sided horses,
rings he dispersed,
and collars cut in
pieces.[1]

36. The nobles drove
through humid ways,
came to a hall,
where Hersir dwelt;
there they found
a slender maiden,
fair and elegant,
Erna her name.

37. They demanded her,
and conveyed her home,
to Jarl espoused her;
she under the linen[2]
went.
They together lived,
and well throve,
had offspring,
and old age enjoyed.

38. Bur was the eldest,
Barn the second,
Jod and Adal,
Arfi, Mög,
Nid and Nidjung.
They learned games;
Son and Svein
swam and at tables
played.
One was named Kund,
Kon was the youngest.

39. There grew up
Jarl's progeny;
horses they broke,
curved shields,
cut arrows,
brandished spears.

40. But the young Kon
understood runes,
æfin-runes,
and aldr-runes;
he moreover knew
men to preserve,
edges to deaden,
the sea to calm.

41. He knew the voice of birds,
how fires to mitigate,
assuage and quench`
sorrows to allay.
He of eight men had
the strength and energy.

42. He with Rig Jarl
in runes contended,
artifices practiced,
and superior proved;
then acquired
Rig to be called,
and skilled in runes.

43. The young Kon rode
through swamps and forests,
hurled forth darts,
and tamed birds.

44. Then sang the crow,
sitting lonely on a bough!
"Why wilt thou, young Kon:
tame the birds?
Rather shouldst thou,
young Kon!
on horses ride
and armies overcome.

45. Nor Dan nor Danp
halls more costly had,
nobler paternal seats,
then ye had.
They well knew how
the keel to ride,
the edge to prove,
wounds to inflict.

The rest is wanting.

[1] A common practice: the pieces served as money.
[2] The nuptial veil.

14: Ægisdrekka, eða Lokasenna, eða Lokaglepsa: Ægir's Compotation or Loki's Altercation.

Ægir, who is also name Gýmir, had brewed beer for the Æsir, after he had got the great kettle, as has been already related. To the entertainment came Odin and his wife Frigg. Thor did not come, being in the East, but his wife Sif was there, also Bragi and his wife Idun, and Tý, who was one-handed, Fenrisulf having bitten off his hand while being bound. Besides these were Niörd and his wife Skadi, Frey and Freyja, and Odińs son Vidar. Loki too was there, and Freýs attendants, Byggvir and Beyla. Many other Æsir and Alfar were also present. Ægir had two servants, Fimafeng and Eldir. Bright gold was there used instead of fire-light. The beer served itself to the guests. The place was a great sanctuary. The guests greatly praised the excellence of Ægiŕs servants. This Loki could not hear with patience, and so slew Fimafeng; whereupon the Æsir shook their shields, exclaimed against Loki, chased him into the forest, and then returned to drink. Loki came again, and found Eldir standing without, whom he thus addressed:

1. Tell me, Eldir!
ere thou thy foot settest
one step forward,
on what converse
the sons of the triumphant gods
at their potation?

Eldir
2. Of their arms converse,
and of their martial fame,
the sons of the triumphant gods.
Of the Æsir and the Alfar
that are here within
not one has a friendly
word for thee.

Loki
3. I will go
into Ægiŕs halls,
to see the compotation.

Strife and hate
to the Æsir's sons I bear,
and will mix their mead
with bale.

Eldir

4. Knowest thou not that
if thou goest
into Ægir's halls
to see the compotation,
but contumely and
clamour
pourest forth on the
kindly powers,
they will wipe it all off on
thee.

Loki

5. Knowest thou not,
Eldir,
that if we two
with bitter words contend,
I shall be rich
in answers,
if thou sayest too much?

Loki then went into the hall, but when those present saw who was come in, they all sat silent.

Loki

6. I Lopt am come thirsty
into this hall,
from a long journey,
to beseech the Æsir
one draught to give me
of the bright mead.

7. Why gods! are ye so
silent,
so reserved,
that ye cannot speak?
A seat and place
choose for me at your
board,
or bid me hie me hence.

Bragi

8. A seat and place
will the Æsir never
choose for thee at their
board;
for well the Æsir know
for whom they ought to
hold
a joyous compotation.

Loki

9. Odin! dost thou
remember
when we in early days
blended our blood
together?
When to taste beer

thou didst constantly
refuse,
unless to both´twas
offered?

Odin

10. Rise up, Vidar!
and let the wolf́s sire
sit at our compotation;
that Loki may not utter
words of contumely
in Ægiŕs hall.

Vidar then rising, presented Loki with drink, who before drinking thus addressed.

11. Hail, Æsir!
Hail, Asyniur!
And ye, all-holy gods!
all, save that one As,
who sits within there,
Bragi, on yonder bench.

Bragi
12. A horse and falchion
I from my stores will give
thee,
and also with a ring
reward thee,
if thou the Æsir wilt not
requite with malice.
Provoke not the gods
against thee.

Loki
13. Of horse and rings
wilt thou ever, Bragi!
be in want.
Of the Æsir and the Alfar,
that are here present,
in conflict thou art the
most backward,
and in the play of darts
most timid.

Bragi
14. I know that were I
without,
as I am now within,
the hall of Ægir,
I thy head would
bear in my hand,
and so for lying punish
thee.

Loki
15. Valiant on thy seat art
thou, Bragi!
but so thou shouldst not
be,
Bragi, the bencȟs pride!
Go and fight,

if thou art angry;
a brave man sits not
considering.

Idun
16. I pray thee, Bragi!
let avail the bond of
children,
and of all adopted sons,
and to Loki speak not
in reproachful words,
in Ægir's hall.

Loki
17. Be silent, Idun!
of all women I declare
thee
most fond of men,
since thou thy arms,
carefully washed, didst
twine
round thy brother's
murderer.

Idun
18. Loki I address not
with opprobrious words,
in Ægir's hall.
Bragi I soothe,
by beer excited.
I desire not that angry ye
fight.

Gefion
19. Why will ye, Æsir
twain,
here within,
strive with reproachful
words?
Lopt perceives not
that he is deluded,
and is urged on by fate.

Loki
20. Be silent, Gefion!
I will now just mention,
how that fair youth
thy mind corrupted,
who thee a necklace gave,
and around whom thou
thy limbs didst twine?

Odin
21. Thou art raving, Loki!
and hast lost thy wits,
in calling Gefion's anger
on thee;
for all men's destinies,
I ween, she knows
as thoroughly as I do.

Loki
22. Be silent, Odin!
Thou never couldst allot
conflicts between men:
oft hast thou given to
those

to whom thou oughtest
not -
victory to cowards.

Odin
23. Knowest thou that I
gave
to those I ought not -
victory to cowards?
Thou was eight winters
on the earth below,
a milch cow and a
woman,
and didst there bear
children.
Now that, methinks,
betokens a base nature.

Loki
24. But, it is said, thou
wentest
with tottering steps in
Samsö,
and knocked at houses as
a Vala.
In likeness of a fortune
teller,
thou wentest among
people;
Now that, methinks,
betokens a base nature.

Frigg
25. Your doings
ye should never
publish among men,
what ye, Æsir twain,
did in days of yore.
Ever forgotten be meńs
former deeds!

Loki
26. Be thou silent, Frigg!
Thou art Fjörgyńs
daughter,
and ever hast been fond
of men,
since Ve and Vili, it is
said,
thou, Vidriŕs wife, didst
both to thy bosom take.

Frigg
27. Know thou that if I
had,
a Ægiŕs halls,
a son like Baldr,
out thou shouldst not go
from the Æsiŕs sons:
thou should'st have been
fiercely assailed.

Loki
28. But wilt thou, Frigg!
that of my wickedness
I more recount?
I am the cause
that thou seest not

Baldr riding to the halls.

Freyja
29. Mad art thou, Loki!
in recounting
thy foul misdeeds.
Frigg, I believe,
knows all that happens,
although she says it not.

Loki
30. Be thou silent, Freyja!
I know thee full well;
thou art not free from
vices:
of the Æsir and the Alfar,
that are herein,
each has been thy
paramour.

Freyja
31. False is thy tongue.
Henceforth it will, I think,
prate no good to thee.
Wroth with thee are the
Æsir,
and the Asyniur.
Sad shalt thou home
depart.

Loki
32. Be silent, Freyja!
Thou art a sorceress,
and with much evil
blended;
since against thy brother
thou
the gentle powers excited.
And then, Freyja! what
didst thou do?

Niörd
33. It is no great wonder,
if silk-clad dames
get themselves husbands,
lovers;
but ́tis a wonder that a
wretched As,
that has borne children,
should herein enter.

Loki
34. Be silent, Niörd!
Thou wast sent eastward
hence,
a hostage from the gods.
Hýmiŕs daughter had thee
for a utensil,
and flowed into thy
mouth.[1]

Niörd
35. ́Tis to me a solace,
as I a long way hence
was sent, a hostage from
the gods,
that I had a son,

whom no one hates,
and accounted is a chief
among the Æsir.

Loki
36. Cease now, Niörd!
in bounds contain thyself;
I will no longer keep it
secret:
it was with thy sister
thou hadst such a son;
hardly worse than thyself.

Tý
37. Frey is best
of all the exalted gods
in the Æsir's courts:
no maid he makes to
weep,
no wife of man,
and from bonds looses
all.

Loki
38. Be silent, Tý!
Thou couldst never settle
a strife 'twixt two;
of thy right hand also
I must mention make,
which Fenrir from thee
tore.

Tý
39. I of a hand am
wanting,
but thou of honest fame;
sad is the lack of either.
Nor is the wolf at ease:
he in bonds must bide,
until the gods' destruction.

Loki
40. Be silent, Tý;
to thy wife it happened
to have a son by me.
Nor rag nor penny ever
hadst thou, poor wretch!
for this injury.

Frey
41. I the wolf see lying
at the river's mouth,
until the powers are swept
away.
So shalt thou be bound,
if thou art not silent,
thou framer of evil.

Loki
42. With gold thou
boughtest
Gýmir's daughter,
and so gavest away thy
sword:
but when Muspell's sons
through the dark forest
ride,

thou, unhappy, wilt not
have wherewith to fight.

Byggvir
43. Know that were I of
noble race,
like Inguńs Frey,
and had so fair a
dwelling,
than marrow softer I
would bray
that ill-boding crow,
and crush him limb by
limb.

Loki
44. What little thing is
that I see
wagging its tail,
and snapping eagerly?
At the ears of Frey
thou shouldst ever be,
and clatter under mills.

Byggvir
45. Byggvir I am named,
and am thought alert,
by all gods and men;
therefore am I joyful
here,
that all the sons of Hropt
drink beer together.

Loki
46. Be silent, Byggvir!
Thou couldst never
dole out food to men,
when, lying in thy truckle
bed,
thou wast not to be found,
while men were fighting.

Heimdall
47. Loki, thou art drunk,
and hast lost thy wits.
Why dost thou not leave
off, Loki?
But drunkenness
so rules every man,
that he knows not of his
garrulity.

Loki
48. Be silent, Heimdall!
For thee in early days
was that hateful life
decreed:
with a wet back
thou must ever be,
and keep watch as
guardian of the gods.

Skadi
49. Thou art merry, Loki!
Not long wilt thou
frisk with an unbound
tail;
for thee, on a rocḱs point,

with the entrails of thy
ice-cold son,
the gods will bind.

Loki
50. Know, if on a rock's
point,
with the entrails of my
ice-cold son,
the gods will bind me,
that first and foremost
I was at the slaying,
when we assailed Thiassi.

Skadi
51. Know, if first and
foremost
thou wast at the slaying,
when ye assailed Thiassi,
that from my dwellings
and fields shall to thee
ever cold counsels come.

Loki
52. Milder was thou of
speech
to Laufey's son,
when to thy bed thou
didst invite me.
Such matters must be
mentioned,
if we accurately must
recount our vices.

Then Sif came forth, and poured out mead for Loki in an icy cup, saying:

53. Hail to thee, Loki!
and this cool cup receive,
full of old mead:
at least me alone,
among the blameless Æsir race,
leave stainless.

He took the horn, drank, and said:

54. So alone shouldst
thou be,
hadst thou strict and
prudent been
towards thy mate;
but one I know,
and, I think, know him
well,

a favoured rival of Hlorridi,
and that is the wily Loki.

Beyla
55. The fells all tremble:
I think Hlorridi
is from journeying home.
He will bid be quiet
him who here insults
all gods and men.

Loki
56. Be silent, Beyla!
Thou art Byggvir's wife,
and with much evil mingled:
never came a greater monster
among the Æsir's sons.
Thou art a dirty strumpet.

Thor then came in and said:

57. Silence, thou impure being!
My mighty hammer, Mjöllnir,
shall stop thy prating.
I will thy head
from thy neck strike;
then will thy life be ended.

Loki
58. Now the son of earth
is hither come.
Why dost thou chafe so, Thor?
Thou wilt not dare do so,
when with the wolf thou hast to fight,
and he the all-powerful father swallows whole.

Thor
59. Silence, thou impure being!
My mighty hammer, Mjöllnir,
shall stop thy prating.
Up I will hurl thee
to the east region,
and none shall see thee after.

Loki
60. Of thy eastern travels
thou shouldst never
to people speak,
since in a glove-thumb
thou, Einheri! wast doubled up,

and hardly thoughtest
thou was Thor.

Thor
61. Silence, thou impure being!
My mighty hammer, Mjöllnir,
shall stop thy prating;
with this right hand I,
Hrugnir's bane,
will smite thee,
so that thy every bone be broken.

Loki
62. 'Tis my intention
a long life to live,
though with thy hammer
thou dost threaten me.
Skrymir's thongs
seemed to thee hard,
when at the food thou couldst not get,
when, in full health, of hunger dying.

Thor
63. Silence, thou impure being!
My mighty hammer, Mjöllnir,
shall stop thy prating.
Hrungnir's bane
shall cast thee down to Hel,
beneath the grating of the dead.

Loki
64. I have said before the Æsir,
I have said before the Æsir's sons,
that which my mind suggested:
but for thee alone
will I go out;
because I know that thou wilt fight.

65. Ægir! thou hast brewed beer;
but thou never shalt henceforth
a compotation hold.
All thy possessions,
which are herein,
flame shall play over,
and on thy back shall burn thee.

After this Loki, in the likeness of a salmon, cast himself into the waterfall of Franangr, where the Æsir caught him, and bound him with the entrails of his son Nari; but his other son, Narfi, was changed into a wolf. Skadi took a venomous serpent, and fastened it up over Loki's face. The venom trickled down from it. Sigyn, Loki's wife, sat by, and held a basin under the venom; and when the basin was full, carried the venom out. Meanwhile the venom dropped on Loki, who shrank from it so violently that the whole earth trembled. This causes what are not called earthquakes.

[1] The events related in this strophe are probably a mere perversion, by the poet, of what we know of Njord's history.

15: Fiölsvinnsmál.: The Lay of Fiölsvith.

1. From the outward wall
he saw one ascending to
the seat of the giant race.

Fiölsvith
Along the humid ways
haste the back hence,
here, wretch! is no place
for thee.

2. What monster is it
before the fore-court
standing,
and hovering round the
perilous flame?
Whom dost thou seek?
Of what art thou in quest?
Or what, friendless being!
desirest thou to know?

Wanderer
3. What monster is that,
before the fore-court
standing,
who to the wayfarer
offers not hospitality?
Void of honest fame,
prattler! hast thou lived:
but hence hie thee home.

Fiölsvith
4. Fiölsvith is my name;
wise I am of mind,
though of food not
prodigal.
Within these courts
thou shalt never come:
so now, wretch! take
thyself off.

Wanderer
5. From the eye's delight
few are disposed to hurry,
where there is something
pleasant to be seen.
These walls, methinks,
shine around golden halls.
Here I could live
contented with my lot.
Fiölsvith
6. Tell me, youth;
of whom thou art born,
or of what race hath
sprung.

Wanderer
7. Vindkald I am called,
Varkald was my father
named,
his sire was Fiölkald.

8. Tell me, Fiölsvith!

that which I will ask thee,
and I desire to know:
who here holds sway,
and has power over
these lands and costly
halls?

Fiölsvith
9. Menglöd is her name,
her mother her begat
with Svaf, Thorińs son.
She here holds sway,
and has power over
these lands and costly
halls.

Vindkald
10. Tell me, Fiölsvith!
etc.
what the grate is called,
than which among the
gods
mortals never saw a
greater artifice?

Fiölsvith
11. Thrymgiöll it is
called,
and Solblindís
three sons constructed it:
a fetter fastens
eery wayfarer,
who lifts it from its
opening.

Vindkald
12. Tell me, Fiölsvith!
etc.
what that structure is
called,
than which among the
gods
mortals never saw a
greater artifice?

Fiölsvith
13. Gastropnir it is called,
and I constructed it
of Leirbrimir's limbs.
I have so supported it,
that it will ever stand
while the world lasts.

Vindkald
14. Tell me, Fiölsvith!
etc.
what those dogs are
called,
that chase away the
giantesses,
and safety to the fields
restore?

Fiölsvith
15. Gifr the one is called,
the other Geri,
if thou that wouldst
know.

Eleven watches
they will keep,
until the powers perish.

Vindkald
16. Tell me, Fiölsvith!
etc.
whether any man
can enter
while those fierce
assailants sleep?

Fiölsvith
17. Alternate sleep
was strictly to them
enjoined,
since to the watch they
were appointed.
One sleeps by night,
by day the other,
so that no wight can enter
if he comes.

Vindkald
18. Tell me, Fiölsvith!
etc.
whether there is any food
that men can get,
such that they can run in
while they eat?

Fiölsvith
19. Two repasts
lie in Vidofnir's wings,
if thou that wouldst
know:
that is alone such food
as men can give them,
and run in while they eat.
Vindkald

20. Tell me, Fiölsvith!
etc.
what that tree is called
that with its branches
spreads itself
over every land?

Fiölsvith
21. Mimameidr it is
called;
but few men know
from what roots it
springs:
it by that will fall
which fewest know.
Nor fire nor iron will
harm it.

Vindkald
22. Tell me, Fiölsvith!
etc.
to what the virtue is
of that famed tree
applied,
which nor fire nor iron
will harm?

Fiölsvith
23. Its fruit shall
on the fire be laid,
for labouring women;
out then will pass
what would in remain:
so it is a creator of
mankind.

Vindkald
24. Tell me, Fiölsvith!
etc.
what the cock is called
that sits in that lofty tree,
and all-glittering is with
gold?

Fiölsvith
25. Vidofnir he is called;
in the clear air he stands,
in the boughs of Mimás
tree:
afflictions only brings,
together indissoluble,
the swart bird at his
lonely meal.

Vindkald
26. Tell me, Fiölsvith!
etc.
whether there be any
weapon,
before which Vidofnir
may
fall to Heĺs abode?

27. Hævatein the twig is
named,
and Lopt plucked it,
down by the gate of
Death.
In an iron chest it lies
with Sinmoera,
and is with nine strong
locks secured.

Vindkald
28. Tell me, Fiölsvith!
etc.
whether he will alive
return,
who seeks after,
and will take, that rod?

Fiölsvith
29. He will return
who seeks after,
and will take, the rod,
if he bears that
which few possess
to the dame of the glassy
clay.

Vindkald
30. Tell me, Fiölsvith!
etc.

whether there is any
treasure,
that mortals can obtain,
at which the pale giantess
will rejoice?

Fiölsvith
31. The bright sickle
that lies in Vidofnir's
wings,
thou in a bag shalt bear,
and to Sinmoera give,
before she will think fit
to lend an arm for
conflict.

Vindkald
32. Tell me, Fiölsvith!
etc.
what this hall is called,
which is girt round
with a curious flickering
flame?

Fiölsvith
33. Hyr it is called,
and it will long
tremble as on a lance's
point.
This sumptuous house
shall, for ages hence,
be but from hearsay
known.

Vindkald
34. Tell me, Fiölsvith!
etc.
which of the Æsir's sons
has that constructed,
which within the court I
saw?

Fiölsvith
35. Uni and Iri,
Bari and Ori,
Var and Vegdrasil,
Dorri and Uri,
Delling and Atvard,
Lidskialf, Loki.

Vindkald
36. Tell me, Fiölsvith!
etc.
what that mount is called
on which I see
a splendid maiden stand?

Fiölsvith
37. Hyfiaberg 'tis called,
and long has it a solace
been
to the bowed-down and
sorrowful:
each woman becomes
healthy,
although a year's disease
she have,
if she can but ascend it.

Vindkald
38. Tell me, Fiölsvith!
etc.
how those maids are called,
who sit at Menglöd's knees
in harmony together?

Fiölsvith
39. Hlif the first is called,
the second is Hlifthursa,
the third Thiodvarta,
Biört and Blid,
Blidr, Frid,
Eir and Örboda.

Vindkald
40. Tell me, Fiölsvith!
etc.
whether they protect
those who offer to them,
if it should, be needful?

Fiölsvith
41. Every summer
in which men offer to them,
at the holy place,
no pestilence so great shall come
to the sons of men,
but they will free each from peril.

Vindkald
42. Tell me, Fiölsvith!
etc.
whether there is any man
that may in Menglöd's
soft arms sleep?

Fiölsvith
43. There is no man
who may in Menglöd's
soft arms sleep,
save only Svipdag;
to him the sun-bright maid
is for wife betrothed.

Vindkald
44. Set the doors open!
Let the gate stand wide;
here thou mayest Svipdag see;
but yet go learn
if Menglöd will
accept my love.

Fiölsvith
45. Hear, Menglöd!
A man is hither come:
go and behold the stranger;
the dogs rejoice;

the house is opened.
I think it must be
Svipdag.

Menglöd
46. Fierce ravens shall,
on the high gallows,
tear out thy eyes,
if thou art lying,
that hither from afar is
come
the youth unto my halls.

47. Whence art thou
come?
Whence hast thou
journeyed?
How do thy kindred call
thee?
Of thy race and name
I must have a token,
if I was betrothed to thee.

Svipdag
48. Svipdag I am named,
Solbiart was my father
named;
thence the winds on the
cold ways drove me.
Urd's decree
may no one gainsay,
however lightly uttered.

Menglöd
49. Welcome thou art:
my will I have obtained;
greeting a kiss shall
follow.
A sight unlooked-for
gladdens most persons,
when one the other loves.

50. Long have I sat
on my loved hill,
day and night
expecting thee.
Now that is come to pass
which I have hoped,
that thou, dear youth,
again
to my halls art come.

Svipdag
51. Longing I have
undergone
for thy love;
and thou, for my
affection.
Now it is certain,
that we shall pass
our lives together.

16: Hyndluliόð.: The Lay of Hyndla.

Freyja rides with her favourite Ottar to Hyndla, a Vala, for the purpose of obtaining information respecting Ottaŕs geneology, such information being required by him in a legal dispute with Angantyr. Having obtained this, Freyja further requests Hyndla to give Ottar a portion (minnisöl) that will enable him to remember all tha thas been told him. This she refuses, but is forced to comply by Freyja having encircled her cave with flames. She gives him the potion, but accompanied by a malediction, which is by Freyja turned to a blessing.

Freyja
1. Wake, maid of maids!
Wake, my friend!
Hyndla! Sister!
who in the cavern
dwellest.
Now there is a dark of
darks;
we will both
to Valhall ride,
and to the holy fane.

2. Let us Heriafather pray
into our minds to enter,
he gives and grants
gold to the deserving.
He gave to Hermod
a helm and corslet,
and from him Sigmund
a sword received.

3. Victory to his sons he
gives,
but to some riches;
eleoquence to the great,
and to men, wit;
fair wind he gives to
traders,
but poesy to skallds;
valour he gives
to many a warrior.

4. She to Thor will offer,
she to him will pray,
that to thee he may
be well disposed;
although he bears ill will
to Jötun females.

5. Now of thy wolves
take one
from out the stall;
let him run
with runic rein.[1]

Hyndla
6. Sluggish is thy hog
the god's way to tread:

Freyja
7. I will my noble
palfrey saddle.

Hyndla
8. False art thou, Freyja!
who tempest me:
by thy eyes thou showest
it,
so fixed upon us;
while thou thy man hast
on the dead-road,[2]
the young Ottar,
Innstein's son.

Freyja
9. Dull art thou, Hyndla!
methinks thou dreamest,
since thou sayest that my
man
is on the dead-road with
me;
there where my hog
sparkles
with its golden bristles,
hight Hildisvini,
which for me made
the two skilful dwarfs,
Dain and Nabbi.
From the saddle we will
talk:
let us sit,
and of princely
families discourse,
of those chieftains
who from the gods
descend.
They have contested
for the dead's gold,
Ottar the young
and Angantýr.

10. A duty 'tis to act
so that the young prince
his paternal heritage may
have,
after his kindred.

11. An offer-stead to me
he raised,
with stones constructed;
now is that stone
as glass become.
With the blood of oxen
he newly sprinkled it.
Ottar ever trusted
in the Asyniur.

12. Now let us reckon up
the ancient families,
and the races of
exalted men.
Who are the Skiöldings?
Who are the Skilfings?
Who the Ödlings?
Who the Ylfings?
Who the höld-born?
Who the hers-born?
The choicest race of men
under heaven?

Hyndla
13. Thou, Ottar! art
of Innstein born,
but Innstein was
from Alf the Old,
Alf was from Ulf.
Ulf from Sæfari,
but Sæfari
from Svan the Red.

14. Thy father had a
mother,
for her necklaces famed,
she, I think, was named
Hledis the priestess;
Frodi her father was,
and her mother Friant:
all that stock is reckoned
among chieftains.
15. Ali was of old
of men the strongest,
Halfdan before him,
the highest of the
Skiöldungs;
(Famed were the wars
by those chieftains led)
his deeds seemed to soar
to the skirts of heaven.

16. By Eimund aided,
chief of men,
he Sigtrygg slew
with the cold steel.
He Almveig had to wife,
first of women.
They begat and had
eighteen sons.

17. From them the
Skiöldungs,
from them the Skilfings,
from them the Ödlings,
from them the Ynglings,
from them the höld-born,
from them the hers-born,
the choicest race of men
under heaven.
All that race is thine,
Ottar Heimski!

18. Hildegun
her mother was,
of Svafa born
and a sea-king.
All that race is thine,

Ottar Heimski!
Carest thou to know?
Wishest thou a longer
narrative?

19. Dag wedded Thora,
mother of warriors;
of that race were born
the noble champions,
Fradmar, Gyrd,
and the Frekis both,
Am, Jösur, Mar,
Alf the Old.
Carest thou this to know?
Wishest thou a longer
narrative?

20. Ketil their friend was
named,
heir of Klyp;
he was maternal grandsire
of thy mother.
Then was Frodi
yet before Kari,
but the eldest born
was Alf.

21. Nanna was next,
Nökkvís daughter;
her son was
thy father's kinsman,
ancient is that kinship.
I knew both
Brodd and Hörfi.
All that race is thine,
Ottar Heimski!

22. Isolf, Asolf,
Ölmod́s sons
and Skurhild́s
Skekkiĺs daugher;
thou shalt yet count
chieftains many.
All that race is thine,
Ottar Heimski!

23. Gunnar, Balk,
Grim, Ardskafi,
Jarnskiöld, Thorir,
Ulf, Ginandi,
Bui and Brami,
Barri and Reifnir,
Tind and Tyrfing,
the two Haddingis.
All that race is thine,
Ottar Heimski!

24. To toil and tumult
were the sons
of Arngrim born,
and of Eyfura:
ferocious berserkir,
calamity of every kind,
by land and sea,
like fire they carried.
All that race is thine,
Ottar Heimski!

25. I knew both
Brodd and Hörfi,
they were in the court
of Hrolf the Old;
all descended
from Jörmunrek,
son-in-law of Sigurd.
(Listen to my story)
the dread of nations,
him who Fafnir slew.

26. He was a king,
from Völsung sprung,
and Hiördis
from Hrödung;
but Eylimi
from the Ödlings.
All that race it thine,
Ottar Heimski!

27. Gunnar and Högni,
sons of Giuki;
and Gudrun likewise,
their sister.
Guttorm was not
of Giuki's race,
although he brother was
of them both.
All that race is thine,
Ottar Heimski!

28. Harald Heildetönn,
born of Hrærekir
Slöngvanbaugi;
he was a son of Aud,
Aud the rich
was Ivar's daugther;
but Radbard was
Randver's father.
They were heroes
to the gods devoted.
All that race is thine,
Ottar Heimski!

29. There were eleven
Æsir reckoned,
when Baldr on
the pile was laid;
him Vali showed himself
worthy to avenge,
his own brother:
he the slayer slew.
All that race is thine,
Ottar Heimski!

30. Baldr's father was
son of Bur:
Frey to wife had Gerd,
she was Gymir's
daugther,
from Jötuns sprung
and Aurboda;
Thiassi also
was their relation,
that haughty Jötun;
Skadi was his daughter.

31. We tell thee much,

and remember more:
I admonish thee thus
much to know.
Wishest thou yet a longer
narrative?

32. Haki was not the
worst
of Hvedna's sons,
and Hiövard
was Hvednás father;
Heid and Hrossthiof were
of Hrimnir's race.

33. All the Valas are
from Vidolf;
all the soothsayers
from Vilmeidr,
all the sorcerers
from Svarthöfdi;
all the Jötuns
come from Ymir.

34. We tell thee much,
and more remember,
I admonish thee thus
much to know.
Wishest thou yet a longer
narrative?

35. There was one born,
in times of old,
with wondrous might
endowed,
of origin divine:
nine Jötun maids
gave birth
to the gracious god,
at the worlds margin.

36. Gialp gave him birth,
Greip gave him birth,
Eistla gave him birth,
and Angeia;
Ulfrun gave him birth,
and Eyrgiafa,
Imd and Atla,
and Jarnsaxa.

37. The boy was
nourished
with the strength of earth,
with the ice-cold sea,
and with Son's blood.
We tell thee much,
and more remember.
I admonish thee thus
much to know.
Wishest thou a yet longer
narrative?

38. Loki begat the wolf
with Angrboda,
but Sleipnir he begat
with Svadilfari:
one monster seemed
of all most deadly,
which from Byleist's

brother sprang.

39. Loki, scorched up[3]
in his heart's affections,
had found a half-burnt
woman's heart.
Loki became guileful
from that wicked woman;
thence in the world
are all giantesses come.

40. Ocean towers with
storms
to heaven itself,
flows o'er the land;
the air is rent:
thence come snows
and rapid winds;
then it is decreed
that the rain should cease.

41. There was one born
greater than all,
the boy was nourished
with the strength of earth;
he was declared a ruler,
mightiest and richest,
allied by kinship
to all princes.

42. Then shall another
come,
yet mightier,
although I dare not
his name declare.
Few may see
further forth
than when Odin
meets the wolf.

Freyja
43. Bear thou the
memory-cup
to my guest,
so that he may all
the words repeat
of this discourse,
on the third morn,
when he and Angantýr
reckon up races.

Hyndla
44. Go thou quickly
hence,
I long to sleep;
more of my wondrous
power
thou gettest not from me.
Thou runnest, my hot
friend,
out at nights,
as among he-goats
the she-goat goes.

45. Thou hast run thyself
mad,
ever longing;
many a one has stolen

under thy girdle.
Thou runnest, my hot
friend,
out at nights,
as among he-goats
the she-goat goes.

Freyja
46. Fire I strike
over thee, dweller of the
wood!
so that thou goest not
ever away from hence.

Hyndla
47. Fire I see burning,
and the earth blazing;
many will have
their lives to save.
Bear thou the cup
to Ottar's hand,
the mead with venom
mingled,
in an evil hour!

Freyja
48. Thy malediction
shall be powerless;
although thou, Jötun-
maid!
dost evil threaten.
He shall drink
delicious draughts.
All the gods I pray
to favour Ottar.

[1] That is, with a rein inscribed with runes.
[2] The road to Valhall
[3] The sense of this and of the following line is not apparent; they stand thus in the original: Loki of hiarta lyndi brendu, fann hann hâlfsviþinn hugstein konu, for which Grimm (Myth, Vorrede XXXVII) would read, Loki ât hiarta lundi brenda, etc. Lokius comedit cor in nemore assum, invenit semiustum mentis lapidem mulieris. I believe the difficulty is beyond help.

17: Gróugaldr.: The Incantation of Groa.

Son
1. Wake up, Groa!
wake up, good woman!
at the gates of death I wake thee!
if thou remembrest,
that thou thy son badest
to thy grave_mound to come.

Mother
2. What now troubles
my only son?
With what affliction art thou burthened,
that thou thy mother callest,
who to dust is come,
and from human homes departed?

Son
3. A hateful game
thou, crafty woman, didst set before me,
whom my father has in his bosom cherished,
when thou bides me go
no one knows whither,
Menglöd to meet.

Mother
4. Long is the journey,
long are the ways,
long are meńs desires.
If it so fall out,
that hou thy will obtainest,
the event must then be as it may.

Son
5. Sing to me songs
which are good.
Mother! protect thy son.
Dead on my way
I fear to be.
I seem to young in years.

Mother
6. I will sing to thee first
one that is thought most useful,
which Rind sang to Ran;
that from thy shoulders
thou shouldst cast
what to thee seems irksome:
let thyself thyself direct.

7. A second I will sing to thee,

as thou hast to wander
joyless on the ways.
May Urd's protection
hold thee on every side,
where thou seest
turpitude.

8. A third I will sing to
thee.
If the mighty rivers
to thy life's peril fall,
Horn and Rud,
may they flow down to
Hel,
and for thee ever be
diminished.

9. A fourth I will sing to
thee.
If foes assail thee
ready on the dangerous
road,
their hearts shall fail
them,
and to thee be power,
and their minds to peace
be turned.

10. A fifth I will sing to
thee.
If bonds be
cast on thy limbs,
friendly spells I will let
on thy joints be sung,
and the lock from thy
arms shall start,
(and from thy feet the
fetter.)

11. A sixth I will sing to
thee.
If on the sea thou comest,
more stormy than men
have known it,
air and water
shall in a bag attend thee,
and a tranquil course
afford thee.

12. A seventh I will sing
to thee.
If on a mountain high
frost should assail thee,
deadly cold shall not
thy carcase injure,
nor draw thy body to thy
limbs.

13. An eighth I will sing
to thee.
If night overtake thee,
when out on the misty
way,
that the dead Christian
woman
no power may have
to do thee harm.

14. A ninth I will sing to thee.
If with a far_famed
spear_armed Jötun
thou words exchangest,
of words and wit
to thy mindful heart
abundance shall be given.

15. Go now ever
where calamity may be,
and no harm shall
obstruct thy wishes.
On a stone fast in the earth
I have stood within the door,
while songs I sang to thee.

16. My son! bear hence
thy mother's words,
and in thy breast let them dwell;
for happiness abundant
shalt thou have in life,
while of my words thou art mindful.

18: Solarlióð.: The Song of the Sun.

This singular poem, the authorship of which is, in some manuscripts, assigned to Sæmund himself, may be termed a Voice from the Dead, given under the form of a dream, in which a deceased father is supposed to address his son from another world. The first 7 strophes seem hardly connected with the following ones, which, as far as the 32nd consist chiefly in aphorisms with examples, some closely resembling those in the Havamal. In the remaining portion is given the recital of the last illness of the supposed speaker, his death, and the scenes his soul passed through on the way to its final home.

The composition exhibits a strange mixture of Christianity and Heathenism, whence it would seem that the poet's own religion was in a transition state. Of the allusions to Heathenism it is, however, to be observed that they are chiefly to persons and actions of which there is no trace in the Odinic mythology, as known to us, and are possibly the fruits of the poet's own imagination. The title of the poem is no doubt derived from the allusion to the Sun at the beginning of the strophes 39-45.

For an elaborate and learned commentary, with an interlinear version of "the Song of the Sun", the reader may consult "Les Chants de Sol", by Professor Bergmann, Strassbourg & Paris, 1858.

1. Of life and property
a fierce freebooter
despoiled mankind;
over the ways
beset by him
might no one living pass.

2. Alone he ate
most frequently,
no one invited he to his repast;
until weary,
and with failing strength,
a wandering guest

came from the way.

3. In need of drink
that way-worn man,
and hungry feigned to be:
with trembling heart
he seemed to trust
him who had been so
evil-minded.

4. Meat and drink
to the weary one he gave,
all with upright heart;
on God he thought,
the traveller's wants
supplied;
for he felt he was an evil-
doer.

5. Up stood the guest,
he evil meditated,
he had not been kindly
treated;
his sin within him
swelled,
he while sleeping
murdered
his wary cautious host.

6. The God of heaven
he prayed for help,
when being struck he
woke;
but he was doomed the
sins of him
on himself to take,
whom sackless he had
slain.

7. Holy angels came
from heaven above,
and took to them his soul:
in a life of purity
it shall ever live
with the almighty God.

8. Riches and health
no one may command,
though all go smoothly
with him.
To many that befalls
which they least expect.
No one may command his
tranquility.

9. Unnar and Sævaldi
never imagined
that happiness would fall
on them,
yet naked they became,
and of all bereft,
and, like wolves, ran to
the forest.

10. The force of pleasure
has many a one bewailed.

Cares are often caused by women;
pernicious they become,
although the mighty God
them pure created.

11. United were
Svafud and Skarthedin,
neither might without the other be,
until to frenzy they were driven
for a woman;
she was destined for their perdition.

12. On account of that fair maid,
neither of them cared
for games or joyous days;
no other thing
could they in memory bear
then that bright form.

13. Sad to them were
the gloomy nights,
no sweet sleep might they enjoy:
but from that anguish
rose hate intense
between the faithful friends.

14. Hostile deeds
are in most places
fiercely avenged.
To the holm they went,[1]
for that fair woman,
and each one found his death.

15. Arrogance should no one entertain:
I indeed have seen
that those who follow her,
for the most part,
turn from God.

16. Rich were both,
Radey and Vebogi,
and thought only of their well-being;
now they sit
and turn their sores
to various hearths.

17. They in themselves confided,
and though themselves
alone to be
above all people;
but their lot
Almighty God was pleased
otherwise to appoint.

18. A life of luxury they
led,
in may ways,
and had gold for sport.
Now they are requited,
so that they must walk
between frost and fire.

19. To thy enemies
trust thou never,
although they speak thee
fair:
promise them good:
'tis good to have another's
injury
as a warning.

20. So it befell
Sörli the upright,
when he placed himself in
Vigolf's power;
he confidently trusted
him,
his brother's murderer,
but he proved false.

21. Peace to them he
granted,
with heart sincere;
they in return promised
him gold,
feigned themselves
friends.,
while they together
drank;
but then came forth their
guile.

22. Then afterwards,
on the second day,
when they in Rýgiardal
rode,
they with swords
wounded him
who sackless was,
and let his life go forth.

23. His corpse they
dragged
(on a lonely way,
and cut up piecemeal)
into a well,
and would it hide;
but the holy Lord
beheld from heaven.

24. His soul summoned
home
the true God
into his joy to come;
but the evil doers
will, I ween, late
be from torments called.

25. Do thou pray the Disir
of the Lord's words

to be kind to thee in
spirit:
for a week after,
all shall then go happily,
according to thy will.

26. For a deed of ire
that thou has perpetrated,
never atone with evil:
the weeping thou shalt
sooth with benefits:
that is salutary to the soul.

27. On God a man
shall for good things call,
on him who has mankind
created.
Greatly sinful is
every man
who late finds the Father.

28. To be solicited, we
opine,
is with all earnestness
for that which is lacking:
of all things may be
destitute
he who for nothing asks:
few heed the wants of the
silent.

29. Late I came,
though called betimes,
to the supreme Judge's
door;
thitherward I yearn;
for it was promised me,
he who craves it shall of
the feast partake.

30. Sins are the cause
that sorrowing we depart
from this world:
no one stands in dread,
if he does no evil:
good it is to be blameless.

31. Like unto wolves
all those seem
who have a faithless
mind:
so he will prove
who has to go
through ways strewed
with gleeds.

32. Friendly counsels,
and wisely composed,
seven
I have imparted to thee:
consider thou them well,
and forget them never:
they are all useful to
learn.

33. Of that I will speak,
how happy I was
in the world,

and secondly,
how the sons of men
reluctantly become
corpses.

34. Pleasure and pride
deceive the sons of men
who after money crave;
shining riches
at last become a sorrow:
many have riches driven
to madness.

35. Steeped in joys
I seemed to men;
for little did I see before
me:
our worldly sojourn
has the Lord created
in delights abounding.

36. Bowed down I sat,
long I tottered,
of life was most desirous;
but He prevailed
who was all-powerful:
onward are the ways of
the doomed.

37. The cords of Hel
were tightly
bound round my sides;
I would rend them,
but they were strong.
"Tis easy free to go.

38. I alone knew,
how on all sides
my pains increased.
The maids of Hel each
eve
with horror bade me
to their home.

39. The sun I saw,
true star of day,
sink in its roaring home;
but Hel's grated doors
on the other side I heard
heavily creaking.

40. The sun I saw
with blood-red beams
beset:
(fast was I then from this
world declining)
mightier she appeared,
in many ways
than she was before.

41. The sun I saw,
and it seemed to me
as if I saw a glorious god:
I bowed before her,
for the last time,
in the world of men.

42. The sun I saw:

she beamed forth so
that I seemed nothing to
know;
but Giöll's streams
roared from the other side
mingled much with
blood.

43. The sun I saw,
with quivering eyes,
appalled and shrinking;
for my heart
in great measure was
dissolved in languor.

44. The sun I saw
seldom sadder;
I had then almost from
the world declined:
my tongue was
as wood become,
and all was cold without
me.

45. The sun I saw
never after,
since that gloomy day;
for the mountain-waters
closed over me,
and I went called from
torments.

46. The star of hope,
when I was born,
fled from my breast
away;
high it flew,
settled nowhere,
so that it might find rest.

47. Longer than all
was that one night,
when stiff on my straw I
lay;
then becomes manifest
the divine word:
"Man is the same as
earth."

48. The Creator God can
it estimate and know,
(He who made heaven
and earth)
how forsaken
many go hence,
although from kindred
parted.

49. Of his works
each has the reward:
happy is he who does
good.
Of my wealth bereft,
to me was destined
a bed strewed with sand.
50. Bodily desires
men oftentimes seduce,

of them has many a one
too much:
water of baths
was of all things to me
most loathsome.

51. In the Norns' seat
nine days I sat,
thence I was mounted on
a horse:
there the giantess's sun
shone grimly
through the dripping
clouds of heaven.

52. Without and within,
I seemed to traverse all
the seven nether worlds:
up and down,
I sought an easier way,
where I might have the
readiest paths.

53. Of that is to be told,
which I first saw,
when I to the worlds of
torment came:-
scorched birds,
which were souls,
flew numerous as flies.

54. From the west I saw
Von's dragons fly,
and Glæval's paths
obscure:
their wings they shook;
wide around me seemed
the earth and heaven to
burst.

55. The sun's hart I saw
from the south coming,
he was by two together
led:
his feet stood on the
earth,
but his horns
reached up to heaven.

56. From the north riding
I saw
the sons of Nidi,
they were seven in all:
from full horns,
the pure mead they drank
from the heaven-god's
well.

57. The wind was silent,
the waters stopped their
course;
then I heard a doleful
sound:
for their husbands
false-faced women
ground earth for food.

58. Gory stones
those dark women
turned sorrowfully;
bleeding hearts hung
out of their breasts,
faint with much affliction.

59. Many a man I saw
wounded go
on those gleed-strewed
paths;
their faces seemed
to me all reddened
with reeking blood.

60. Many men I saw
to earth gone down,
who holy service might
not have;
heathen stars
stood above their heads,
painted with deadly
characters.

61. I saw those men
who much envy harbour
at another's fortune;
bloody runes
were on their breasts
graved painfully.

62. I there saw men
many not joyful;
they were all wandering
wild:
this he earns,
who by this world's vices
is infatuated.

63. I saw those men
who had in various ways
acquired other's property:
in shoals they went
to Castle-covetous,
and burthens bore of lead.

64. I saw those men
who many had
of life and property
bereft:
through the breasts
of those men passed
strong venomous
serpents.

65. I saw those men
who the holy days
would not observe:
their hands were
on hot stones
firmly nailed.

66. I saw those men
who from pride
valued themselves too
highly;
their garments

ludicrously were
in fire enveloped.

67. I saw those men
who had many
false words of others
uttered:
Hel's ravens
from their heads
their eyes miserably tore.

68. All the horrors
thou wilt not get to know
which Hel's inmates
suffer.
Pleasant sins
end in painful penalties:
pains ever follow
pleasure.

69. I saw those men
who had much given
for God's laws;
pure lights were
above their heads
brightly burning.

70. I saw those men
who from exalted mind
helped the poor to aid:
angels read
holy books
above their heads.

71. I saw those men
who with much fasting
had
their bodies wasted:
God's angels
bowed before them:
that is the highest joy.

72. I saw those men
who had put food
into their mothers' mouth:
their couches were
on the rays of heaven
pleasantly placed.

73. Holy virgins
had cleanly washed
the souls from sin
of those men,
who for a long time had
themselves tormented.

74. Lofty cars I saw
towards heaven going;
they were on the way to
God:
men guided them
who had been murdered
wholly without crime.

75. Almighty Father!
greatest Son!
holy Spirit of heaven!
Thee I pray,

who hast us all created;
free us all from miseries.

76. Biugvör and Listvör
sit at Herðiŕs doors,
on resounding seat;
iron gore
falls from their nostrils,
which kindles hate among
men.

77. Odin's wife
rows in earth's ship,
eager after pleasures;
her sails are
reefed late,
which on the ropes of
desire are hung.

78. Son! I thy father
and Solkatla's sons
have alone obtained for
thee
that horn of hart,
which from the grave-
mound bore
the wise Vigdvalin.

79. Here are runes
which have engraven
Niörd́s daughters nine,
Radvör the eldest,
and the youngest
Kreppvör,
and their seven sisters.

80. How much violence
have they perpetrated
Svaf and Svaflogi!
bloodshed they have
excited,
and wounds have sucked,
after an evil custom.

81. This lay,
which I have taught thee,
thou shalt before the
living sing,
the Sun-Song,
which will appear
in many parts no fiction.

82. Here we part,
but again shall meet
on the day of men's
rejoicing.
Oh Lord!
unto the dead grant peace,
and to the living comfort.

83. Wondrous lore
has in dream to thee been
sung,
but thou hast seen the
truth:
no man has been
so wise created

that has before heard the Sun-Song.

[1] That is, they engaged in single combat; the spot for such encounters being called a holm, consisting of a circular space marked out by stones.

19: Völundarkviða: The Lay of Völund.

There was a king in Sweden named Nidud: he had two sons and a daughter, whose name was Bödvild. There were three brothers, sons of a king of the Finns, one was called Slagfid, the second Egil, the third Völund. They went on snow-shoes and hunted wild-beasts. They came to Ulfdal, and there made themselves a house, where there is a water called Ulfsíar. Early one morning they found on the border of the lake three females sitting and spinning flax. Near them lay their swan-plumages: they were Valkyriur. Two of them, Hladgud-Svanhvit and Hervör-Alvit, were daughters of King Hlödver; the third was Ölrún, a daughter of Kiár of Valland. They took them home with them to their dwelling. Egil had Ölrún, Slagfid Svanhvít, and Völund Alvit. They lived there seven years, when they few away seeking conflicts, and did not return. Egil then went on snow-shoes in search of Ölrún, and Slagfid in search of Svanhvit, but Völund remained in Ulfdal. He was a most skilful man, as we learn from old traditions. King Nidud ordered him to be seized, so as it is here related.

1. Maids flew from the south,
through the murky wood,
Alvit the young,[1]
fate to fulfil.
she a swań's plumage bore;
but the third,
their sister,
the white neck clasped
of Völund.

2. One of them,
of maidens fairest,
to his comely breast
Egil clasped.
Svanhvit was the second,

3. There they stayed
seven winters through;
but all the eighth
were with longing seized;
and in the ninth

fate parted them.
The maidens yearned
for the murky wood,
the young Alvit,
fate to fulfil.

4. From the chase came
the ardent hunters,
Slagfid and Egil,
found their house
deserted,
went out and in,
and looked around.
Egil went east
after Ölrún,
and Slagfid west
after Svanhvit;

5. But Völund alone
remained in Ulfdal.
He the red gold set
with the hard gem,
well fastened all the rings
on linden bast,
and so awaited
his bright consort,
if to him
she would return.

6. It was told to Nidud,
the Niararś lord,
that Völund alone
remained in Ulfdal.
In the night went men,
in studded corslets,
their shields glistened
in the waning moon.

7. From their saddles they
alighted
at the housés gable,
thence went in
through the house.
On the bast they saw
the rings all drawn,
seven hundred,
which the warrior owned.

8. And they took them
off,
and they put them on,
all save one,
which they bore away.
Came then from the chase
the ardent hunter,
Völund, gliding[2]
on the long way.

9. To the fire he went,
beaŕs flesh to roast.
Soon blazed the
brushwood,
and the arid fir,
the wind-dried wood,
before Völund.

10. On the bearskin sat,
his rings counted,

the Alfar's companion:
one was missing.
He thought that Hlödver's
daughter had it,
the young Alvit,
and that she was returned.

11. So long he sat
until he slept;
and he awoke
of joy bereft:
on his hands he felt
heavy constraints,
and round his feet
fetters clasped.

12. "Who are the men
that on the rings'
possessor
have laid bonds?
and me have bound?"

13. Then cried Nidud,
the Niarars' lord:
"Whence gottest thou,
Völund!
Alfar's chief![3]
our gold,
in Ulfdal?"

14. "No gold was here
in Grani's path,[4]
far I thought our land
from the hills of Rhine.
I mind me that we more
treasures possessed,
when, a whole family,
we were at home.

15. Hladgud and Hervör
were of Hlödver born;
know was Ölrún,
Kiar's daughter,
she entered
into the house,
stood on the floor,
her voice moderated:
"Now is he[5] not
mirthful,
who from the forest
comes."

King Nidud gave to his daughter Bödvild the ring which had been taken from the bast in Völund's house; but he himself bore the sword that had belonged to Völund. The queen said:

16. His teeth he shows,

when the sword he sees,
and Bödvild's ring
he recognizes:
threatening are his eyes
as a glistening serpent's:
let be severed
his sinews' strength;
and set him then
in Sævarstad.

This was done; he was hamstrung and then set on a certain small island near the shore, called Sævarstad. He there forged for the king all kinds of jewellery work. No one was allowed to go to him, except the king. Völund said:

17. "The sword shines
in Nidud's belt,
which I whetted
as I could most skilfully,
and tempered,
as seemed to me most
cunningly.
That bright blade for ever
is
taken from me:
never shall I see it
borne into Völund's
smithy.

18. Now Bödvild wears
my consort's
red-gold rings:[6]
for this I have no
indemnity."
He sat and never slept,
and his hammer plied;
but much more speedy
vengeance
devised on Nidud.

19. The two young sons
of Nidud ran
in at the door to look,
in Sævarstad.
To the chest they came,
for the keys asked;
manifest was their
grudge,
when therein they looked.

20. Many necklaces were there,
which to those youths appeared
of the red gold to be,
and treasures.
"Come ye two alone,
to-morrow come;
that gold shall
be given to you.

21. Tell it not to the maidens,
nor to the household folk,
nor to any one,
that ye have been with me."
Early called
one the other,
brother, brother:
"Let us go see the rings."

22. To the chest they came,
for the keys asked;
manifest was their grudge,
when therein they looked.
Of those children[7] he
the heads cut off,
and under the prison's mixen
laid their bodies.[8]

23. But their skulls
beneath the hair
he in silver set,
and to Nidud gave;
and of their eyes
precious stones he formed,
which to Nidud's
wily wife he sent.

24. But of the teeth
of the two
breast-ornaments he made,
and to Bödvild sent.
Then did Bödvild
praise the ring:
to Völund brought it,
when she had broken it:
"I dare to no one tell it,
save alone to thee."

Völund
25. "I will so repair
the fractured gold,
that to thy father
it shall fairer seem,
and to thy mother
much more beautiful,
and to thyself,
in the same degree."

26. He then brought her beer,

that he might succeed the
better,
as on her seat
she fell asleep.
"Now have I
my wrongs avenged,
all save one
in the wood
perpetrated."[9]

27. "I wish," said Völund,
"that on my feet I were,
of the use of which
Nidud's men have
deprived me."
Laughing Völund
rose in the air:
Bödvild weeping
from the isle departed.
She mourned her lover's
absence,
and for her father's wrath.

28. Stood without
Nidud's wily wife;
then she went in
through the hall;
but he on the enclosure
sat down to rest.
"Art thou awake
Niarars' lord!"

29. "Ever am I awake,
joyless I lie to rest,
when I call to mind
my children's death:
my head is chilled,
cold are to me thy
counsels.
Now with Völund
I desire to speak."

30. "Tell me, Völund,
Alfars' chief!
of my brave boys
what is become?"

31. "Oaths shalt thou
first to me swear,
by board of ship,
by rim of shield,
by shoulder of steed,
by edge of sword,
that thou wilt not slay
the wife of Völund,
nor of my bride
cause the death;
although a wife I have
whom ye know,
or offspring
within thy court.

32. To the smithy go,
which thou has made,
there wilt thou the
bellows find
with blood besprinkled.
The heads I severed

of thy boys,
and under the prison's
mixen
laid their bodies.

33. But their skulls
beneath the hair
I in silver set,
and to Nidud gave;
and of their eyes
precious stones I formed,
which to Nidud's
wily wife I sent.

34. Of the teeth
of the two,
breast-ornaments I made,
and to Bödvild sent.
Now Bödvild goes
big with child,
the only daughter
of you both."

35. "Word didst thou
never speak
that more afflicted me,
or for which I would
more severely punish
thee.
There is no man so tall
that he from thy horse can
take thee,
or so skilful
that he can shoot thee
down,
thence where thou
floatest
up in the sky."

36. Laughing Völund
rose in air,
but Nidud sad
remained sitting.

37. "Rise up Thakrád,
my best of thralls!
bid Bödvild,
my fair-browed daughter,
in bright attire come,
with her sire to speak.

38. Is it, Bödvild! true
what has been told to me,
that thou and Völund
in the isle together sat?"

39. "True it is, Nidud!
what has been told to
thee,
that Völund and I
in the isle together sat,
in an unlucky hour:
would it had never been!
I could not
against him strive,
I might not
against him prevail."

[1] Here two lines, mentioning Svanhvit and Ölrun, appear to me to be lost. But see Str. 3 l. 9.
[2] On snow-shoes.
[3] The designation of Alfars' chief, or prince, applied to Völund, who, as we learn from the prose introduction, was a son of a king of the Finns, may perhaps be accounted for by the circumstance that the poem itself hardly belongs to the Odinic Mythology, and was probably composed when the system was in its decline and giving place to the heroic or romantic. Bp. Müller (Sagabibl. II, p. 158) would derive Völund from Alfheim, an ancient name of a district in Norway bordering on Sweden.
[4] Sigurd's horse: See Sig. II. Intro.
[5] The he refers to Völund, who speaks of himself in the 3d person. This 15th strophe is to all appearance an interpolation.
[6] We had previously (Str. 8, 10) been informed that one ring only had been taken.
[7] Lit. cubs.
[8] Lit. feet.
[9] The translation of this line is founded solely on a conjectural emendation of the text. The wrong alluded to may be hamstringing.

MODERN-DAY POEMS ABOUT THE GODS

Valhalla: The Myths of Norseland; A Saga, in Twelve Parts by Julia Clinto Jones

Part First

Creation

In the dim morning-dawn of Time,
Éer yet was made the green Earth fair,
With Muspel bright, and dark Niflheim,
Ginunga, still as windless air,--
These three,--two Worlds of Fire and Night
With the Abyss,--ruled in their might.

Great Surtur, with his burning sword,
Southward, at Muspeĺs gate kept ward,
And flashes of celestial flame,
Life-giving, from the Fire-World came;
While in the North, in Niflheim dread,
Dwelt Nidhögg, Dragon of the Dead;
Death-dealing frosts and vapors rise
From that black Mist-World, full of sights.
Between the two, Ginunga lay,
A yawning chasm void of day.
The salt rime-drops from Niflheiḿs streams,
Quickended by Msupeĺs living beams,
Met in Ginungágloomy space,
And Ymir bore, of Jötun race,
Who of himself Hrimthursar had,--
Frost-Giants they, and Jötunś bad.

The Cow, Audhumla, having nursed
The Jötun Ymir, licked the rime;
Just wrath to wreak on the accursed,
Then forth sprang Buri, the Divine.
From Bör, his son, came Aesir three,
Odin, and Vili, and great Vè,
Who, slaying Ymir in fierce war,
Drowned in his blood the Hrimthursar.

Now was conceived the god-like plan;--
The Spirit, Light, and mighty Fire,
Those Aesir three, their task began,--
Creatiońs wondrous work entire.
From Asgard́s Hill, their heavenly home,
The sons of Bör triumphant come!
Into Ginunga, Ymir hurled;
Out of his parts they formed the Worlds;
His body, Earth; his blood, the Sea;
Mountains, his bones; each hair, a tree;
They of his skull created sky,
Above the Earth fair archéd high,
Adorned with sparks from Muspel bright,--
The Sun, and Moon, and stars of light;
While, for defence´gainst Jötun raid,
A breast-work of his eye-brows made,
And called it Midgard, and acrost
From Asgard, threw the bridge Bifröst,
The Rainbow-bridge of colors three,--
That joined with Heaven, Earth might be.
Around the Earth they caused to swell
Deep seas upon whose utmost strand,
Jötuns escaped they gave to dwell
In black and fearful nether land.

Of Jötun race sprang black-browed Night,
Who unto bright-eyed Day gave birth;
Him Aesir placed in car of light
Darkness to chase away from Earth;
Hence Night and Day alternate course
The heavńs in circle-wise, perforce.
Night rides before on dark Hrimfax,
Who hoar-frost from his bridle shakes;
While, from Skinfaxís mane so fair,
Day scatters light óer earth and air.
Lest Jötun wolves should them devour,
To swiftest flight they bend each power.

The Sun, beneath the sultry noon,
Held, high in Heaven, her horseś́s rein;
And, with her pale companion, Moon,
Waited until the gods should deign
To mark their path, their powers to tell,
And place the stars from bright Muspel.

Born in the flesh of Ymir old,
Four dwarfs the mighty Aesir set
Four corners of the sky to hold;
While, where the outmost boundaries met,
The giant Hrae, in eagle guise
Sat in the north,-- when he shall rise,
Each mighty wing-stroke will give birth
To storms that desolate the Earth.

Within, below, óershadowing all,
The Life-Tree, Igdrasil, upreared
Its sacred boughs óver Asgarḿs Hall,
Alike by gods and Jötun feared.
Its Nornir sat by Odin's gate,

Sjjinning the thread of Time and Fate;
While deeper down was Mimir's Well
On which was laid rare Wisdom's spell ;
Its deepest root did Nidhögg gnaw,
Dragon of Death! forever more.
Hovered aloft the Eagle, Life,
While deep below lurked Death and Strife.

From high Valhalla's hall of might.
The Aesir looked the whole Earth o'er,
Did in their handiwork delight;
And then, upon the lone sea-shore
Seeing two trees, the Ash and Elm,
They chose them rulers of this realm,
Lest all the fair Creation vast
Be wasted, lonely, to the last.
Odin on them the Spirit poured,
And sense was their's by Vili's word;
With flesh, and speech, and sight were they
Endowed by power of mighty Vè.
He Ask, she Embla, they by name,
First Man and Woman now became.
On Midgard did the glorious Three
Place human life and destiny.

And now the gods' great work was o'er.
Creation, beautiful, complete.
The vaulted sky, the sea-girth shore
Lay, stretched along at Odin's feet.
But even in this early morn,
Faintly foreshadowed, was the dawn
Of that fierce struggle, deadly shock,
Which yet should end in Ragnarock;
When Good and Evil, Death and Life,

Beginning now, end then their strife.

by Julia Clinton Jones, 1878

Part Second

Valhalla

All is ended! all is done, —
Every thing beneath the sun;
While above, — the stars, the sky,--
Even Valhal, home on high
Of the gods', in Asgard's land, —
Full-perfected now doth stand.

Assemble, ye gods!
In Valhalla's high hall
Odin awaits ye,
Seats stand for ye all.

Valhalla's high hall, 'gainst wild tempest proof,
Spears are its pillars, and shields are its roof !
Battle-axes carve the feast,
Coats of mail for ev'ry guest
Drape the walls, support the board;
Valhalla, home of Odin, God,
On Asgard's height, is the delight
Of Aesir, working deeds of might.

The Eagle of great Igdrasil
High hovers o'er the sacred Hill,
Bird of Life !
While waves of strife
Round the gates of Asgard pour, —
Loud hear Thund, the Death-Stream, roar !
'Thro' the dreadful tumult made.
Fallen heroes hither wade,
Brought to Odin by Valkyr,

Battle-maidens held most dear.
O'er sea and thro' air,
'Mid lightnings' fierce glare,
Bright shields bearing.
Each maid wearing
Gleaming armor, side by side,
Down thro' lurid sky they ride.
When to Asgard back they come,
Tyr and Vidar welcome home ;
Valhal's wide hall
Has room for all !
Odin loves not empty seat;
Fairest maids the victors greet,
Fill full high with mead the bowl, —
Deeply drinks each warrior soul.

High in Valhal sits God Odin ;
By his side, in place of pride,
Decked with falcon plumes is Friga, —
Queen of gods, and Odin's bride ;
Aesir's Mother,
Fjörgyn's daughter!
Future is to her revealed
Useless, for her lips are sealed.

And now, at last
Thro' Heav'n the blast
Rings clear from Heimdal's mighty horn.
O'er earth and air its sound is borne.
Loud summons the Aesir,—
Gods of the earth and air, —
To Valhalla's glorious feast;
Fading faint the sound has ceased.

First, Thor with the bent brow,
In red beard muttering low.
Darting fierce lightnings from eye-balls that glow,
Comes, while each chariot-wheel
Echoes in thunder-peal,
As his dread hammer-shock
Makes Earth and Heaven rock,
Clouds rifting above, while Earth quakes below.

Fairest of all gods, beautiful Baldur!
Bright-browed and pure One, best loved of Aesir !
Light from his shining face
Streams over Asgard's race;
Rising from realms of night,
Bears he in car of light,
Bears he from realms afar,
Brilliantly beaming, joy to Valhalla!

Why trembles Friga on her throne
When comes blind Hoedur, Odin's son?
Lo! strong and silent drawing near,
The Mother shrinks from him in fear,
For of veiled Futurity
Pierces she the mystery;
Baldur's fate to her revealed
Useless, since her lips are sealed.

Now Loki comes, cause of ill!
Men and Aesir curse him still.
Long shall the gods deplore,
Even till Time be o'er,
His base fraud on Asgard's Hill.
While, deep in Jötunheim, most fell,
Are Fenrir, Serpent, and dread Hel, —

Pain, Sin and Death, his children three, —
Brought up and cherished ; thro' them he
Tormentor of the world shall be.

Lovely Gerda, Goddess rare!
Snow white arms and bosom fair
Gleaming soft o'er sea and air!
With her brilliant beaming blush,
Glowing lights thro' cloud-waves rush,
While Auroras from her hair
Quiver 'round the ether dome;
Shooting o'er the Northern skies
Radiant arrows from her eyes,
As to Odin's joyous home.
She, the Bride of Frey, doth come.

Great Frey himself hastens hither,
Lord of warm, life-giving weather !
Soft-dropping rains
O'er smiling plains,
And dew-drops shed
On Nature's bed,
Fall from his chariot, fleet and bright,
As speeds he on to halls of light.

Bright Iduna, Maid immortal !
Standing at Valhalla's portal.
In her casket has rich store
Of rare apples, gilded o'er ;
Those rare apples, not of Earth,
Ageing Aesir give fresh birth.

When e'er the fearful Day be past, —
That Day, of Odin's pow'r the last, —

She, unharmed shall stand the shock,
Rising over Ragnarock,
Defying Surtur, God of Fire,
Conqu'ring Serpent, Hel and Fenrir;
Then, to Gimli's golden dome,
Lead the purer Aesir home.

Amid the summons loud.
Rising o'er Earth and cloud,
Swelling, then lying faint on ambient air,
In rich melodious strain
The rune-notes' sweet refrain
Falls ling'ring, from the golden harp-strings rare !
Ecstatic notes!
Each, liquid floats
In welcome as the Aesir come ;
Circling round Odin's home,
Up to Valhalla's dome,
Triumphant, exultant, they rise ;
E'er they reel and rebound
In full billows of sound,
Thrilling greetings thro' trembling skies, —
Rare greetings o'er rain-bow arch,
As hither the Aesir march,
Still Bragi doth sing;
Higher and louder,
Clearer and prouder,
Entrancing chords ring!
Seated at Odin's feet.
Pouring forth floods of sweet
Silvery sound,
Bragi, on Idun's breast.
Singing shall ever rest ;
Soft strains from skilled finger-tips.

High themes from wise rune-graved lips
Echo around !
Delighting with his minstrelsy
The gods amid their revelry,
Until Surtur's fiery brand
Ruin flings o'er sea and land ;
Then, passed the Twilight of the gods,
E'er shall he dwell in pure abodes,
And, beyond all reach of sadness,
He shall pour forth notes of gladness.

More triumphant then the rune,
Sweeter far will be the tune
Than now in Valhal
At high festival,
When with Iduna, then shall he
The Aesir greet full joyously,
As the fierce strife on Vigrid's plain
Rolls away,
And Odin's race shall meet again
In brighter day.

Feasting and pleasure,
Joy without measure
In Valhalla hold full sway;
While, throughout the happy day,
To and fro goes Hermodur, —
O'er the Earth, and thro' the air
Swift and sure, as messenger,
Odin's mandates oft doth bear.

For even in the flowing bowl
Shall ne'er forget the god-like soul ;
Aesir great

All await
Until Heimdal sounds his call.

Valhalla's feast
Enchains no guest !
When there is need,
No sparkling mead,
Nor maiden's kiss,
Nor Asgard's bliss
Keeps them in Valhalla's hall.

To their power belongs
To quell evil, right wrongs !
Earth lifts to them her pleading hands.
For them, Air stills his tempest bands.
While Dwarf with Jötun trembling stands ;--
All bow before their high commands,
By purity made strong.

So the gods in glorious state,
Dwell within Valhalla's gate.
Cursed be the woeful hour
When shall creep in Jötun power,
When Good and Ill, in deadly shock
Shall battle in dread Ragnarock.

Julia Clinton Jones, 1878

Part Third

Einheriar's Song

Feasting sit the mighty Aesir
In Valhalla's golden splendor :
There, on snow-white arm reclining,
Garlands gay is Freya twining ;
" Mercy," singeth Baldur bright,
" Is the ornament of might.
As wreaths bedeck the victor's shield,
So Mercy crowns him on the field."

Throned high is Odin great ;
Well he loves the Hero-feast :
Wounds adorn each warrior guest.
In that radiant hall of state
Decorated seats are set,
Still with gore the swords are wet.
No craven there
To sit may dare !
In the brightness of the gods,
In those blessed, grand abodes,
Heroes feast, on couches lying,
Brave in life, most blest in dying.

Close beside him, in the Feast-hall,
Stand the beauteous Maids of War,
Who from the stricken field shall call
Bands of strong Einheriar.
Grave they wait, with bright shields gleaming,
Thoughtful, brazen spears in hand,
Of those chosen Norse-sons dreaming,
Soon to feast with Odin's band.

Whispered Odin, " Soon the gray Wolf
In Valhalla shows his face ;
Who can tell how soon in Vingolf
He shall ravage Asgard's race ?
Still seats are empty. Go ye forth
Thro' the kingdoms of the North ;
Bold warriors who have bravely fought,
Mighty deeds have nobly wrought,
Choose ye from the misty Norse-land,
Allies, at our Throne to stand ;
So, when fierce Fenrir comes in might.
They may aid us in the fight.
Heroic deed claims god-like meed,
Of valiant hearts have Aesir need.
Daughters of War !
Scent ye afar
Where red battle doth rage.
The steam of the carnage.
Who on the death-plain
Hath striven to gain
Peace for his country, and fame for his gods,
Bring here on your shields to blessed abodes,
E'er in victorious festival
To sup with us in high Valhal."

Swift thro' the startled air,
Like lightning flashing,
Thro' war-clouds dashing,
Speed the Valkyriar !
Brazen armor gleaming bright,
Glittering far with Glory's light,
Skuld, their leader, upward lifting
Pointing finger, where, thro' rifting

Crimson clouds, the path is lying
To the gods in glorious dying.

Louder the battle roars !
As rain the life-blood pours !
Shivers the barbed lance !
Sharp swords like meteors glance!
Each fiery heart
Pierced by Death's dart
Exults with sluggish life to part !
Fiercer yet see warriors battling,
Twanging bows and quivers rattling ;
Thro' the field, mad chargers rushing,
Ruthless hoofs the fallen crushing ;
O'er red earth, with strong spears crashing,
Gold haired sons of vahant sires
Like their northern blasts are dashing;
In each breast, Berserker fires
Spring hot to life
At sound of strife,
Smell of blood their sinews bracing,
Film of death from glazed eyes chasing ;
Leaping mad thro' hostile bands,
Seizing victory with fierce hands.
Clutching in wild grasp, the spear
Which shall wide their heart-strings tear ;
Triumphant, feel the welcome wound
That, sure, the seat of life has found ;
Falling on the field of slaughter
Wildly screaming joyful laughter.
Exultant, that in Saga's song,
Undying, should their deeds belong ;
Impatient, hail the maids who bear
Their souls aloft on blood-shields rare.

Downward thro' gore and carnage swooping,
Valkyriar, o'er the death-field stooping, —
The field of fame, —
In Odin's name,
Choose from the slain
On whom the hero-mark is plain.
On their brows press icy kisses,
Hold them close in cold embraces,
Snatch them from the arms of Death,
Woo back life with Glory's breath.
Back streams their golden hair
As thro' the trembling air.
Up to the Aesir,
The bold Valkyriar
On gory shields their spirits bear.
Heimdal waits at Asgard's portal,
Leads to Idun, Maid Immortal.
Gaping wounds are bound by Eyra
Ee'r they feast with blue-eyed Freya.
Then, loud the song of triumph rings, —
'Tis Bragi, lo ! the rune who sings !

Bragís Song

"Skoal to the Heroes, from battle returning !
Loud sung for aye be each death-dealing blow ;
With scorning, to Hel, the craven ones spurning,
Shield-bearing Valkyrs exultantly go.
Agape are the wounds, proud crimson marks glowing,
Gashes of glory on Heroes who die ;
Precious to Odin, the purple tide flowing,
Each red drop, a wine-draught, runes ev'ry sigh.
Fires of Conquest, the dun skies are lighting,

Vidar is chaunting victorious strain ;
Hail to our Feast-Hall ! great Heimdal, inviting,
On Gjallar-horn sounds triumphant refrain.
Mercy and Might round each bold heart are twining,
Adorning each soul like shield-graven blooms ;
Gondula and Skuld, with Rota, combining.
Bear them to Vingolf, thro' Death's welcome glooms.
Odin awaits them, in splendor proud sitting.
There gather the gods in high festival ;
Vidar and Thor shall receive as befitting
Einheriar led to golden Valhal.
Radiant couches for them are preparing.
Banquets that strengthen the warrior-soul ;
Maidens alluring full beakers are bearing, —
Love mingling with wine in o'erflowing bowl.
Softly recline they on warm bosoms, thrilling
Every quick pulse of the swift throbbing heart ;
Fulla for Friga their mead-cups high filling, —
Joy is imperfect where Love hath no part.
Safely surrounded by Passion's sweet longing,
Feast they and rest they till dawning of light ;
Pleasure and banquet to Valor belonging,
Feasting shall strengthen strong sinews of Might.
Then when the car of fair Day is uprising
From dense murky depths of cloud-land below.
On Idavöld's plain, in warfare surprising,
Till eve shall they strive, in prowess shall grow.
So, when the gray wolf to Asgard be coming,
And Jötun hosts rage in wild tempest shock,
For Odin they'll fight, in Day of dark dooming,
And battle for him, in dread Ragnarock."

So Bragi ends ; thro' list'ning air
Rise, swell, and die, the rune-notes rare.

Around the Hall, on seats of gold
Recline at ease Einheriar bold.
Bright maids, caressing, pour the mead,
While Saga chaunts each warlike deed ;
On Bragi's breast, Iduna leans,
Fair Gerda's blush thro' Valhal gleams,
And Friga welcomes to her side
The Hero-band, great Odin's pride.
In joy and feasting, passes night ;
Their souls, with dawn rejoice in fight ;
They, blest, shall dwell in fair abodes
Till comes the Twilight of the gods ;
'Gainst Hela, and 'her hosts of Dead,
They then shall strive in battle dread.

Julia Clinton Jones, 1878

Part Fourth

Loki, the Mischief Maker

Neath Valhalla's glorious dome,
In the Aesir's heavenly home,
Hither, hence, they ceaseless roam,
Rest to find, their labors done ;
Rest and pleasure
Without measure !
Finished task is pleasure won.
In fair Duty's perfect round.
Godlike souls are ever found.

From beaming day till cloudless night
The gods compete in works of might ;
Great Friga's bounteous smiles delight
And warm the Earth ; Frey, from his height.
Sunshine and rain
O'er hill and plain,
Sends to the Earth,
That plenteous birth
From Nature's womb may deck his fane.
Lovely Gerda's brilliant blushes,
Lights auroral, quiv'ring flushes.
From Frey's proud throne, thro' evening air.
Tremble in ether wavelets rare.
The grateful Earth looks up with love
To bright Valhalla's dome above ;
While, in dark Jötunheim most drear,
Giants and dwarfs shrink down in fear.

Love is the rule of all
In Valhalla's high hall !

Love is the Lord ! Love never fails !
Meekness and strength,
Mingled at length,
By Love poised in Odin's just scales.
So Love ruled all
Till Loki's fall,—
Loki, thro' whom Death, Sin and Woe
Should ravage Heaven, and Earth below.
One with Odin at the first
When the grand Creation burst
From the Aesir's glorious plan ;
One with him when Time began ;
One with him in godlike thought :
One with him in good deeds wrought ;
At every feast
His honored guest ;
His foster-brother,
Of Jötun mother ;
Fair of face, seductive grace.
Fair, as tho' of Aesir race, —
Fell he from his high estate.
Sinking in the depths of Earth,
There had Loki second birth, —
Born of Laufey, frail and base ;
His father, Wind,
Fickle, unkind ;
Dwelt he within Utgard's gate.
Thro' Jötun change, his holy fire
Burnt fiercer into wrong desire,
Mingling with evil ones, became
An earthly, devastating flame.

Deep below, on dragon's bed,
Brought he forth his children dread,

Frightful, fearful, fiendish brood !
Loving evil, hating good ;
Wily Serpent, raging Fenrir,
Dark Hel most awful, scourges drear,
Shapes so terrible,
Forms too horrible
For aught but wretched Guilt to see,
Yet ever in the world to be ;
While in fierce Loki's deepest soul
Held he most dear these offspring foul.

Now back to Asgard having come,
The gods receive the traitor home.
Little the mighty yEsir dream
Their brother be not all he seem.
But prone to hate
Their better state ;
Ah ! bitter have the high gods cursed
The evil stock which Loki nursed !
Goes he where the Aesir go,
Working still as secret foe
To undo their mighty deeds ;
Leaves them at their greatest needs.
Now soon in Asgard peace is dead !
From Valhalla rest has fled.
Creeping in
Shapes of sin,
Lust of gold and greed of gain,
Dim the light on Ida's plain.
Darkly, densely gather there
Forms that seem of thinnest air.
But as yet that show all fair; — -
Hateful forms, by Loki brought,
Which shall render Asgard naught!

Ever by stealth
Works he himself,
Foul and fiendish like his race ;
All woes that fall
On Odin's hall
Can be traced to Loki base.
From out Valhalla's portal
'Twas he who pure Iduna lured, —
Whose casket fair
Held apples rare
That render gods immortal, —
And in Thiassi's tower immured.
By his mocking, scornful mien.
Soon, in Valhal it was seen
'Twas the traitor Loki's art
Which had led Idun apart
To gloomy tower.
And Jötun power.
In eagle guise he wrought the wrong ;
In like disguise the wrathful throng
Of Aesir force him bring the maid
Safe under Asgard's mighty shade,
Guarded by god-like power most strong.

Once did the traitor rank conspire
'Gainst Asgard's mighty host entire ;
At one fell blow
To wreak dread woe.
Tho' trusted by the Aesir still,
'Twas Loki planned the hateful ill.
To Asgard came an architect,
And castle offered to erect, —
A castle high

Which should defy
Deep Jotun guile and giant raid ;
And this most wily compact made, —
Fair Freya, with the Moon and Sun
As price the fortress being done.
Darkened, indeed, and gloomy all
Earth, Asgard, and Valhalla's hall.
Should aught the Moon or Sun befall ;
Barren the earth, breathless the air,
If they should lose loved Freya's care !

Deceitful wile,
Seducing guile
So well had veiled the deep-laid scheme,
The gods could not detect, nor dream
Which one of all Valhalla's throng
Had been the author of the wrong,
Till, like a flash, the memory came, —
'Twas Loki did the payment name !
Horror and fear the gods beset ;
Finished almost the castle stood !
In three days more
The work be o'er ;
Then must they make their contract good,
And pay the awful debt.

Horror and fear
At danger near
Sudden to fiercest anger turned ;
Each god-like soul now eager burned
To force him break the contract dread,
Or vengeance wreak on Loki's head.
Guile and fear are kindred ever,
Brothers they, who may not sever !

To appease the Aesir ire
Loki bent to their desire,
That crafty builder's strongest stay,
The magic steed, to wile away.
Subtile and full of strange device,
As a young mare did he entice
The horse afar to unknown shore
Thus could the plotter harm no more.
Thro' all the night,
Till morning's light,
Swift after Svadelfari fleet
The Builder sped with anxious feet.

But useless all ! By Loki foiled,
His anger on the gods recoiled.
As further work himself could naught
Without the magic aid he brought.
Now, casting all disguise aside,
Amidst the gods in angry pride, —
While crumbling sank the half-built tower,-
In giant form and Jötun power
He stood ! Wild terror seized on all,
Lest ruin should on Asgard fall.

Dread hour for Valhal ! help was none
When Asgard's stoutest stay was gone !
The vengeful Jötun, tow'ring high,
With scoffing taunt and furious cry.
Shook gate and roof— e'en upper sky, —
Grasped at the Sun,
While pallid Moon
Coursed swiftly by !
Then on the trembling ALsir turned,
And forward dashed ;

In thunders crashed
Portal and wall, defences they
Too feeble all in such affray, —
Like reeds from out his path he spurned.

But, joy ! great Thor, returning slow
From road and toil
And frequent broil.
In wearied march
Up rainbow arch,
Heard the foul insults of the foe.
Frantic at the outrage wrought.
Maddened by the ruin sought.
As storm-wind sudden, on he swept.
Like thunder-bolt on Jötun leapt !
As on the giant foe he sprang,
'Gainst rib and thigh great Mjolnir rang,
With mighty stroke
His skull he broke,—
Then hurled him down to Hel below.

So Thor restored Valhalla's peace.
But ills in Asgard did not cease ;
Uneven balanced Odin's scales.
Kindness on evil nature fails,
Meekness naught avails !
Odin's self, distraught
By the trouble wrought.
Early and late e'er sought from Fate
Wisdom to rule in god-like state.

Julia Clinton Jones, 1878

Mimir's Well

In the dread Frost-Giants' dwelling,
In the realm of Jötunheim,
By the sacred Life Tree swelling,
Filled with mysteries of Time,
The Fountain sprang of Mimir wise, —
Mimir, knowing good and ill,—
While from those silver waves would rise
Mists that watered Igdrasil.

Thoughtful there sat Wisdom's son.
Warder of the Well
In whose waters dwell
Future, past and present lore,
From which Nornir evermore
Deeply drank. He, knowing One,
Whene'er the early dawn was breaking.
And Jötunheim from sleep awaking,
His constant thirst these waters slaking.
Would his very heart-strings steep
In full horn drawn from the deep.

With silv'ry beard which far below
His girdle fell in glist'ning flow.
With wrinkled brow yet flashing eye,
Sat Bragi old, stern Mimir nigh.
He, worthy son of Odin high.
Who held the gift of minstrelsy.
When, sudden, from the sacred Well
Up would light foam and vapor swell,
Or when o'erlapping wave.
Springing from deepest cave,
Outflung its misty spray,

Then to his golden harp would stray
His quiv'ring hand, and forth would roll
Such strains as straight enchant the soul
And hold, spell-bound, the listener's ear :
Rich runic rhymes
Of olden times,
High words of ancient lore,
Deep words from wisdom's store;—
While still thro' all the lofty measure,
With soft sounds breathing clear
Of Love's delight and godlike pleasure,
Were mingled notes of woe,
Tho' sadly, sweetly low,
The burden, wierd, unearthly wailing.
As tho' doomed spirits, unavailing,
Lost raptures mourned; then tones faint failing
Would rise again, with harp high sounding.
Thro' all the silent air resounding.
And louder, longer e'er swelled high.
Inspiring themes of poesy, —
Deeds of the gods that yet should be,
And deeds that were of Eld.
By Bragi's deep-rune-written tongue
Oft were such magic song-notes sung ;
Oft with his harp, in vesture white.
He would the Aesir proud delight.
For Inspiration's power he held

Hither came the awful Vala,
Seeress from the land of Hela,
Counsel wise to take ;
Here her thirst would slake.
Often, too, came Aesir hither ;
Often sent the Jötuns whither

Welled the fount of Wisdom fast,
Draining deep the horn of Knowledge,
Solving secrets of the Past.
Vapors, rising from the Well's edge,
Shadows of the Future cast.

Now, great Odin, just and true,
God of gods, on Asgard's hill,
Tho' his ravens faithful flew,
Bringing news from all earth through,
Tho' he quaffed from Urda's bowl
Wisdom's draughts that feast the soul,
Tho' by Sökvabek he stayed
With fair Saga, all-wise maid, —
Knowledge still
Lacked the God to right the ill.

Anxious, troubled, full of thought
To undo the evils wrought,
Gloomy, grieving,
Great God Odin
Uprising from Valhalla's throne.
Slow, the pillared Feast Hall leaving,
Engraven deep with runes within.
Sad, parting from those halls of light.
Forth rode he out into the night,
Down to dark Jötunheim alone.

Rode he long and rode he fast.
First, beneath the great Life Tree,
At the sacred Spring, sought he
Urdar, Norna of the Past ;
But her backward seeing eye
Could no knowledge now supply.

Across Verdandi's page there fell
Dark shades that ever woes foretell ;
The shadows which 'round Asgard hung
Their baleful darkness o'er it flung ;
The secret was not written there
Might save Valhal, the pure and fair.
Last, youngest of the sisters three,
Skuld, Noma of Futurity,
Implored to speak, stood silent by, —
Averted was her tearful eye.
And now, deprived of guiding light,
Onward rode Odin thro' the night.

When to the Fountain's brink he came.
The God invoked the Sage's name.
Arising slow
Respect to show
To Odin great, the Aesir chief,
Stood Mimir wise,
Whose piercing eyes
Saw that the Father sought relief
From some sharp trouble, fear or grief.

Straight to him, then, Al-father spoke.
With questioning words the silence broke.
" Oh ! all wise Mimir !
Sprung of the Aesir,
Wise wert thou e'er of old,
Prophet and seer ! unfold
What mysteries the Fates may hold !
Darkened Valhalla's hall.
The gods, confounded all !
Shame and disgrace o'er Asgard's race
Hang like an evil shrouding pall.

Where is our perfect quiet gone ?
Why has the peace of Asgard flown ?
Whence come the ills, the wrongs that fill
With strife and care our happy Hill ?
Has yet a god wrought this disgrace ?
Or springs it from the Jötun race ?
Speak thou ! for thou cans't tell !
Speak ! Watcher o'er the Well !
For, by the oath of gods.
Whatever rich rewards
Thou seek, they shall be thine ; —
Thou hast my pledge divine !"

Then spoke Mimir, stern and slow,
Filling high his golden' horn,
While deep murmurings, muttered low.
Up from out the Well were borne, —
Surges of all-knowing Time,
Utt'ring faint their solemn chime :
" Odin, drink ! this beaker drain !
Every drop a Fate shall be ;
Spill not one ! great God, in vain
Misty veil shall lift for thee.

Yet e'er these waters can be thine,
Sure pledge of payment must be mine ;-
Not helmet bright, nor corslet strong,
For they to war and strife belong ;
No jewels rare, nor golden store ;
Thine eye in pledge leave evermore."

" Uneven sway thy scales.
Blind meekness ever fails
To balance crafty strength, —

The strength that springs from ill,--
Behold ! at length
From guile and lies
Pure peace e'er flies.
Strength is evil, vain is will.
Meekness, weakness, — each is sin.
While false Loki's brood within
Ye shall cherish and shall nourish.
Giving thus ill deeds to flourish.
Be Loki's brood outcast,
In deepest depths chained fast ;
Else on the cow'ring world
Shall torments fierce be hurled !
Ruined shall fall proud Asgard's wall,
Void be each throne, — guestless each hall !
Thro' the Serpent, Hel, and Fenrir
Shall come destruction, deep and drear.
But, battle with them as ye will,
Dread Ragnarock thro' them comes still.
Too long has Loki dwelt within,
Too long have Aesir cherished sin ;
Too late ! too late, great God ! too late !
Unchangeable the words of Fate.
Ward off the ills, if so ye may, —
But Ragnarock ye cannot stay !
On Baldur's brilliant crest
What shining glories rest !
White vestured God !
Love is his sword,
Peace is his battle-cry !
But even now false Loki waits
Within the shade of Asgard's gates ;
Lo ! even now the Tempter stands
By Hoedur blind, with guiding hands.

The hour is drawing nigh !
Alas ! full soon shall Asgard's light
Be quenched and lost in blackest night !
Then triumphs Loki base !
Ravens his fearful race !
Terrible shall be the hour
When is loosed their baleful power !
Thee, thee shall hideous Fenrir slay
With cruel fangs that awful Day
When Earth shall burn, gods pass away.
All this great Friga knoweth well.
But heron's crown forbids to tell, —
The pluméd crown, Forgetfulness,
Condemns her lips to silentness.

" Quaff once again, O God !
But mark thou well each word.
Not strength of Thor, or heart of Tyr,
'Gainst Serpent, Hel, or fierce Fenrir,
Can aught alone. Let all Aesir
Rise in their might, cast out to night
Loki's foul brood ; then, in the light
Of Justice high, let judgment fall
With equal measure upon all.
Restored Valhalla's purity,
Thus Ragnarock delayed may be.
Return thou, Odin, e'er too late !
Hear, and obey the words of Fate."

So ended Mimir, while the swell
Of sigh-like murmurs from the well
Ceased with his voice ; then all was still.
Back Odin rode to Asgard's Hill,
Where, in Valhalla's shield-hung hall,

Assembled were the Aesir all
To learn what might from Fate befall.
Again, when early dawn was breaking.
And Jötunheim from sleep awaking,
Then Mimir, in the morn's first glowing.
Going to the fountain's edge.
Drank ever of the clear mead flowing
In his horn, o'er Odin's pledge.

Julia Clinton Jones, 1878

Part Sixth

Casting out of Lokís Brood

Deep down in the realms of night,
Hideous powers dwelt in might,
Brought forth on the dragon's bed,
With dwarf's dew and venom fed ;
Awful, dreadful shapes of terror.
Guilty forms of darkest horror !
Demon birth.
Accursed of Earth !
Well do the Aesir know the sight.
The traitor Loki was their father
By Angurboda, Jötun mother ;
Fierce hate and wrong
With time grown strong ;
The brood triumphant,
In this exultant,
By Fate 'twas given
That they should raven
Proud Asgard's sons and men among.

Seated high among the Aesir,
In Valhalla's shield-hung Hall,
Words of judgment spake God Odin,
Counsel took he with them all.
Fiercely burned the gods' just ire !
Angry-browed, with shoulders bent,
On their rune-graved staves they lent ;
Thro' Loki's art, had peace within
Been slain, while loathsome forms of sin, —
The Wolf, the Serpent, and pale Hel, —
Permitted upon Earth to dwell.

Rising from his Judgment-Seat,
From his spear-supported Throne,
Tow'ring to his fullest height.
Spake great Odin, " Thou most fleet
Tried Hermodur ! quick begone !
Bear my mandate ! speed thou forth
Thro' the wild and frozen North ;
From drear Jötun lands of night
Bring the foul death-dealing blight
To be judged by Aesir might."

'Twas done. The deadly brood
Before the high Throne stood.
Wildly striving,
Wrestling, writhing,
Unwilling, to the Judgment came,
Compelled by power of Odin's name.
Defiant, haughty Loki reared
His lofty head ; with threat'nings dared
Affront the gods ; if so they feared
His power of ill, to cease from wrath,
Resign to him his race of death !
Bold Tyr, undaunted, smote swift blow.
Then hurled the Evil One below.

With venom-dripping crest.
Fierce tail in mad unrest,
Coiling his loathsome length,
Launching forth rings of strength,
Forked tongue, and poisoned breath,
The Serpent, child of Death,
Menaced Valhalla high ;
With heaving throes,

And deaf 'ning blows,
Lashing the very sky.

Close by the Throne now Hela stood
Whose awful aspect chilled the blood ;
Gaunt and pallid,
Grim and livid,
A frightful, ghastly shape was she,
As dead among the dead shall be.
Red lightnings flashed from hollow eyes,
Her dark robes gave forth groans and sighs.
Back shrank the Aesir, pale, aghast.
As thro' their midst the Dread One passed,
All reeking with the fumes of death,
Mad, drunken, wild with frantic wrath ;
Malignant glared she round the Hall,
As, baleful, would she crush them all ;
Shaking in rage her mighty arm,
Burning to work high Asgard harm.

Then thronéd Justice, roused at length,
Seized each the monsters in his grasp,
Awful in ire and wondrous strength ;
In vain they strove 'gainst Odin's clasp !
Swiftly impelled thro' air
In breathless race
They flew thro' space,
Thro' mist and cloud,
With howlings loud.
Cowered the Earth in fear !
While, in Valhalla, at the sight.
Shivered the Gods with faces white.

Into mid-ocean's dark depths hurled,

Grown with each day to giant size.
The Serpent soon enclosed the world.
With tail in mouth, in circle-wise ;
Held harmless still
By Odin's will,
With lurid eye, in strong despair,
Belching forth fierce
Winds that should pierce
With rain and storm, the trembling air.
Up maëlstroms broke.
While thunders woke
With sullen roar,
From shore to shore,
As he, with baffled ire,
Writhed still in vain desire.

By Odin strong,
Avenging wrong,
In ice-bound realms of Niflheim dread,
In gloomy regions of the Dead,
Was hideous Hel
Condemned to dwell.
Hither, to her dark domain.
Came those worthless spirits, slain
By old age, disease, or pain,
Captive, by the Dragon, Death,
Borne on black-hued wings beneath ;
Unmarked by hero-gore.
There wade they evermore
In venom-streams that pour
'Round that dismal habitation ;
All restless driven
Till chains be riven
In the Day of consternation ;

When will those rigid bands
Rush forth from Hela's lands,
And, in the shock
Of Ragnarock,
Thro' Thund's roaring river.
Against the high Aesir,
'Gainst the Einheriar,
Led by Valkyriar,
Shall strive that fearful host,
The armies of the lost.

Elvidner was Hela's hall.
Iron-barred, with massive wall ;
Horrible that palace tall !
Hunger was her table bare ;
Waste, her knife ; her bed, sharp care ;
Burning Anguish spread her feast ;
Bleachéd bones arrayed each guest ;
Plague and Famine sang their runes.
Mingled with Despair's harsh tunes.
Misery and Agony
E'er in Hel's abode shall be !
'Round about Thund's torrent poured ;
Loud without, Garm, Hell-dog, roared ;
While, on the bridge of glass,
To take from whom might pass
The toll of blood,
Grim Modgud stood;
There, Hel shall reign
Till, freed from chain,
In Ragnarock she rave in strife, —
Evil 'gainst Good, and Death 'gainst Life.

Remained for doom Fenrir alone ;

Even Al-father on his throne
Trembled before that Jötun power,
Fearing should come the woeful hour,
Decreed by Nornir,
Foretold by Mimir,
To most high Aesir,
When bright Valhal be plunged in gloom,
The Wolf's red jaws be Odin's tomb.

Exultant in his awful strength
Before the gods he stood at length.
None but hraxe Tyr might dare
To come the Wolf anear.
Twice did the Aesir strive to bind,
Twice did they fetters powerless find ;
Iron or brass of no avail,
Naught, save thro' magic could prevail.
Gleipnir, at last,
By Dark Elves cast.
In Svartalf-heim, with strong spells wrought.
To Odin was by Skirnir brought,
As soft as silk, as light as air.
Yet still of magic power most rare ;
Wound round his limbs in weblike fold,
Full tight did Gleipnir Fenrir hold.
Striving in vain
Freedom to gain,
Each struggle only tighter bound ;
The Wolf lay chainéd on the ground.
With bristling back and gnashing teeth,
The monster rolled the throne beneath ;
The venom froth
From gory mouth
Was scattered by his blistering breath ;

Ever he sought in rage to rise,
Drawn ever back by magic plies ;
With frenzied bite
And furious might.
Would tear apart his fetters light.
Mad howUngs loud
Pierced Asgard proud ;
More frantic grew !
His huge weight threw
From side to side ;
His hideous hide
With dust and gore
Was covered o'er.
With foaming jaws
And outstretched claws
Then glared he, impotent, about ;
With fury heard the taunting shout,
The shrill laughter of the Aesir,
Derision loud of all save Tyr,
Thro' him one-handed evermore.

Bound firm, this scourge of earth.
Fierce Loki's fiercer birth,
On rocky isle
To wait the while,
A sword between his wide jaws thrust, —
The mighty sword of Odin just, —
On earth the hilt, the point aloft,
His howlings oft
Shook earth and main ;
Struggles all vain !
There lies he fast
Till time be past,
And Ragnarock burst forth at last.

In vain, alas ! did vengeance come ;
Doomed, even then, Valhalla's dome.
Too late, too late !
Decrees of Fate,
Unchanged and sure,
Must still endure.
Stern Destiny, who can avoid ?
She, pitiless, shall govern all !
Fair Asgard's gold-thatched roofs must fall
Void be her thrones ; guestless each hall.
Alas ! the hour still came apace
When all of earth and Odin's race
In Ragnarock should be destroyed.

Julia Clinton Jones, 1878

Part Seventh

Thor and the Daughters of Aegir

On their azure pillows lying,
O'er them distant murmurs dying,
Ocean caves beneath replying
From mermaid's horn
To echoes borne
On winged breeze
O'er land and seas
From Asgard, Midgard, Jötunheim.
Gently rocking to and fro,
Aegir's daughters ceaseless go ;
Mantles blue the maidens wear,
Snow-white bosoms gleaming bare,
Sea-grass green their floating hair,
Still onward rolling, keeping time.

Who so fair as the waves,
Aegir's daughters.
Dancing waters !
Lapping lightly on the land,
Sporting softly on the strand,
Chasing one another.
Then the breeze, their brother,
Ruffles their crests,
Scatters their spray,
While their billowy breasts.
Heaving high in their play,
Swell and throb ! In coral caves
Reigns King Aegir,
Feasts the Aesir,
Feasts he, too, the drownéd Ones

Hither brought by Ran, his queen,
Swathed in shrouds of sea-weed green,
Fringed with shells ; while still the sheen
Of pallid limbs and whit'ning bones.
E'er ghastly through the meshes comes
Of the net, in which each day
Unwary sailors catches she,
Grim Sea King's guests below to be.

Who so fierce as the waves,
When, from deep ocean caves,
Aegir shall call,
Shall summon all
To bear his fury on high !
Madly raging, roaring, lashing,
'Gainst steep crags in wild wrath crashing,
Up to Heav'n their spray-clouds dashing,
Mingling sea and sky !

Hither comes Thor,
The Thunderer,
To sport with those maids at rest.
Sleepily lies each maiden calm,
Gently drifting, with snow-white arm
Folded on billowy breast ;
Foam-wreaths over the floating hair,
Swelling surges murmuring e'er
Lullaby songs that soothe to rest.

But fierce Thor,
The Thunderer,
Loves no calm !
Peace has no charm
To lull his soul to rest.

Comes he hither to sport an hour.
In Jötun's land,
With mighty hand,
His Aesir power
Rang in the rock
In tempest shock,
And raised dread fear in giant's breast.
What Odin sought,
That strong Thor wrought ;
And, now returned.
For sport he burned
E'er yet he reached Bilskirnir's bower.

From their rest the maids are waking,
Dimpling smiles o'er soft cheeks breaking,
Sparkling showers from fingers shaking, —
Foamy fingers, light and fair ;
While bright Day from car of gold
Scatters gems of price untold
To bedeck each virgin rare.
Clinging, clasping in caresses.
To his breast the great God presses
Each soft maid, while floating tresses
Wrap him in embraces cold.

Burning Thor, with kisses fierce,
Will their frozen bosoms pierce,
Seizes in enfolding arms ;
Filled with passion, strong desire,
Lustful flames e'er mounting higher,
Presses wildly yielding forms,
Riots on their sparkling charms.
Lightly still the maids caress him.
Closer to their bosoms press him ;

Strange regrets and vague alarms
Wake too late ! now, filled with storms
Of wild wrath, they vainly try
From his mighty arms to fly.
More gently does their lover Thor,
To lie at peace the maids implore ;
But struggling, rising in their rage.
While all the ocean powers engage
To free them from the Thunderer,
At length his wrath they rouse ;
Then ends in strife the rude carouse.
Fiercely the billows strive,
Madly they toss and writhe,
'Neath towers of froth they hide ;
While all the ocean wide
Is lashed in boiling surge.

Aegir sits trembling on his throne,
For power to match with Thor is none.
Now, from their towers the maids emerge,
Now, driven back by tempest scourge.
Rough, wild waters !
True Jötun daughters !
Roaring, wrestling, battling, writhing,
Evil powers 'gainst Aesir striving ;
Now, lost 'neath walls of foaming froth,.
Now, darting swift high billows forth !
Blinded by the spray they pour.
Deafened by their sullen roar.
Mighty Thor,
The Thunderer,
Flashes lightnings, rolls his thunder.
Tears their billowy arms asunder.
Undoes their fiercely clinging clasp.

Upholds them firmly in his grasp.
Upholds them high
'Neath lowering sky,
Rampant raging, shrieking shrill,
Holds them powerless at his will ;
Still the maidens higher lifts.
Dashes 'gainst the frowning cliffs, —
Dashes with his gathered strength !
His wrath appeased, he turns at length.
And muttering in his red beard low,
While glaring still from bended brow.
Home to Bilskirnir wends he slow ;
With mocking laughter doth he go.

Julia Clinton Jones, 1878

Part Eighth

Odińs Visit to the Valä

Of all the gods of Asgard fair
Who did in Valhal's feast-hall meet,
'Mong Aesir twelve who gathered there
To quaff their mead at Odin's feet,
And tell their tales of rare emprize
Beneath the light of Freya's eyes; —
Of all the twelve round Odin's throne,
Baldur, the Beautiful, alone,
The Sun-god, good, and pure, and bright.
Was loved by all, as all love light.

But now strange dreams and omens ill
O'erclouded brows whence light e'er streamed ;
While Midgard all, with Asgard's hill,
Trembled for him, most cherished deemed.
At council grave did hither come
Beneath Valhalla's royal dome,
The anxious Aesir, thus to seek
What harm might hang o'er Baldur meek.

They prayed and offered great reward,
And begged the Earth this charge to make, —
Round Baldur fair a watch and ward
By day and night to ceaseless take.
Friga, his mother, restless went
To every plant, each element,
Each thing, with breath or breathless, she
Bound by an oath to harmless be
To her dear son ; but, woe ! ah, woe !
She passed the sacred mistletoe.

Then up rose Odin, anxious still,
Saddled Sleipnir, of Loki's brood; —
To dark Niflheim, fearing some ill.
Then quickly rode Al-Father good.
Forth in his path sprang Garm, the hound,
Fierce keeper he of Hela's gate;
On rode Odin ; from Earth came sound
Of moaning over Baldur's fate.
Reached he soon the eastern portal
Whence returns no living mortal,
Chaunted loud the Saga's song-spell
Which shades shall call from death and hell.

Forth from the tomb the Väla came,
Foreboding shape of woe and ill;
" What man art thou, — called by what name, —
Who dares disturb my rest at will ?
Dead have I lain long years gone by.
The snows of winter on me lie,
The rains have washed my bleached bones dry,
Long since the worms have ate their fill;
And now thou 'rt come to break my rest, —
Speak ! I must answer thy behest !""

" Vegtam my name is, Valtam's son,
And come I now to question thee;
Behold these seats ! see every one
Bedecked with rings and jewelry ;
For whom prepared ? The mead is set,
The foamina; draught with shield laid o'er; —
For whom the feast ? the guest stays yet !
Can gods withhold from Hela's shore?"

"For Baldur gleams the beaker bright,
His seat is set by Hela's side :
Compelled to speak by power of might,
Silent henceforward I abide.
Hoedur, by Löki's fraud led on,
Blind arbiter of sighs and tears !
Will slay the bright, the mighty One,
And bring the end on Odin's heirs.
But, see! th' avenger, Vali, come,
Sprung from the west, in Rindus' womb.
True son of Odin ! one day's birth !
He shall not stop nor stay on earth
His locks to comb, his hands to lave.
His frame to rest, should rest it crave,
Until his mission be complete,
And Baldur's death find vengeance meet.'"

"Close not thy lips! I further seek
The name of her who will not mourn,
Who will not weep for Baldur meek,
But scornful smiles from eve till dawn."
" Thou art not Wegtam, as I deemed !
Closed are my lips forever more."

" Nor art thou Väla, as thou seemed !
No seeress thou of Hela's shore,
But mother of the giants dread,
Appointed guarders of the dead !"

" Ride on, great Odin ! thou hast found
Answers to all that troubled thee;
I to my cold sleep under ground.
Will lay me calm and quietly.
Compelled, unwilling, have I said;

My words shall weigh on thee as lead.
Never for man shall ope my tomb
Till fatal Ragnarock be come!"

So homeward thro' dark Hela's shade
Odin his upward journey made;
Passed close beside the waters still
That lave the roots of Igdrasil ;
Nor heeded Valkyr's greetings fair.
When now he reached the purer air;
That air to him breathed but one sigh,-
"Baldur the Beautiful must die !"

Baldur ́s Death

With mournful brow and heavy eye,
Came Odin to Valhalla's gate,
And passed the fateful Nornir by,
But found within all joyful state;
For Aesir strong and Vingolf fair
Had met in Baldur's honor there,
And placed him in their midst on high, —
A mark for spear and archery ;
Most god-like of the gods was he,
And proven deathless now to be.

Huge rocks and mighty boulders Thor
Hurled with full force, but without harm ;
And Vidar, with the Thunderer, —
And Njörd, — the Sun-god bore a charm !
Loki alone stood silent by;
Mad, jealous hate was in his eye;
Swift his device, — as ancient dame.
He to the loving Mother came,

And thro' fair words the secret found, —
That all in, on, above the ground,
Except the feeble mistletoe,
Had sworn to shield her son from woe.

Then loud laughed Loki ! swift returned,
The slighted plant within his hand,
Soon the blind Hoedur he discerned;
Then, giving him the tender wand, —
" Wherefore, O Hcedur ! dost not pay
Due honor to this festal day ?
Dost thou not see the Aesir great
Think it not ill to show him state ?
Blind as thou art, I'll lead to where
Bright Baldur stands, a target fair;
Thou knowest well, Creation now
To work no ill has taken vow."

Blind Hoedur threw, — ah, woe ! the dart
By Loki from the frail plant shred,
Pierced fatal to the Sun-god's heart.
Baldur the Beautiful lay dead !

Dead lay the Sun-god. Never more
Should summer-light stream from his brow ;
To do him honor, to the shore
Came Odin, with the Aesir now]
Heroic souls, by Valkyr led,
Ljus-Alfers, Vans, thro' sorrow sped
To swell the train that mourned the dead.
Near, with bent brows, the Thunderer stood;
While Hoedur, bowed 'neath weight of blood,
All shod with silence, slow drew near
To weep with him their brother dear.

On swift Hringhorni's giant prow
Baldur the Beautiful they laid, —
The burning ship must bear him now
Thro' gloomy skies of gathering shade ;
Dull yellow fringe on pale gold shroud
Gleamed coldly 'neath the wintry cloud.
Then Odin lit the funeral pyre, —
Out to the north, in streams of fire,
To Saga's call his spirit sailed,
While Nature's heart his loss bewailed.
Ne'er shall the mild god hasten home
Till fatal Ragnarock be come.

Hermodur's Visit to Hela

Sad Mother ! watching her dear son
Borne by the burning ship away,
Dreamed might be Loki's work undone
Should she to Hela ransom pay.
With veiléd head and mournful brow,
Then did she to the Aesir go,
And sought which of them all would prove
The depth and greatness of his love,
By riding swift to Elvidnir,
Ransom from Hel the White-God dear.
And bring him back, the loved of all,
Safe to his seat in Asgard's hall.

At once Hermodur claimed the quest.
Mounted Sleipnir, who saddled stood,
And never sought he stay nor rest
Till he nine days had been on road ;
Then, on the tenth, he came to where

The bridge of glass hung on a hair
Thrown o'er the river terrible, —
The Giöll, boundary of Hel.
Now here the maiden, Mödgud, stood
Waiting to take the toll of blood, —
A maiden horrible to sight,
Fleshless, with shroud and pall bedight.
As swift Hermodur thundered by, —
"Stop!" quoth the maiden, "give thy name !
Thou hast not hue of those who die;
Only yestreen five dead troops came,
Yet trembled not this bridge so much
Beneath their tread as thy one touch."'

And when he asked, " Did Baldur ride
Down to the dead within her sight ?"
"E'en now," she answered, " at the side
Of Hel he feasts in halls of night."
On rode Hermodur. Fearful Garm,
The Hel-dog, bayed, nor caused alarm ;
The Nornir dread, by Igdrasil,
Could not withstay him 'gainst his will.
So he to dark Elvidnir came.
And there invoked Hel's mighty name, —
Gave Friga's message, told her how
All nature mourned for Baldur now.
And prayed her set the White-god free.
That joy in Asgard's halls might be.

" And is it so?" swift answered Hel;
" Now shall the truth of tliis appear !
If all things loved thy God so well
No loss of Baldur need thou fear.
Let all things from fair Nature's birth,

Breathing or breathless, on the earth,
For him, throughout creation, mourn ;
And then your Sun-God shall return."

Back rode Hermodur to the hall
Where Friga and the Aesir stayed ;
There, filled with hope, he told them all
What promises dark Hela made.
Already light seemed to return,
For did not Nature e'en now mourn ?
What breathing thing, or without breath.
That would not mourn for Baldur's death ?
Quick o'er the earth great Friga sent
Her mandate that all things should weep ;
And gods and Vanir loving lent
Their powerful aid, that all should keep
A day of universal woe
To ransom Baldur from below.

Now, as Hermodur homeward rode
From bearing Friga's message forth.
A giantess, all shameless, strode
From a dark cave that fronts the north.
Veilless her head, undimmed her eye.
A hateful smile her lips shone nigh ; —
'Twas Loki, in the form of Thökt,
Who, evil, at the summons mocked.
" If so thou please, let Nature wail ;
Without my tears 'twill not avail.
Why should I weep, whose heart is dry ?
Weeping and wailing, none will I !
Living or lifeless, ill or well,
Let Baldur bide his time with Hel !"
Then, with loud laughter, Thökt was gone,

But where she stood a stream poured down.

Hermodur sad returned, and slow, —
Through Asgard spread the words of woe,
' Baldur the Beautiful shall ne'er
From Hel return to upper air !
Betrayed by Löki, twice betrayed,
The prisoner of Death is made ;
Ne'er shall he 'scape the place of doom
Till fatal Ragnarock be come !"

Julia Clinton Jones, 1878

Part Ninth

King Aegir's Feast

Now Loki's last, worst work was done.
Triumphant Wrong, exalted high,
O'ershadowed even Odin's throne,
And dimmed the glow o'er Earth and sky.
Weeping and gloom
Fill'd Valhal's dome;
The stars gleamed pale
Thro' Heaven's cloud-veil;
Fair Day reined back his steed of light.
Exultant rode forth Jötun Night;
Lost in the consciousness of woe,
All purposeless the Aesir go.
Withered the Earth !
Creation's birth
Reeled blindly 'neath the staggering blow.
Baldur, defenceless, innocent,
Naught but his shining purity
'Gainst evil deeds as surety,
To Hela's feast by craft was sent.

Evil before,
Now more and more
Evil and base the traitor grew ;
Lower and lower fell he ever,
Only for ill his each endeavor;
Fled from his heart the pure and true ;
A reckless raging
Each power engaging,
Until to all his very name
Symbol of craft and hate became ;

While, still defiant, held he high
His haughty head, 'neath lowering sky.
Yet still, tho' lost, upon his face
At times a grace
Faint glimmered of the ancient day
When he and Odin, one in soul,
Mingled their love in flowing bowl ;
A transient gleam, — a semblance cast
By shad'wy mem'ries of the past, —
Arising dim to fade away.

Now, to assauge the high gods' grief
And bring their mourning some relief,
From coral caves
'Neath ocean waves.
Mighty King Aegir
Invited the Aesir
To festival
In Hlesey's hall;
That, tho' for Baldur, every guest
Was grieving yet,
He might forget
Awhile his woe in friendly feast.

The vexed waves heard the summons given ;
From white lips hissed their wrath to Heaven ;
Who joy or feasting e'er should know
While Baldur sat with Hel below ?
Panting, heaving, restless waters !
Sobbing, moaning, Aegir's daughters !
Bellowing in sullen roar,
Beating on the rock-girt shore,
Tumbling wild in dismal tide,
Whit'ning all the deep sea wide,

The booming surges thundering fell
O'er sunken rocks in hoarse, sad swell,
While the thick mists flaunted high
Funeral banners to the sky.
Weeping waters !
Aegir's daughters,
Unforgetful,
And regretful.
Wailing over Baldur's fate;
While far below
Their mournful flow.
On throne of state
Sat King Aegir,
Who the Aesir
Would feast at banquet rarely great.

Beneath the watery dome,
AVitli crystalline splendor,
In radiant grandeur,
Upreared the sea-god's home.
More dazzling than foam of the waves,
E'er glimmered and gleamed thro' deep caves
The glistening sands of its floor,
Like some placid lake rippled o'er.
Lights opalescent
Glowed phosphorescent
Thro' its sparkling emerald walls ;
Flowers the fairest,
Rich treasures rarest,
Lavish decked its billowy halls;
Bright shells from ocean's bed.
Gem-like, their luster shed,
Twinkling in rays most bright.
Mingled their gleaming

Brilliantly beaming
Rainbow-like light.

Myriad things of ocean.
With soft gliding motion,
Through branched coral grove
Would dartingly rove.
Thro' blooms and o'er palm trees,
'Mid mosses and sea-fan.
Swayed by the cool breeze
In the grottoes of Ran.
While thro' crystal gulfs were gleaming
Ocean depths, with wonders teeming ;
Shapes of terror, huge, unsightly,
Loomed thro' vaulted roof translucent ;
Silver finnéd fish swam lightly,
Sparkling showers scatt'ring brightly, —
Phosphorescent rays pelucent.

Devouring Ran, by Aegir's side,
Smiled, treacherous, thro' the feast-hall wide.
In festive state awaited they
Their Aesir guests to deep Hlesey.
At length a conch-shell, hung on high,
Rang hoarse and loud.
A greeting proud,
As Odin and his numerous train
To hall drew nigh ;
While Heimdal, with great Gjallar-horn,
Answered the notes, on ripples borne,
In clear refrain.

Then Vans and Aesir, mighty gods.
Of Earth, and air, and Asgard, lords —

Advancing with each goddess fair,
A brilliant retinue most rare. —
Attending mighty Odin, swept
Up wave-worn aisle in radiant march,
Thro' pillared crystals, glittering bright,
Fair diamond lamps, dispersing light.
Around them briny breezes crept.
Wafting them on
To Aegir's throne
'Neath billowy arch,
Where fountains flowing, filled with mead,
And goblets wreathed with bright sea-weed,
For them abounded ;
While songs resounded
Loud and high
In welcoming cry.
As near and nearer, drew they nigh.

With burnished gold helm, at their head
Great Odin up the feast-hall led, —
Mighty father of the Aesir !
With his bride, the blue-eyed Friga ;
Azure robes around her flowing.
Heron-crested,
Snow-white breasted,
Love upon her soft lips glowing
For her lord, — her heart's desire.

Freya close beside was treading,
Dazzling rays around her shedding
From the starry wreath of light, —
Sun-worlds, — glowing scarce so bright
As fair Beauty's lovely queen
Hast'ning on thro' crystal sheen.

Sweet Bragi, Njörd, Forseti mild.
And gold-curled Sif, the spouse of Thor,
With Vidar, Frey, and many more,
Up thro' the central nave defiled;
Absent alone the Thunderer.
As close to Aegir's throne they drew,
With ev'ry step the conches blew;
The shrill notes rang,
And skoal loud sang !
Skoal to each guest
At Aegir's feast.

Higher and louder swelled the glee.
Merrier the festivity !
When, suddenly, in shadow fell
A shade from Hel
The hall within;
A figure tall
Crept in by stealth, — a shape of sin !
'Twas Loki reared his hateful form ;
Like lull in storm,
A dismal silence shrouded ail,
And ended the high festival.

Julia Clinton Jones, 1878

Part Tenth

Lokís Punishment

Alone, forlorn,
Apart withdrawn,
An outcast, Loki leant
'Gainst coral feast-seat in the aisle;
On traitor shameless each the while
Reproachful glances bent.

" Now, wherefore art thou hither come,
An unsought guest, in Aegir's home ?
At festival
In banquet hall,
For thee, behold ! no seat is set ;
No flowing mead thy lips shall wet.
Depart ! thou scourge of Asgard's race !
Among the gods thou hast no place."

'Twas Bragi spoke;
From Loki broke
Resounding words of insult vile;
" Confusion on all
Within this hall !
Death to the Aesir !
Ruin to Aegir !
May flames of Surtur
Destroy ye all !
Empty your pleasures,
Worthless your treasures ;
In a brief while
Cometh your fall.
Even now Hela

Glares at Valhalla !
Never, ye gods ! again
Shall meet your festive train
At banquet high.
Lo ! darkened sky
Attests my power.
In woeful hour
Your Baldur fell thro' subtle art ;
I plucked the dart
That, surely, pierced the Sun-God's heart.
When Nature wept,
As Thokt, I kept
My tearless watch, lest he
From Hela's kingdom freed might be.
From earliest dawn
Of Time's young morn.
On Asgard's hill,
My steadfast will
Opposed you in each high endeavor ;
Fair tho' I seemed, —
Friend, as ye deemed, —
A double game I played you ever.
Triumphant, tho' I now give way ;
The stronger ye
This time may be.
Soon, Aesir ! comes the woeful day !
Dread Ragnarock ye none can stay ;
Then my fierce power shall Valhal know.
And Asgard feel me open foe.

" Tremble, ye Aesir !
And you, King Aegir !
Hark how fierce Fenrir
Howls loud and long !

Now, Odin ! speed
Valkyriar,
Your maids of war;
For in Valhalla
Soon is there need
Of brave and strong
Einheriar !
" Ye fair-faced goddesses ! Not one,
By Beauty's light or Wisdom's ray.
Can turn away
The woe begun.
Soon, ravening, shall
Thro' proud Valhal,
And bright Vingolf,
Rage the Gray Wolf!
No seat have I, as welcome guest.
At this your feast !
Where horrors dwell
In halls of Hel,
Behold ! a mightier feast is spread, —
Meats that nourish,
And cause to flourish
The ghastly armies of the Dead.
Above, loud crows your golden Cock !
Once hath the sound
Echoed around !
The third time heralds Ragnarock !"

Scoffing he spoke, and sneering gazed
On throng assembled; — mute, amazed.
They, listening, stood an instant's space.
Then wrath swelled high.
Darkened each eye.
Convulsed each face !

Stung by insulting taunt.
Enraged at odious vaunt,
Quick to his feet each, furious, sprang;
Thro' dome and arch deep curses rang !
When, suddenly, a peal of thunder
Shivered the crystal gulfs asunder;
With lurid ray, fierce lightnings played,
Reflected bright
In diamond light.
'Gainst billowy wall
Of banquet hall,
While winds and waves loud tumult made.
Then quaked the undulating floor,
Quivered each amber lamp,
Each wreath of sea-weed damp ;
Rocked the translucent dome ;
Deep aisles were flecked with foam,
It was the mighty Thunderer, Thor !

Swift drawing nigh
- With flashing eye
And flaming beard,
Wroth, mutt'ring low
'Neath bended brow,
He raised great Mjölnir high;
On traitor vile he glared.
Before the dread
Avenger's tread
Back Loki shrank,
'Mid steel swords' clank,
And, craven ! trembling fled !

Mad for vengeance, wild with hate.
Forth the gods, infuriate,

From gay halls in coral caves,
Rushed thro' surging, swelling waves !
In fearful race,
To Loki chase
The wrathful Aesir gave !
Now, thro' boiling whirlpools darting,
Hissing depths, asunder partuig;
Now, the foaming billows breasting.
Never for a moment resting ;
Until, wearied out at length,
Gathering all his failing strength
Himself to save.
The traitor, to a salmon changing, —
Slipping, sliding,
Doubling, gliding,
Beneath a roaring cascade ranging,
Halted for an instant's space.

In that instant's pause for breathing, —
Waters 'round him frothing, seething,
Sides with fear and flight fast heaving, —
His fierce enemies perceiving
Golden scales thro' foam-clouds flashing,
On him dashing,
Seized and bound him, firmly lashing
Struggling form with horrid coils.
Fettered by the entrails torn
From his own son, Jötun-born,
Laid he, hopeless, in the toils ;
While the Aesir, mocking, taunting,
Chained him — powerless and panting, —
Fast to a triple-pointed rock.
Till freed by final battle-shock.
Ere they left him in his anguish.

O'er his treacherous brow ungrateful,
Skadi hung a serpent hateful,
Venom-drops for aye distilling.
Every nerve with torment filling ;
Thus shall he in horror languish.

By him, still unwearied kneeling,
Sigyn at his tortured side, —
Faithful wife ! with beaker stealing
Drops of venom as they fall, —
Agonizing poison all !
Sleepless, changeless, ever dealing
Comfort, will she still abide;
Only when the cup's o'erflowing
Must fresh pain and smarting cause,
Swift, to void the beaker going,
Shall she in her watching pause.
Then doth Loki
Loudly cry ;
Shrieks of terror,
Groans of horror,
Breaking forth in thunder peals !
With his writhings scared Earth reels.
Trembling and quaking,
E'en high Heav'n shaking !
So wears he out his awful doom,
Until dread Ragnarock be come.

Julia Clinton Jones, 1878

Part Eleventh

Ragnarock

'Twas done ! th' avenging deed was
wrought !
Alas, too late !
Decrees of Fate
With judgment fraught
Must be obeyed.
With Baldur dead
Pure Peace and Innocence had fled ;
When his swift, shining course was stayed,
Then darkness gathered o'er the Earth,
Strife and Corruption sprang to birth.
Tho' Loki lay fast bound below,
The seeds of woe
Were sown broadcast;
Nearer and nearer drew the hour,
Blacker and fiercer grew the power
That should o'erwhelm all things at last.

Grim Fimbul raged, and o'er the world
Tempestuous winds and snow-storms hurled ;
The roaring ocean icebergs ground,
And flung its frozen foam around
E'en to the top of mountain height ;
No warming air,
Nor radiance fair
Of gentle Summer's soft'ning light,
Tempered this dreadful glacial night.

Three other winters howled abroad
With furious storms of ice and hail ;

Beneath the might of fearful gale
Earth trembled ; while, thro' wild abyss,
The seas around, upthundering, roared
To sable skies, with moan and hiss !
Crag hurled on crag with deaf'ning crash ;
Great Igdrasil, beneath the lash
Of tempest shock, all quivering stood ;
The blackened skies were flecked with blood ;
By raging powers of Darkness riven
From their fixed orbits in the heaven,
The pallid stars were ruthless driven
Thro' flying cloud.
Hoarse earthquakes bellowed loud ;
Crumbled the rocks; forests down bowed !
Forth burst the hot volcanic stream ;
Flashed forth the fatal lightning's gleam ;
Streamed sheets of flame to lurid sky;
Devouring tongues of fire rose high,
Did mighty Igdrasil enshroud,
And Time expired in burning flood.

All bonds were burst ;
Troops of accursed
Tore rampant thro' the Earth and air ;
The gloomy hordes of Night roamed free;
The powers that erst from Chaos came —
Fire and Water, Darkness, Death —
'Gainst Earth and Asgard strove in wrath.
More fiercely than the lurid glare
Of conflagration, hideously
Shone on men's faces Murder's flame !
Brother slew brother — father, child ;
Men turned to tigers, mad for gore !
Creation raged ! war followed war ;

Impiety, Injustice piled
Huge heaps of horror to the sky ;
Passion, and Fear, and every crime
Mad riot held thro' this dread time —
Undaunted, reared their pale heads high !

So came, with blood and tempest shock,
Wild Ragnarock !
The Day of Doom —
The hour was come!
Shrill crowed Valhalla's golden Cock !
The crimson bird of Hel replied.
Fierce Fenrir flung his fetters wide,
Deep howling, rushed with ravening jaws.
Nostrils flame flashing, outstretched claws,
Hot eyeballs glaring for his prey ;
On-leaping thro' the gulfs of air,
With jaws agape from Earth to Heaven,
A yawning chasm of red fear !
Well knew the Wolf, that awful Day,
What prey should to his maw be given.

In giant wrath, the Serpent tossed
In ocean depths, till, freed from chain.
He rose upon the foaming main ;
Beneath the lashings of his tail.
Seas, mountain high, swelled o'er the land ;
Then, darting mad the waves acrost,
Pouring forth bloody froth like hail,
Spurting with poisoned, venomed breath
Foul, deadly mists o'er all the Earth,
Thro' thundering surge, he sought the strand.

Over the lurid ocean flew

The Death-ship, Nagelfari, dread,
Filled with Hrimthursar, led by Hrym,
Bearing huge rocks ; the winds that blew
And sped it on this final time,
Were dying sighs of mortal dead.

Now at the head of Hel's pale host,
Those livid armies of the lost,
The unchained Loki furious came.
Grimmer and closer, thro' the gloom
On pressed they to the plain of Doom.
Scorching on high, rolled pillared flame ;
With bayings that thro' Nature pierced,
From Gnipa, Garm, the Hel-Dog, burst ;
In mad, chaotic rout,
Thro' baleful light,
The powers of Night
Reeled and careered about !

Amid the hideous din,
Confusion dire,
The blackened Heav'ns were rent in twain ;
Thro' the jaggéd rift,
With dazzling radiance swift,
Streamed the World of Fire !
'Gainst the hosts of Sin,
On hastening to broad Vigrid's plain,
The blazing sons of Muspel rode ;
Thro' gloomy clouds their pathway glowed.
Down thro' the fields of air,
With glittering armor fair,
In battle order bright,
They sped, while seething flame
From rapid hoof strokes came.

Leading his gleaming band, rode Surtur,
Mid the red ranks of raging fire ;
His very sword a ray of light
Snatched from the Sun !
Flinging on high
Flame banners flaunting to the sky,
Onward they came at headlong pace ;
The Rainbow Bridge, 'neath furious race.
Shivered and sank — its work was done !

White as the winter snows.
Great Heimdal now arose —
Valhalla's Warder,
High Heaven's Guarder ! —
Siezed his huge trump and boldly blew.
Loudly and long thro' Asgard rang
Great Gjallar-horn, with startling clang !
That summons well the Aesir knew !
Then, for the third time, crowed the Cock,
Assembling all for Ragnarock !

As thro' the Heavens the summons rang,
Swift to their Chief the Aesir sprang !
Fresh armor seized from steel-draped hall ;
Exulting loud in awful joy
That conflict mighty should employ
Once more their might,
E'en though the fight
Should end in Asgard's fatal fall ;
For, high o'er Vigrid's gory plain.
The Aesir saw fair Gimli's fane.

Little delay was in that hour :
Great Odin gathered all his power !

Ah ! well for him that to his feasts
Had bidden he such warrior guests.
Now, wakened by Valkyriar,
Brave armies of Einheriar
With stiffened fingers bound on swords ;
With shield and lance,
'Mid bright spears' glance,
Pressed on amid the hastening gods.
Then, gold-helmed Odin at their head,
Valhalla's hosts to Vigrid led ;
With polished armor shining bright,
And cuirass gleaming thro' the night.
On to the final battle sped.
Close by his side, the Thunderer.
With Odin, Fenrir closed in strife !
Awful and strong
That contest long,
For death and life !
Powerless to aid was mighty Thor ;
'Gainst him the fell World-Serpent raged,
And all his Aesir powers engaged !

Blood-stained the helmet's burnished gold !
In struggles mad o'er Earth they rolled.
At last, huge Fenrir's wide-stretched jaw
Engulfed the God in grizzly maw;
Thus, by foul Loki's fearful son,
Was greatest ill to Asgard done.

Lo ! Vidar, as avenger, came
Of Odin's fame !
The Monster in his mighty grasp,
Resistless clasp,
He seized; loud howlings broke,

And far, affrighted echoes woke.
Upon his writhing foe
Planting his iron shoe.
Rending and tearing with vast strength,
Until, at length,
Split he Fenrir's jaws asunder !

The reft sky shook with deep death growls,
And sharp, prolongéd, hideous howls
Like harsh peals of angry thunder.
Scarce conquered was the Gray Wolf dread,
E'er, with the life blood oozing slow
From wound dealt forth by dying foe,
On Fenrir foul fell Vidar, dead.

Caught in the loathsome toils
Of Jormungandur's coils,
Thro' all this fearful war
No aid could bear the Thunderer :
The Serpent, armed with fatal sting,
Loud clanking now with scaly side,
Fierce fold on fold out-lapping wide,
With toss and fling
To crush the Aesir-champion tried.
At length,
With wondrous strength,
Great Thor the horrid coils off flung ;
Beneath the blows of Mjölnir dread,
The savage Monster, stricken dead,
In jet-black gore lay weltering.
But, in that awful combat, stung
By venomed fang, nine steps and more
Back recoiled the unconquered Thor,
And in his last World-Victory died.

Once, high in Valhal held a god,
But now, a fallen shape abhorred.
Condemned for ill
Stern doom to fill,
Full long had Loki writhed enchained,
Tormented, tortured, agonized ;
Stretched at gigantic length,
Useless his Jötun strength,
Tearing at iron fetters fast ;
Heavings and howlings — all in vain !
There had he tossed long ages past,
Revolving schemes of deeds accursed.
Wild hopes of wrath and vengeance nursed ;
For these, alone, he freedom prized,
That, with his pristine power regained,
He hatred fierce might wreak at last ;
Joyful to him was Vigrid's plain.

Roused to fresh ire at Fenrir's fall,
Up-towered in rage his figure tall,
Breathing defiance deep and loud,
Leading ahead Hel's ghostly crowd,
With vengeful lust, the Aesir sought.
Swift o'er the field,
With brazen shield,
And lance in rest,
Great Heimdal rushed to meet the foe
'Mid streams of gore,
While shout and roar
And thund'rous blow
Convulsed the earth, the aether split ;
There, thro' the rift with flames alit,
Bright Muspel's sons in awful gaze,

One instant glaring in amaze,
Marked how in frenzied fight they fought.
Then, in death-struggle, wildly pressed,
Infuriate, grappling breast to breast,
In vengeful arms they, gasping, reeled.

The universal fury swelled
Fiercer on high !
The vaulted sky,
High arched with flame,
Resounded with the deaf'ning clang
Which, deep below, in earthquakes rang.
Millions advancing hosts repelled,
Whom millions met and fought, unquelled !
From air, and earth, and sea, there came
Throngs until now in bondage held ;
Down from their cloudy prisons swept
The sons of Aegir, fettered kept
By thunderbolt and lightning's chain.
From seething whirlpools of the main,
Up Aegir sprang with Ran's dank train
Of pallid Drowned ; while ravening waves,
Huge, rearing high their foaming breasts,
Destruction bearing on their crests,
To battle rushed from ocean caves.
Terrific conflict! each on field,
Alone, could devastation wield.
Host surged on host; then, rallying, flew
To join more fierce the strife anew.
No thought of flight !
On his own might
Each in this mad'ning hour relied.
Down to her very central point
Trembled the earth ; thro' every joint

Of pale Creation's quiv'ring frame,
Confusion wild, and warring came :
Till, darting down from scorching sky,
Great Surtur flung his fiery brand !
In conflagration flared the land.
Shrivelled like scroll the heaven high ;
Above, below, surrounding fire
Still mounting higher.
Played lurid 'gainst the crumbling home
Of Valhal's gods in Asgard's dome.

Ended the frightful war.
Alone, as conqueror,
Stood Surtur, Victor!
With ruined Nature's birth,
Down sank the blackened Earth
In boiling sea.
All smould'ring fell !
That which from Chaos came,
To Chaos back returned ;
Disastrously,
In the eclipse of Asgard's lords.
Faded the twilight of the gods.
At length one universal flame.
Enwrapping distant spheres, high burned;
Laid on one mighty funeral pyre,
Forth flashed in fierce consuming fire,
In World-blaze dread, — Earth, Heaven and Hell !

Julia Clinton Jones (publ. 1878)

Part Twelvth

Regeneration

O Chaos wild again
Reigned o'er Creation's fane.
Foul Loki's brood had given birth
To fear in Heav'n, and crime on Earth.
So deep had sunk corruption's stain, —
So far had spread dark sin and pain, —
That Death alone
Could e'er atone :
While thro' the flames of Surtur's sword
Alone could peace be yet restored.
When that dread World-blaze flared on high,
Mingling in ruin earth and sky,—
The lurid glow, still mounting higher,
Shone forth— a god-sent purifier.

'Twas past. The Fire-God's work was done.
Died down the flame;
Weak Nature's shame
Submerged in depths of shoreless sea;
The charred skies, the smoke-wreaths gray.
With battle's din, had passed away;
Day had begun !
All gloriously
Thro' Heaven's broad fields of trackless light,
With splendors bursting thro' the night,
The fairer daughter of the Sun
Rode forth on her celestial way
Round ether main,
Where starry isles strew thick the plain ;
One dazzling blaze

Of cloudless days
Flooded all worlds with ecstacy.

Triumphantly
Stept forth the High and Mighty One
From mansions of Eternity,
Where rests for aye His golden throne;
To Whom Time was a moment's birth;
Strong with the strength of Heaven and Earth,
Victorious o'er sin and pain,
With wondrous majesty shall reign
in judgment's solemn panoply.

Then the Life-giving Spirit spoke;
And sudden broke
Up from the bosom of the sea,
Most beateously,
The vernal Earth, ambrosial ;
Fair as the smile of new-born light,
And fairer far than when at dawn
Of young Creation's early morn,
Up-springing from chaotic night.
She sang her praise to proud Valhal.

Raising on high her forehead fair
Crowned with sweet flowers of beauty rare,
She smiled up to the crystal arch,
Laughing with fountain's gurgling plash,
And mountain streamlet's joyous dash;
While shining planets far,
Moving in liquid harmony
Around the Throne of Him most High,
Pausing awhile in measured march,
Poured down a flood of softened beams,

C'aught from blest Gimli's golden gleams,
To greet their sister star.

Decked in bright robes of living green,
Enamelled o'er with flow'rets' sheen.
Sweet Nature stood restored.
Ripe unsown harvests clothed the hills;
The murmuring rills
Refreshing dews o'er meadows poured ;
The mantling vines, luxurious, hung
With purple treasures richly fraught ;
While sunbeams wrought,
The leafy bowers of shade among,
A network rare of gold with dusk ;
Wide gardens of sweet-smelling musk,
With jassamine and roses' scent,
To perfumed air more perfume lent ;
Thick woods, whose boughs of fragrance flung
Their spicy odors to the breeze.
Rose in fresh coolness o'er the vale,
And gently swayed to balmy gale ;
The bending trees,
With burnished fruit, were weighted deep;
While, from the steep,
Rivers of joy rolled down each dale;
On the sweet breeze that gently swelled
From groves of cassia and of palm,
Forth tuneful voices gaily welled
From feathered songsters of the air.
Whose gorgeous plumes, in colors bright,
Flashed jewelled gleams of rainbow light,
Mingled with roseate sunbeams fair.
Caressing breaths of heavenly balm
Young Nature lapped in blesséd calm ;

While throbbing pulses of the Farth
Beat high at her glad second birth.

Thro' all that doomful Day
When .Surtur's flames destroyed the world,
.And back to Chaos Nature hurled,
Two gentle beings lay
Concealed in Mimir's wood —
Hodminir's forest deep; — unscathed,
Unshaken by the tempest shock,
in dreamless slumbers sweetlv swathed,
They, all unharmed, passed 'neath the brand,
That burning sword which o'er all waved,
Devouring else, air, sea, and land, —
Alone, of all Creation, saved
From that resistless fire and flood
Of Time-destroying Ragnarock.

Unconscious thro' that hideous strife,
Awakened now to blissful life,
Guileless and lovely, they arose
In new-born strength and purity.
All passion passed, with care and woes;
Calmed now convulsed Creation's throes
To peaceful rest and surity.
Thro' all that night of horror dread
On dews of morning they were fed;
Now, lifting up their joyful eyes
In rapturous wonder and surprise,
They gazed around
From ether vault to teeming ground.
Above, the broad horizon's zone
With orient effulgence shone ;
Beneath, the bounteous Earth sent up

Unfading grass, and flow'ret's cup,
Filled with the wine of early dawn ;
With dew-drops gemmed, each emerald blade
Within its gleaming, liquid light
The image of the heavens displayed;
Eternal spring breathed thro' the morn,
And cast o'er all her halo bright.

So beauteous lay, — so tranquilly, —
The virgin daughter of the sea,
That the two souls who on her gazed,
Themselves most innocent and fair,
All perfect 'mid perfection rare,
By myriad blooming charms amazed,
Received with joy this dwelling place.
High altars to the gods they reared,
Pure Gimli's fane they loved and feared ;
So, blest and happy, chosen were
As parents of a nobler race.

Upon the perfume-breathing plain
Of Idavöller, where before
Stood Asgard's gold-roofed halls of yore,
The joyous Aesir met again ;
Conquerors from awful fight,
Grown pure thro' fire, grown strong with strife,
Passed thro' dread death to endless life,
As thro' dark bars to fane of light :
For Loki's reign was o'er.
No more
Should foul wrong, loathsome, side by side
With peace and purity abide.
Broken the power of Hel ;
Freed from her gloomy chain,

Baldur again
Rose, luminous, from realms of night.
All shapes of Ill, as rolled away
The Twilight gloom before his ray,
Back to their bonds appalléd fell :
On Vigrid's plain all evil died.
That great Atonement-Day,
In godlike love, thro' godlike might.
Led back the Aesir, purified,
To firmer thrones and brighter halls
Than e'er were found in Asgard's walls.
Love smiled thro' all the universe ;
Arm linked in arm, in sweet converse,
Baldur, with Hcedur seated nigh,
In perfect peace and harmony,
Glad greetings gave exultantly,
As up the heights to Ida's plain
The happy Aesir rose again,
In the clear dawn, triumphantly.

With crystal walls, gold-fretted roof,
A new-built Valhal, tempest-proof.
Towered aloft ;
Without, within, all rich and rare,
Steel to make strong, and jewels fair
All lavish spread
O'er pavement broad, and vaulted dome ;
While music soft
Floated, full voiced, high overhead,
Guiding the Aesir to their home.
Again the beakers deep brimmed o'er ;
Again the great gods' wondrous lore
And mighty deeds of Eld were sung ;
With runic rhyme

Of earlier time
Again the pillared Feast-Hall rung.
But now no Battle-Maidens stood
Round Odin's Throne, at hero-feast,
With gory armor, shields of blood ;
All useless now Valkyriar,
War brought forth no Einheriar,
For war had ceased.
High o'er young Earth and Ida's plain,
By Gimli's fane—
Close by the Throne of Him Most High—
With folded wings, stood Victory ;
While sweetly thro' each sounding sphere,
In tones that swelled on waves of air,
He spoke, commanding " Peace ! "
Gave chains to Death — to Pain, surcease.

Wide thrown, lo ! Gimli's golden gate
On most harmonious hinges swang,
As, from His Everlasting Seat,
Arrayed in majesty complete.
The Judge Eternal, glorious, came,
Weighing, supreme, all things create,
Empires of Earth, of Heaven, of Hell !
To farthest orbs His judgments rang.
As from His lips just sentence fell,
The fetid ranks of Sin shrank down
Beneath His frown,
Thro' radiant vault of ether sky,
To Hel's domain of misery,
On wings of hideous Nidhogg borne,
In Nastrond's fearful stream to lie,
'Neath serpents' fangs, in lurid flame,
By Fenrir torn,

Bound fast in adamantine chain
In frightful depths of endless pain ;—
Such was their doom of agony,
Of fear and shame.

More awful was their second doom.
Exiled forever from His face,
Removéd far in anguished gloom ;
To know, above on starry plain.
In glories shown fair Gimli's fane,
Where joy ecstatic bathed the good
In endless flood ;
\\'hile they, condemned, could gain no place
E'en at His feet —
Never the faintest ray might snatch,
Nor e'en the dimmest shadow catch
Of raptures sweet.

Seated, now, in Gimli's portal.
As before at Asgard's gate,
Fair Iduna, Maid Immortal,
Shall the purer Aesir wait.
Songs of joyance ever singing,
Skoals of triumph, sweet and clear,
Thro' the vaulted dome are ringing,
Echoing thro' crystal sphere.

"Passed is the gloom of night,
Finished the fearful fight,
Welcome, thrice welcome ! to glories on high.
For striving and sadness,
Now taste ye pure gladness ;
Lo ! thro' the radiant, orient sky,
From Gimli's wide portal,

What splendors immortal
Flash o'er your pathway, to Heav'n drawing nigh.
Joy, joy to you, blest ones !
Behold ! for you gold thrones
Fixed 'neath the dome of Eternity rise ;
The stars of the morning
Sing sweet in the dawning !
Rest after conflict, the soul's dearest prize.
Mount, then, ye heroes all,
Hasten to Gimli's hall ;
Near you, on golden wing, Victory flies ! "

Pausing awhile, more clear and high
Awoke the notes triumphantly.
On tuneful hinge, with music sweet,
Back roll the gates most glorious
The entering conquerors to greet.
Then, bending from his lofty seat,
The Judge Supreme,
With smiles that e'er through Gimli gleam,
Now welcomes these, victorious,
Led by Iduna to His feet.

Bowed low before th" Eternal I'hrone,
A loftier measure still she sings ;
Ten thousand harps with sounding strings
Ascribe all praise to Him alone,
His justice, might and wisdom own.
Thro' list'ning orbs the chorus rings ;
The hosts of Heav'n entrancéd stand
Still in their paths, while echoes grand
Roll in huge waves of ceaseless sound
Those countless burning worlds around.

Too high, too pure, that wondrous strain,
For Earth to catch e'en faint refrain :
Yet Still the exultant song rolls on
For victory won !
The Twilight passed — dread Ragnarock
Passed, with its furious battle shock —
All joyful beams, with brillant ray,
Regeneration's glorious Day !

Julia Clinton Jones (publ. 1878)

Balder Dead, An Episode, Matthew Arnold (British poet and critic, 1822-1888), publ. 1855 in "Poems, Second Series"

I
SENDING

SO on the floor lay Balder dead; and round
Lay thickly strewn swords axes darts and spears
Which all the Gods in sport had idly thrown
At Balder, whom no weapon pierc'd or clove:
But in his breast stood fixt the fatal bough
Of mistletoe, which Lok the Accuser gave
To Hoder, and unwitting Hoder threw:
'Gainst that alone had Balder's life no charm.
And all the Gods and all the Heroes came
And stood round Balder on the bloody floor
Weeping and wailing; and Valhalla rang
Up to its golden roof with sobs and cries:
And on the tables stood the untasted meats,
And in the horns and gold-rimm'd skulls the wine:
And now would Night have fall'n, and found them yet
Wailing; but otherwise was Odin's will:
And thus the Father of the Ages spake:—

'Enough of tears, ye Gods, enough of wail!
Not to lament in was Valhalla made.
If any here might weep for Balder's death
I most might weep, his Father; such a son
I lose today, so bright, so lov'd a God.
But he has met that doom which long ago
The Nornies, when his mother bare him, spun,
And Fate set seal, that so his end must be.
Balder has met his death, and ye survive:

Weep him an hour; but what can grief avail?
For you yourselves, ye Gods, shall meet your doom,
All ye who hear me, and inhabit Heaven,
And I too, Odin too, the Lord of all;
But ours we shall not meet, when that day comes,
With woman's tears and weak complaining cries—
Why should we meet another's portion so?
Rather it fits you, having wept your hour,
With cold dry eyes, and hearts compos'd and stern,
To live, as erst, your daily life in Heaven:
By me shall vengeance on the murderer Lok,
The Foe, the Accuser, whom, though Gods, we hate,
Be strictly car'd for, in the appointed day.
Meanwhile, to-morrow, when the morning dawns,
Bring wood to the seashore to Balder's ship,
And on the deck build high a funeral pile,
And on the top lay Balder's corpse, and put
Fire to the wood, and send him out to sea
To burn; for that is what the dead desire.'

So having spoke, the King of Gods arose
And mounted his horse Sleipner, whom he rode,
And from the hall of Heaven he rode away
To Lidskialf, and sate upon his throne,
The Mount, from whence his eye surveys the world.
And far from Heaven he turn'd his shining orbs
To look on Midgard, and the earth, and men:
And on the conjuring Lapps he bent his gaze
Whom antler'd reindeer pull over the snow;
And on the Finns, the gentlest of mankind,
Fair men, who live in holes under the ground:
Nor did he look once more to Ida's plain,
Nor towards Valhalla, and the sorrowing Gods;
For well he knew the Gods would heed his word,

And cease to mourn, and think of Balder's pyre.

But in Valhalla all the Gods went back
From around Balder, all the Heroes went;
And left his body stretch'd upon the floor.
And on their golden chairs they sate again,
Beside the tables, in the hall of Heaven;
And before each the cooks who serv'd them plac'd
New messes of the boar Serimner's flesh,
And the Valkyries crown'd their horns with mead.
So they, with pent-up hearts and tearless eyes,
Wailing no more, in silence ate and drank,
While Twilight fell, and sacred Night came on.

But the blind Hoder left the feasting Gods
In Odin's hall, and went through Asgard streets,
And past the haven where the Gods have moor'd
Their ships, and through the gate, beyond the wall.
Though sightless, yet his own mind led the God.
Down to the margin of the roaring sea
He came, and sadly went along the sand
Between the waves and black o'erhanging cliffs
Where in and out the screaming seafowl fly;
Until he came to where a gully breaks
Through the cliff wall, and a fresh stream runs down
From the high moors behind, and meets the sea.
There in the glen Fensaler stands, the house
Of Frea, honour'd Mother of the Gods,
And shows its lighted windows to the main.
There he went up, and pass'd the open doors:
And in the hall he found those women old,
The Prophetesses, who by rite eterne
On Frea's hearth feed high the sacred fire
Both night and day; and by the inner wall

Upon her golden chair the Mother sate,
With folded hands, revolving things to come:
To her drew Hoder near, and spake, and said:—

'Mother, a child of bale thou bar'st in me.
For, first, thou barest me with blinded eyes.
Sightless and helpless, wandering weak in Heaven;
And, after that, of ignorant witless mind
Thou barest me, and unforeseeing soul:
That I alone must take the branch from Lok,
The Foe, the Accuser, whom, though Gods, we hate,
And cast it at the dear-lov'd Balder's breast
At whom the Gods in sport their weapons threw—
'Gainst that alone had Balder's life no charm.
Now therefore what to attempt, or whither fly?
For who will bear my hateful sight in Heaven?—
Can I, O Mother, bring them Balder back
Or—for thou know'st the Fates, and things allow'd—
Can I with Hela's power a compact strike,
And make exchange, and give my life for his?'

He spoke: the Mother of the Gods replied:—
'Hoder, ill-fated, child of bale, my son,
Sightless in soul and eye, what words are these?
That one, long portion'd with his doom of death,
Should change his lot, and fill another's life,
And Hela yield to this, and let him go!
On Balder Death hath laid her hand, not thee;
Nor doth she count this life a price for that.
For many Gods in Heaven, not thou alone,
Would freely die to purchase Balder back,
And wend themselves to Hela's gloomy realm.
For not so gladsome is that life in Heaven
Which Gods and Heroes lead, in feast and fray,

Waiting the darkness of the final times,
That one should grudge its loss for Balder's sake,
Balder their joy, so bright, so lov'd a God.
But Fate withstands, and laws forbid this way.
Yet in my secret mind one way I know,
Nor do I judge if it shall win or fail:
But much must still be tried, which shall but fail.'

And the blind Hoder answer'd her, and said:—
'What way is this, O Mother, that thou show'st?
Is it a matter which a God might try?'

And straight the Mother of the Gods replied:—
'There is a way which leads to Hela's realm,
Untrodden, lonely, far from light and Heaven.
Who goes that way must take no other horse
To ride, but Sleipner, Odin's horse, alone.
Nor must he choose that common path of Gods
Which every day they come and go in Heaven,
O'er the bridge Bifrost, where is Heimdall's watch,
Past Midgard Fortress, down to Earth and men;
But he must tread a dark untravell'd road
Which branches from the north of Heaven, and ride
Nine days, nine nights, towards the northern ice,
Through valleys deep-engulph'd, with roaring streams.
And he will reach on the tenth morn a bridge
Which spans with golden arches Giall's stream,
Not Bifrost, but that bridge a Damsel keeps,
Who tells the passing troops of dead their way
To the low shore of ghosts, and Hela's realm.
And she will bid him northward steer his course:
Then he will journey through no lighted land,
Nor see the sun arise, nor see it set;
But he must ever watch the northern Bear

Who from her frozen height with jealous eye
Confronts the Dog and Hunter in the south,
And is alone not dipt in Ocean's stream.
And straight he will come down to Ocean's strand;
Ocean, whose watery ring enfolds the world,
And on whose marge the ancient Giants dwell.
But he will reach its unknown northern shore,
Far, far beyond the outmost Giant's home,
At the chink'd fields of ice, the waste of snow:
And he will fare across the dismal ice
Northward, until he meets a stretching wall
Barring his way, and in the wall a grate.
But then he must dismount, and on the ice
Tighten the girths of Sleipner, Odin's horse,
And make him leap the grate, and come within.
And he will see stretch round him Hela's realm,
The plains of Niflheim, where dwell the dead,
And hear the roaring of the streams of Hell.
And he will see the feeble shadowy tribes,
And Balder sitting crown'd, and Hela's throne.
Then he must not regard the wailful ghosts
Who all will flit, like eddying leaves, around;
But he must straight accost their solemn Queen,
And pay her homage, and entreat with prayers,
Telling her all that grief they have in Heaven
For Balder, whom she holds by right below:
If haply he may melt her heart with words,
And make her yield, and give him Balder back.'

She spoke: but Hoder answer'd her and said:—
'Mother, a dreadful way is this thou show'st.
No journey for a sightless God to go.'

And straight the Mother of the Gods replied:—

'Therefore thyself thou shalt not go, my son.
But he whom first thou meetest when thou com'st
To Asgard, and declar'st this hidden way,
Shall go, and I will be his guide unseen.'

She spoke, and on her face let fall her veil,
And bow'd her head, and sate with folded hands.
But at the central hearth those Women old,
Who while the Mother spake had ceased their toil,
Began again to heap the sacred fire:
And Hoder turn'd, and left his mother's house,
Fensaler, whose lit windows look to sea;
And came again down to the roaring waves,
And back along the beach to Asgard went,
Pondering on that which Frea said should be.

But Night came down, and darken'd Asgard streets.
Then from their loathed feast the Gods arose,
And lighted torches, and took up the corpse
Of Balder from the floor of Odin's hall,
And laid it on a bier, and bare him home
Through the fast-darkening streets to his own house
Breidablik, on whose columns Balder grav'd
The enchantments, that recall the dead to life:
For wise he was, and many curious arts,
Postures of runes, and healing herbs he knew;
Unhappy: but that art he did not know
To keep his own life safe, and see the sun:—
There to his hall the Gods brought Balder home,
And each bespake him as he laid him down:—

'Would that ourselves, O Balder, we were borne
Home to our halls, with torchlight, by our kin,
So thou might'st live, and still delight the Gods.'

They spake: and each went home to his own house.
But there was one, the first of all the Gods
For speed, and Hermod was his name in Heaven;
Most fleet he was, but now he went the last,
Heavy in heart for Balder, to his house
Which he in Asgard built him, there to dwell,
Against the harbour, by the city wall:
Him the blind Hoder met, as he came up
From the sea cityward, and knew his step;
Nor yet could Hermod see his brother's face,
For it grew dark; but Hoder touch'd his arm:
And as a spray of honeysuckle flowers
Brushes across a tired traveller's face
Who shuffles through the deep dew-moisten'd dust,
On a May evening, in the darken'd lanes,
And starts him, that he thinks a ghost went by—
So Hoder brush'd by Hermod's side, and said:—

'Take Sleipner, Hermod, and set forth with dawn
To Hela's kingdom, to ask Balder back;
And they shall be thy guides, who have the power.'

He spake, and brush'd soft by, and disappear'd.
And Hermod gaz'd into the night, and said:—

'Who is it utters through the dark his hest
So quickly, and will wait for no reply?
The voice was like the unhappy Hoder's voice.
Howbeit I will see, and do his hest;
For there rang note divine in that command.'

So speaking, the fleet-footed Hermod came
Home, and lay down to sleep in his own house,

And all the Gods lay down in their own homes.
And Hoder too came home, distraught with grief,
Loathing to meet, at dawn, the other Gods:
And he went in, and shut the door, and fixt
His sword upright, and fell on it, and died.

But from the hill of Lidskialf Odin rose,
The throne, from which his eye surveys the world;
And mounted Sleipner, and in darkness rode
To Asgard. And the stars came out in Heaven,
High over Asgard, to light home the King.
But fiercely Odin gallop'd, mov'd in heart;
And swift to Asgard, to the gate, he came
And terribly the hoofs of Sleipner rang
Along the flinty floor of Asgard streets;
And the Gods trembled on their golden beds
Hearing the wrathful Father coming home;
For dread, for like a whirlwind, Odin came:
And to Valhalla's gate he rode, and left
Sleipner; and Sleipner went to his own stall:
And in Valhalla Odin laid him down.

But in Breidablik Nanna, Balder's wife,
Came with the Goddesses who wrought her will,
And stood round Balder lying on his bier:
And at his head and feet she station'd Scalds
Who in their lives were famous for their song;
These o'er the corpse inton'd a plaintive strain,
A dirge; and Nanna and her train replied.
And far into the night they wail'd their dirge:
But when their souls were satisfied with wail,
They went, and laid them down, and Nanna went
Into an upper chamber, and lay down;
And Frea seal'd her tired lids with sleep.

And 'twas when Night is bordering hard on Dawn,
When air is chilliest, and the stars sunk low,
Then Balder's spirit through the gloom drew near,
In garb, in form, in feature as he was
Alive, and still the rays were round his head
Which were his glorious mark in Heaven; he stood
Over against the curtain of the bed,
And gaz'd on Nanna as she slept, and spake:—

'Poor lamb, thou sleepest, and forgett'st thy woe.
Tears stand upon the lashes of thine eyes,
Tears wet the pillow by thy cheek; but thou,
Like a young child, hast cried thyself to sleep.
Sleep on: I watch thee, and am here to aid.
Alive I kept not far from thee, dear soul,
Neither do I neglect thee now, though dead.
For with to-morrow's dawn the Gods prepare
To gather wood, and build a funeral pile
Upon my ship, and burn my corpse with fire,
That sad, sole honour of the dead; and thee
They think to burn, and all my choicest wealth,
With me, for thus ordains the common rite:
But it shall not be so: but mild, but swift,
But painless shall a stroke from Frea come,
To cut thy thread of life, and free thy soul,
And they shall burn thy corpse with mine, not thee.
And well I know that by no stroke of death,
Tardy or swift, wouldst thou be loath to die,
So it restor'd thee, Nanna, to my side,
Whom thou so well hast lov'd; but I can smooth
Thy way, and this at least my prayers avail.
Yes, and I fain would altogether ward
Death from thy head, and with the Gods in Heaven

Prolong thy life, though not by thee desir'd:
But Right bars this, not only thy desire.
Yet dreary, Nanna, is the life they lead
In that dim world, in Hela's mouldering realm;
And doleful afire the ghosts, the troops of dead,
Whom Hela with austere control presides;
For of the race of Gods is no one there
Save me alone, and Hela, solemn Queen:
And all the nobler souls of mortal men
On battle-field have met their death, and now
Feast in Valhalla, in my Father's hall;
Only the inglorious sort are there below,
The old, the cowards, and the weak are there,
Men spent by sickness, or obscure decay.
But even there, O Nanna, we might find
Some solace in each other's look and speech,
Wandering together through that gloomy world.
And talking of the life we led in Heaven,
While we yet liv'd, among the other Gods.'

He spake, and straight his lineaments began
To fade: and Nanna in her sleep stretch'd out
Her arms towards him with a cry; but he
Mournfully shook his head, and disappear'd.
And as the woodman sees a little smoke
Hang in the air, afield, and disappear—
So Balder faded in the night away.
And Nanna on her bed sunk back: but then
Frea, the Mother of the Gods, with stroke
Painless and swift, set free her airy soul,
Which took, on Balder's track, the way below:
And instantly the sacred Morn appear'd.

II

JOURNEY TO THE DEAD

FORTH from the East, up the ascent of Heaven,
Day drove his courser with the Shining Mane;
And in Valhalla, from his gable perch,
The golden-crested Cock began to crow:
Hereafter, in the blackest dead of night,
With shrill and dismal cries that Bird shall crow,
Warning the Gods that foes draw nigh to Heaven;
But now he crew at dawn, a cheerful note,
To wake the Gods and Heroes to their tasks.
And all the Gods, and all the Heroes, woke.
And from their beds the Heroes rose, and donn'd
Their arms, and led their horses from the stall,
And mounted them, and in Valhalla's court
Were rang'd; and then the daily fray began.
And all day long they there are hack'd and hewn
'Mid dust, and groans, and limbs lopp'd off, and blood;
But all at night return to Odin's hall
Woundless and fresh: such lot is theirs in Heaven.
And the Valkyries on their steeds went forth
Toward Earth and fights of men; and at their side
Skulda, the youngest of the Nornies, rode:
And over Bifrost, where is Heimdall's watch,
Past Midgard Fortress, down to Earth they came:
There through some battle-field, where men fall fast,
Their horses fetlock-deep in blood, they ride,
And pick the bravest warriors out for death,
Whom they bring back with them at night to Heaven,
To glad the Gods, and feast in Odin's hall.

But the Gods went not now, as otherwhile,
Into the Tilt-Yard, where the Heroes fought,

To feast their eyes with looking on the fray:
Nor did they to their Judgement-Place repair
By the ash Igdrasil, in Ida's plain,
Where they hold council, and give laws for men:
But they went, Odin first, the rest behind,
To the hall Gladheim, which is built of gold;
Where are in circle rang'd twelve golden chairs,
And in the midst one higher, Odin's throne:
There all the Gods in silence sate them down;
And thus the Father of the Ages spake:—

Go quickly, Gods, bring wood to the seashore,
With all, which it beseems the dead to have
And make a funeral pile on Balder's ship.
On the twelfth day the Gods shall burn his corpse.
But Hermod, thou, take Sleipner, and ride down
To Hela's kingdom, to ask Balder back.'

So said he; and the Gods arose, and took
Axes and ropes, and at their head came Thor,
Shouldering his Hammer, which the Giants know:
Forth wended they, and drove their steeds before:
And up the dewy mountain tracks they far'd
To the dark forests, in the early dawn;
And up and down and side and slant they roam'd:
And from the glens all day an echo came
Of crashing falls; for with his hammer Thor
Smote 'mid the rocks the lichen-bearded pines
And burst their roots; while to their tops the Gods
Made fast the woven ropes, and hal'd them down,
And lopp'd their boughs, and clove them on the sward,
And bound the logs behind their steeds to draw,
And drove them homeward; and the snorting steeds
Went straining through the crackling brushwood down,

And by the darkling forest paths the Gods
Follow'd, and on their shoulders carried boughs.
And they came out upon the plain, and pass'd
Asgard, and led their horses to the beach,
And loos'd them of their loads on the seashore,
And rang'd the wood in stacks by Balder's ship;
And every God went home to his own house.

But when the Gods were to the forest gone
Hermod led Sleipner from Valhalla forth
And saddled him; before that, Sleipner brook'd
No meaner hand than Odin's on his mane,
On his broad back no lesser rider bore:
Yet docile now he stood at Hermod's side,
Arching his neck, and glad to be bestrode,
Knowing the God they went to seek, how dear.
But Hermod mounted him, and sadly far'd,
In silence, up the dark untravell'd road
Which branches from the north of Heaven, and went
All day; and Daylight wan'd, and Night came on.
And all that night he rode, and journey'd so,
Nine days, nine nights, towards the northern ice,
Through valleys deep-engulph'd, by roaring streams:
And on the tenth morn ho beheld the bridge
Which spans with golden arches Giall's stream,
And on the bridge a Damsel watching arm'd,
In the strait passage, at the further end,
Where the road issues between walling rocks.
Scant space that Warder left for passers by;
But, as when cowherds in October drive
Their kine across a snowy mountain pass
To winter pasture on the southern side,
And on the ridge a wagon chokes the way,
Wedg'd in the snow; then painfully the hinds

With goad and shouting urge their cattle past,
Plunging through deep untrodden banks of snow
To right and left, and warm steam fills the air—
So on the bridge that Damsel block'd the way,
And question'd Hermod as he came, and said:—

'Who art thou on thy black and fiery horse
Under whose hoofs the bridge o'er Giall's stream
Rumbles and shakes? Tell me thy race and home.
But yestermorn five troops of dead pass'd by
Bound on their way below to Hela's realm,
Nor shook the bridge so much as thou alone.
And thou hast flesh and colour on thy cheeks
Like men who live and draw the vital air;
Nor look'st thou pale and wan, like men deceas'd,
Souls bound below, my daily passers here.'

And the fleet-footed Hermod answer'd her:—
'O Damsel, Hermod am I call'd, the son
Of Odin; and my high-roof'd house is built
Far hence, in Asgard, in the City of Gods:
And Sleipner, Odin's horse, is this I ride.
And I come, sent this road on Balder's track:
Say then, if he hath cross'd thy bridge or no?'

He spake; the Warder of the bridge replied:—
'O Hermod, rarely do the feet of Gods
Or of the horses of the Gods resound
Upon my bridge; and, when they cross, I know.
Balder hath gone this way, and ta'en the road
Below there, to the north, toward Hela's realm.
From here the cold white mist can be discern'd,
Not lit with sun, but through the darksome air
By the dim vapour-blotted light of stars,

Which hangs over the ice where lies the road.
For in that ice are lost those northern streams
Freezing and ridging in their onward flow,
Which from the fountain of Vergelmer run,
The spring that bubbles up by Hela's throne.
There are the joyless seats, the haunt of ghosts,
Hela's pale swarms; and there was Balder bound.
Ride on; pass free: but he by this is there.'

She spake, and stepp'd aside, and left him room.
And Hermod greeted her, and gallop'd by
Across the bridge; then she took post again.
But northward Hermod rode, the way below:
And o'er a darksome tract, which knows no sun,
But by the blotted light of stars, he far'd;
And he came down to Ocean's northern strand
At the drear ice, beyond the Giants' home:
Thence on he journey'd o'er the fields of ice
Still north, until he met a stretching wall
Barring his way, and in the wall a grate.
Then he dismounted, and drew tight the girths,
On the smooth ice, of Sleipner, Odin's horse,
And made him leap the grate, and came within.
And he beheld spread round him Hela's realm,
The plains of Niflheim, where dwell the dead,
And heard the thunder of the streams of Hell.
For near the wall the river of Roaring flows,
Outmost: the others near the centre run—
The Storm, the Abyss, the Howling, and the Pain:
Those flow by Hela's throne, and near their spring.
And from the dark flock'd up the shadowy tribes:
And as the swallows crowd the bulrush-beds
Of some clear river, issuing from a lake,
On autumn days, before they cross the sea;

And to each bulrush-crest a swallow hangs
Swinging, and others skim the river streams,
And their quick twittering fills the banks and shores—
So around Hermod swarm'd the twittering ghosts.
Women, and infants, and young men who died
Too soon for fame, with white ungraven shields;
And old men, known to Glory, but their star
Betray'd them, and of wasting age they died,
Not wounds: yet, dying, they their armour wore,
And now have chief regard in Hela's realm.
Behind flock'd wrangling up a piteous crew,
Greeted of none, disfeatur'd and forlorn—
Cowards, who were in sloughs interr'd alive:
And round them still the wattled hurdles hung
Wherewith they stamp'd them down, and trod them deep,
To hide their shameful memory from men.
But all he pass'd unhail'd, and reach'd the throne
Of Hela, and saw, near it, Balder crown'd,
And Hela sat thereon, with countenance stern;
And thus bespake him first the solemn Queen:—

'Unhappy, how hast thou endur'd to leave
The light, and journey to the cheerless land
Where idly flit about the feeble shades
How didst thou cross the bridge o'er Giall's stream,
Being alive, and come to Ocean's shore?
Or how o'erleap the grate that bars the wall?'

She spake: but down off Sleipner Hermod sprang,
And fell before her feet, and clasp'd her knees;
And spake, and mild entreated her, and said:—

'O Hela, wherefore should the Gods declare
Their errands to each other, or the ways

They go? the errand and the way is known.
Thou know'st, thou know'st, what grief we have in Heaven
For Balder, whom thou hold'st by right below:
Restore him, for what part fulfils he here?
Shall he shed cheer over the cheerless seats,
And touch the apathetic ghosts with joy?
Not for such end, O Queen, thou hold'st thy realm.
For Heaven was Balder born, the City of Gods
And Heroes, where they live in light and joy:
Thither restore him, for his place is there.'

He spoke; and grave replied the solemn Queen:—
'Hermod, for he thou art, thou Son of Heaven!
A strange unlikely errand, sure, is thine.
Do the Gods send to me to make them blest?
Small bliss my race hath of the Gods obtain'd.
Three mighty children to my Father Lok
Did Angerbode, the Giantess, bring forth—
Fenris the Wolf, the Serpent huge, and Me:
Of these the Serpent in the sea ye cast,
Who since in your despite hath wax'd amain,
And now with gleaming ring enfolds the world:
Me on this cheerless nether world ye threw
And gave me nine unlighted realms to rule:
While on his island in the lake, afar,
Made fast to the bor'd crag, by wile not strength
Subdu'd, with limber chains lives Fenris bound.
Lok still subsists in Heaven, our Father wise,
Your mate, though loath'd, and feasts in Odin's hall;
But him too foes await, and netted snares,
And in a cave a bed of needle rocks,
And o'er his visage serpents dropping gall.
Yet he shall one day rise, and burst his bonds,
And with himself set us his offspring free,

When he guides Muspel's children to their bourne.
Till then in peril or in pain we live,
Wrought by the Gods: and ask the Gods our aid?
Howbeit we abide our day: till then,
We do not as some feebler haters do,
Seek to afflict our foes with petty pangs,
Helpless to better us, or ruin them.
Come then; if Balder was so dear belov'd,
And this is true, and such a loss is Heaven's—
Hear, how to Heaven may Balder be restor'd.
Show me through all the world the signs of grief:
Fails but one thing to grieve, here Balder stops:
Let all that lives and moves upon the earth
Weep him, and all that is without life weep:
Let Gods, men, brutes, beweep him; plants and stones.
So shall I know the lost was dear indeed,
And bend my heart, and give him back to Heaven.'

She spake; and Hermod answer'd her, and said:—
'Hela, such as thou say'st, the terms shall be.
But come, declare me this, and truly tell:
May I, ere I depart, bid Balder hail
Or is it here withheld to greet the dead?'

He spake; and straightway Hela answer'd him:—
'Hermod, greet Balder if thou wilt, and hold
Converse: his speech remains, though he he dead.'

And straight to Balder Hermod turn'd, and spake:—
'Even in the abode of Death, O Balder, hail!
Thou hear'st, if hearing, like as speech, is thine,
The terms of thy releasement hence to Heaven:
Fear nothing but that all shall be fulfill'd.
For not unmindful of thee are the Gods

Who see the light, and blest in Asgard dwell;
Even here they seek thee out, in Hela's realm.
And sure of all the happiest far art thou
Who ever have been known in Earth or Heaven:
Alive, thou wert of Gods the most belov'd:
And now thou sittest crown'd by Hela's side,
Here, and hast honour among all the dead.'

He spake; and Balder utter'd him reply,
But feebly, as a voice far off; he said:—

'Hermod the nimble, gild me not my death.
Better to live a slave, a captur'd man,
Who scatters rushes in a master's ball,
Than be a crown'd king here, and rule the dead.
And now I count not of these terms as safe
To be fulfill'd, nor my return as sure,
Though I be lov'd, and many mourn my death:
For double-minded ever was the seed
Of Lok, and double are the gifts they give.
Howbeit, report thy message; and therewith,
To Odin, to my Father, take this ring,
Memorial of me, whether sav'd or no:
And tell the Heaven-born Gods how thou hast seen
Me sitting here below by Hela s side,
Crown'd, having honour among all the dead.'

He spake, and rais'd his hand, and gave the ring.
And with inscrutable regard the Queen
Of Hell beheld them, and the ghosts stood dumb.
But Hermod took the ring, and yet once more
Kneel'd and did homage to the solemn Queen;
Then mounted Sleipner, and set forth to ride
Back, through the astonish'd tribes of dead, to Heaven.

And to the wall he came, and found the grate
Lifted, and issued on the fields of ice;
And o'er the ice he far'd to Ocean's strand,
And up from thence, a wet and misty road,
To the arm'd Damsel's bridge, and Giall's stream.
Worse was that way to go than to return,
For him: for others all return is barr'd.
Nine days he took to go, two to return;
And on the twelfth morn saw the light of Heaven.
And as a traveller in the early dawn
To the steep edge of some great valley comes
Through which a river flows, and sees beneath
Clouds of white rolling vapours fill the vale,
But o'er them, on the farther slope, descries
Vineyards, and crofts, and pastures, bright with sun—
So Hermod, o'er the fog between, saw Heaven.
And Sleipner snorted, for he smelt the air
Of Heaven: and mightily, as wing'd, he flew.
And Hermod saw the towers of Asgard rise:
And he drew near, and heard no living voice
In Asgard; and the golden halls were dumb.
Then Hermod knew what labour held the Gods:
And through the empty streets he rode, and pass'd
Under the gate-house to the sands, and found
The Gods on the seashore by Balder's ship.

III

FUNERAL

THE GODS held talk together, group'd in knots,
Round Balder's corpse, which they had thither borne;
And Hermod came down towards them from the gate.
And Lok, the Father of the Serpent, first
Beheld him come, and to his neighbour spake:—

'See, here is Hermod, who comes single back
From Hell; and shall I tell thee how he seems
Like as a farmer, who hath lost his dog,
Some morn, at market, in a crowded town—
Through many streets the poor beast runs in vain,
And follows this man after that, for hours;
And, late at evening, spent and panting, falls
Before a stranger's threshold, not his home,
With flanks a-tremble, and his slender tongue
Hangs quivering out between his dust-smear'd jaws,
And piteously he eyes the passers by:
But home his master comes to his own farm,
Far in the country, wondering where he is—
So Hermod comes to-day unfollow'd home.'

And straight his neighbour, mov'd with wrath, replied:—
'Deceiver, fair in form, but false in heart,
Enemy, Mocker, whom, though Gods, we hate—
Peace, lest our Father Odin hear thee gibe.
Would I might see him snatch thee in his hand,
And bind thy carcase, like a bale, with cords,
And hurl thee in a lake, to sink or swim.
If clear from plotting Balder's death, to swim;
But deep, if thou devisedst it, to drown,
And perish, against fate, before thy day!'

So they two soft to one another spake.
But Odin look'd toward the land, and saw
His messenger; and he stood forth, and cried:
And Hermod came, and leapt from Sleipner down,
And in his Father's hand put Sleipner's rein,
And greeted Odin and the Gods, and said:—

‘Odin, my Father, and ye, Gods of Heaven!
Lo, home, having perform’d your will, I come.
Into the joyless kingdom have I been,
Below, and look’d upon the shadowy tribes
Of ghosts, and commun’d with their solemn Queen;
And to your prayer she sends you this reply:—
Show her through all the world the signs of grief:
Fails but one thing to grieve, there Balder stops.
Let Gods, men, brutes, beweep hint, plants and stones.
So shall she know your loss was dear indeed,
And bend her heart, and give you Balder back.’

He spoke; and all the Gods to Odin look’d:
And straight the Father of the Ages said:—

‘Ye Gods, these terms may keep another day.
But now, put on your arms, and mount your steeds,
And in procession all come near, and weep
Balder; for that is what the dead desire.
When ye enough have wept, then build a pile
Of the heap’d wood, and burn his corpse with fire
Out of our sight; that we may turn from grief,
And lead, as erst, our daily life in Heaven.’

He spoke; and the Gods arm’d: and Odin donn’d
His dazzling corslet and his helm of gold,
And led the way on Sleipner: and the rest
Follow’d, in tears, their Father and their King.
And thrice in arms around the dead they rode,
Weeping; the sands were wetted, and their arms,
With their thick-falling tears: so good a friend
They mourn’d that day, so bright, so lov’d a God.
And Odin came, and laid his kingly hands
On Balder’s breast, and thus began the wail:—

'Farewell, O Balder, bright and lov'd, my Son!
In that great day, the Twilight of the Gods.
When Muspel's children shall beleaguer Heaven,
Then we shall miss thy counsel and thy arm.'

Thou camest near the next, O Warrior Thor!
Shouldering thy Hammer, in thy chariot drawn,
Swaying the long-hair'd Goats with silver'd rein;
And over Balder's corpse these words didst say:—

'Brother, thou dwellest in the darksome land,
And talkest with the feeble tribes of ghosts,
Now, and I know not how they prize thee there,
But here, I know, thou wilt be miss'd and mourn'd.
For haughty spirits and high wraths are rife
Among the Gods and Heroes here in Heaven,
As among those, whose joy and work is war:
And daily strifes arise, and angry words:
But from thy lips, O Balder, night or day,
Heard no one ever an injurious word
To God or Hero, but thou keptest back
The others, labouring to compose their brawls.
Be ye then kind, as Balder too was kind:
For we lose him, who smooth'd all strife in Heaven.'

He spake: and all the Gods assenting wail'd.
And Freya next came nigh, with golden tears:
The loveliest Goddess she in Heaven, by all
Most honour'd after Frea, Odin's wife:
Her long ago the wandering Oder took
To mate, but left her to roam distant lands;
Since then she seeks him, and weeps tears of gold:
Names hath she many; Vanadis on earth
They call her; Freya is her name in Heaven:

She in her hands took Balder's head, and spake:—

'Balder, my brother, thou art gone a road
Unknown and long, and haply on that way
My long-lost wandering Oder thou hast met,
For in the paths of Heaven he is not found.
Oh, if it be so, tell him what thou wert
To his neglected wife, and what he is,
And wring his heart with shame, to hear thy word.
For he, my husband, left me here to pine,
Not long a wife, when his unquiet heart
First drove him from me into distant lands.
Since then I vainly seek him through the world,
And weep from shore to shore my golden tears,
But neither god nor mortal heeds my pain.
Thou only, Balder, wert for ever kind,
To take my hand, and wipe my tears, and say:—
Weep not, O Freya, weep no golden tears!
One day the wandering Oder will return,
Or thou wilt find him in thy faithful search
On some great road, or resting in an inn,
Or at a ford, or sleeping by a tree.—
So Balder said; but Oder, well I know,
My truant Oder I shall see no more
To the world's end; and Balder now is gone;
And I am left uncomforted in Heaven.'

She spake; and all the Goddesses bewail'd.
Last, from among the Heroes one came near,
No God, but of the Hero-troop the chief—
Regner, who swept the northern sea with fleets,
And rul'd o'er Denmark and the heathy isles,
Living; but Ella captur'd him and slew:
A king, whose fame then fill'd the vast of Heaven,

Now time obscures it, and men's later deeds:
He last approach'd the corpse, and spake, and said:—

'Balder, there yet are many Scalds in Heaven
Still left, and that chief Scald, thy brother Brage,
Whom we may bid to sing, though thou art gone:
And all these gladly, while we drink, we hear,
After the feast is done, in Odin's hall:
But they harp ever on one string, and wake
Remembrance in our soul of wars alone,
Such as on earth we valiantly have wag'd,
And blood, and ringing blows, and violent death:
But when thou sangest, Balder, thou didst strike
Another note, and, like a bird in spring,
Thy voice of joyance minded us, and youth,
And wife, and children, and our ancient home.
Yes, and I too remember'd then no more
My dungeon, where the serpents stung me dead,
Nor Ella's victory on the English coast;
But I heard Thora laugh in Gothland Isle;
And saw my shepherdess, Aslauga, tend
Her flock along the white Norwegian beach:
Tears started to mine eyes with yearning joy
Therefore with grateful heart I mourn thee dead.'

So Regner spake, and all the Heroes groan'd.
But now the sun had pass'd the height of Heaven,
And soon had all that day been spent in wail;
But then the Father of the Ages said:—

'Ye Gods, there well may be too much of wail.
Bring now the gather'd wood to Balder's ship;
Heap on the deck the logs, and build the pyre.'

But when the Gods and Heroes heard, they brought
The wood to Balder's ship, and built a pile,
Full the deck's breadth, and lofty; then the corpse
Of Balder on the highest top they laid,
With Nanna on his right, and on his left
Hoder, his brother, whom his own hand slew.
And they set jars of wine and oil to lean
Against the bodies, and stuck torches near,
Splinters of pine-wood, soak'd with turpentine;
And brought his arms and gold, and all his stuff,
And slew the dogs which at his table fed,
And his horse, Balder's horse, whom most he lov'd,
And threw them on the pyre, and Odin threw
A last choice gift thereon, his golden ring.
They fixt the mast, and hoisted up the sails,
Then they put fire to the wood; and Thor
Set his stout shoulder hard against the stern
To push the ship through the thick sand: sparks flew
From the deep trench she plough'd—so strong a God
Furrow'd it—and the water gurgled in.
And the Ship floated on the waves, and rock'd:
But in the hills a strong East-Wind arose,
And came down moaning to the sea; first squalls
Ran black o'er the sea's face, then steady rush'd
The breeze, and fill'd the sails, and blew the fire.
And, wreath'd in smoke, the Ship stood out to sea.
Soon with a roaring rose the mighty fire,
And the pile crackled; and between the logs
Sharp quivering tongues of flame shot out, and leapt,
Curling and darting, higher, until they lick'd
The summit of the pile, the dead, the mast,
And ate the shrivelling sails; but still the Ship
Drove on, ablaze, above her hull, with fire.
And the Gods stood upon the beach, and gaz'd:

And, while they gaz'd, the Sun went lurid down
Into the smoke-wrapt sea, and Night came on.
Then the wind fell, with night, and there was calm.
But through the dark they watch'd the burning Ship
Still carried o'er the distant waters on
Farther and farther, like an Eye of Fire.
And as in the dark night a travelling man
Who bivouacs in a forest 'mid the hills,
Sees suddenly a spire of flame shoot up
Out of the black waste forest, far below,
Which woodcutters have lighted near their lodge
Against the wolves; and all night long it flares:—
So flar'd, in the far darkness, Balder's pyre.
But fainter, as the stars rose high, it burn'd;
The bodies were consum'd, ash chok'd the pile
And as in a decaying winter fire
A charr'd log, falling, makes a shower of sparks—
So, with a shower of sparks, the pile fell in,
Reddening the sea around; and all was dark.
But the Gods went by starlight up the shore
To Asgard, and sate down in Odin's hall
At table, and the funeral-feast began.
All night they ate the boar Serimner's flesh,
And from their horns, with silver rimm'd, drank mead,
Silent, and waited for the sacred Morn.

And Morning over all the world was spread.
Then from their loathèd feast the Gods arose,
And took their horses, and set forth to ride
O'er the bridge Bifrost, where is Heimdall's watch,
To the ash Igdrasil, and Ida's plain:
Thor came on foot; the rest on horseback rode.
And they found Mimir sitting by his Fount
Of Wisdom, which beneath the ashtree springs;

And saw the Nornies watering the roots
Of that world-shadowing tree with Honey-dew:
There came the Gods, and sate them down on stones:
And thus the Father of the Ages said:—

'Ye Gods, the terms ye know, which Hermod brought.
Accept them or reject them; both have grounds.
Accept them, and they bind us, unfulfill'd,
To leave for ever Balder in the grave,
An unrecover'd prisoner, shade with shades.
But how, ye say, should the fulfilment fail?—
Smooth sound the terms, and light to be fulfill'd;
For dear-belov'd was Balder while he liv'd
In Heaven and Earth, and who would grudge him tears?
But from the traitorous seed of Lok they come,
These terms, and I suspect some hidden fraud.
Bethink ye, Gods, is there no other way?—
Speak, were not this a way, the way for Gods?
If I, if Odin, clad in radiant arms,
Mounted on Sleipner, with the Warrior Thor
Drawn in his car beside me, and my sons,
All the strong brood of Heaven, to swell my train,
Should make irruption into Hela's realm,
And set the fields of gloom ablaze with light,
And bring in triumph Balder back to Heaven?'

He spake; and his fierce sons applauded loud.
But Frea, Mother of the Gods, arose,
Daughter and wife of Odin; thus she said:—

'Odin, thou Whirlwind, what a threat is this!
Thou threatenest what transcends thy might, even thine.
For of all powers the mightiest far art thou,
Lord over men on Earth, and Gods in Heaven;

Yet even from thee thyself hath been withheld
One thing; to undo what thou thyself hast rul'd.
For all which hath been fixt, was fixt by thee:
In the beginning, ere the Gods were born,
Before the Heavens were builded, thou didst slay
The Giant Ymir, whom the Abyss brought forth,
Thou and thy brethren fierce, the Sons of Bor,
And threw his trunk to choke the abysmal void:
But of his flesh and members thou didst build
The Earth and Ocean, and above them Heaven:
And from the flaming world, where Muspel reigns,
Thou sent'st and fetched'st fire, and madest lights,
Sun Moon and Stars, which thou hast hung in Heaven,
Dividing clear the paths of night and day:
And Asgard thou didst build, and Midgard Fort:
Then me thou mad'st; of us the Gods were born:
Then, walking by the sea, thou foundest spars
Of wood, and framed'st men, who till the earth,
Or on the sea, the field of pirates, sail:
And all the race of Ymir thou didst drown,
Save one, Bergelmer; he on shipboard fled
Thy deluge, and from him the Giants sprang;
But all that brood thou hast remov'd far off,
And set by Ocean's utmost marge to dwell:
But Hela into Niflheim thou threw'st,
And gav'st her nine unlighted worlds to rule,
A Queen, and empire over all the dead.
That empire wilt thou now invade, light up
Her darkness, from her grasp a subject tear?—
Try it; but I, for one, will not applaud.
Nor do I merit, Odin, thou should'st slight
Me and my words, though thou be first in Heaven
For I too am a Goddess, born of thee,
Thine eldest, and of me the Gods are sprung;

And all that is to come I know, but lock
In my own breast, and have to none reveal'd.
Come then; since Hela holds by right her prey,
But offers terms for his release to heaven,
Accept the chance;—thou canst no more obtain.
Send through the world thy messengers: entreat
All living and unliving things to weep
For Balder; if thou haply thus may'st melt
Hela, and win the lov'd one back to Heaven.'

She spake, and on her face let fall her veil,
And bow'd her head, and sate with folded hands.
Nor did the all-ruling Odin slight her word;
Straightway he spake, and thus address'd the Gods:

'Go quickly forth through all the world, and pray
All living and unliving things to weep
Balder, if haply he may thus be won.'

When the Gods heard, they straight arose, and took
Their horses, and rode forth through all the world.
North south east west they struck, and roam'd the world,
Entreating all things to weep Balder's death:
And all that liv'd, and all without life, wept.
And as in winter, when the frost breaks up,
At winter's end, before the spring begins,
And a warm west wind blows, and thaw sets in—
After an hour a dripping sound is heard
In all the forests, and the soft-strewn snow
Under the trees is dibbled thick with holes.
And from the boughs the snowloads shuffle down;
And in fields sloping to the south dark plots
Of grass peep out amid surrounding snow,
And widen, and the peasant's heart is glad—

So through the world was heard a dripping noise
Of all things weeping to bring Balder back:
And there fell joy upon the Gods to hear.

But Hermod rode with Niord, whom he took
To show him spits and beaches of the sea
Far off, where some unwarn'd might fail to weep—
Niord, the God of storms, whom fishers know
Not born in Heaven; he was in Vanheim rear'd,
With men, but lives a hostage with the Gods:
He knows each frith, and every rocky creek
Fring'd with dark pines, and sands where seafowl scream:—
They two scour'd every coast, and all things wept.
And they rode home together, through the wood
Of Jarnvid, which to east of Midgard lies
Bordering the Giants, where the trees are iron;
There in the wood before a cave they came
Where sate, in the cave's mouth, a skinny Hag,
Toothless and old; she gibes the passers by:
Thok is she call'd; but now Lok wore her shape:
She greeted them the first, and laugh'd, and said:—

'Ye Gods, good lack, is it so dull in Heaven.
That ye come pleasuring to Thok's Iron Wood?
Lovers of change ye are, fastidious sprites.
Look, as in some boor's yard a sweet-breath'd cow
Whose manger is stuff'd full of good fresh hay
Snuffs at it daintily, and stoops her head
To chew the straw, her litter, at her feet—
So ye grow squeamish, Gods, and sniff at Heaven.'

She spake; but Hermod answer'd her and said:—
'Thok, not for gibes we come, we come for tears.

Balder is dead, and Hela holds her prey,
But will restore, if all things give him tears.
Begrudge not thine; to all was Balder dear.'

But, with a louder laugh, the Hag replied:—
'Is Balder dead? and do ye come for tears?
Thok with dry eyes will weep o'er Balder's pyre.
Weep him all other things, if weep they will—
I weep him not: let Hela keep her prey!'

She spake; and to the cavern's depth she fled,
Mocking: and Hermod knew their toil was vain.
And as seafaring men, who long have wrought
In the great deep for gain, at last come home,
And towards evening see the headlands rise
Of their own country, and can clear descry
A fire of wither'd furze which boys have lit
Upon the cliffs, or smoke of burning weeds
Out of a till'd field inland;—then the wind
Catches them, and drives out again to sea:
And they go long days tossing up and down
Over the grey sea ridges; and the glimpse
Of port they had makes bitterer far their toil—
So the Gods' cross was bitterer for their joy.

Then, sad at heart, to Niord Hermod spake:—
'It is the Accuser Lok, who flouts us all.
Ride back, and tell in Heaven this heavy news.
I must again below, to Hela's realm.'

He spoke; and Niord set forth back to Heaven.
But northward Hermod rode, the way below;
Tho way he knew: and travers'd Giall's stream,
And down to Ocean grop'd, and cross'd the ice,

And came beneath the wall, and found the grate
Still lifted; well was his return foreknown.
And once more Hermod saw around him spread
The joyless plains, and heard the streams of Hell.
But as he enter'd, on the extremest hound
Of Niflheim, he saw one Ghost come near,
Hovering, and stopping oft, as if afraid;
Hoder, the unhappy, whom his own hand slew:
And Hermod look'd, and knew his brother's ghost,
And call'd him by his name, and sternly said:—

'Hoder, ill-fated, blind in heart and eyes!
Why tarriest thou to plunge thee in the gulph
Of the deep inner gloom, but flittest here,
In twilight, on the lonely verge of Hell,
Far from the other ghosts, and Hela's throne?
Doubtless thou fearest to meet Balder's voice,
Thy brother, whom through folly thou didst slay.'

He spoke; but Hoder answer'd him, and said:—
'Hermod the nimble, dost thou still pursue
The unhappy with reproach, even in the grave?
For this I died, and fled beneath the gloom,
Not daily to endure abhorring Gods,
Nor with a hateful presence cumber Heaven—
And canst thou not, even here, pass pitying by?
No less than Balder have I lost the light
Of Heaven, and communion with my kin:
I too had once a wife, and once a child,
And substance, and a golden house in Heaven:
But all I left of my own act, and fled
Below, and dost thou hate me even here?
Balder upbraids me not, nor hates at all,
Though he has cause, have any cause; but he,

When that with downcast looks I hither came,
Stretch'd forth his hand, and, with benignant voice,
Welcome, he said, if there be welcome here,
Brother and fellow-sport of Lok with me.
And not to offend thee, Hermod, nor to force
My hated converse on thee, came I up
From the deep gloom, where I will now return;
But earnestly I long'd to hover near,
Not too far off, when that thou camest by,
To feel the presence of a brother God,
And hear the passage of a horse of Heaven,
For the last time: for here thou com'st no more.'

He spake, and turn'd to go to the inner gloom.
But Hermod stay'd him with mild words, and said:—
'Thou doest well to chide me, Hoder blind.
Truly thou say'st, the planning guilty mind
Was Lok's; the unwitting hand alone was thine.
But Gods are like the sons of men in this—
When they have woe, they blame the nearest cause.
Howbeit stay, and be appeas'd; and tell—
Sits Balder still in pomp by Hela's side,
Or is he mingled with the unnumber'd dead?'

And the blind Hoder answer'd him and spake:—
'His place of state remains by Hela's side,
But empty: for his wife, for Nanna came
Lately below, and join'd him; and the Pair
Frequent the still recesses of the realm
Of Hela, and hold converse undisturb'd.
But they too doubtless, will have breath'd the balm
Which floats before a visitant from Heaven,
And have drawn upwards to this verge of Hell.'

He spake; and, as he ceas'd, a puff of wind
Roll'd heavily the leaden mist aside
Round where they stood, and they beheld Two Forms
Make towards them o'er the stretching cloudy plain.
And Hermod straight perceiv'd them, who they were,
Balder and Nanna; and to Balder said:—

'Balder, too truly thou foresaw'st a snare.
Lok triumphs still, and Hela keeps her prey.
No more to Asgard shalt thou come, nor lodge
In thy own house, Breidablik, nor enjoy
The love all bear towards thee, nor train up
Forset, thy son, to be belov'd like thee.
Here must thou lie, and wait an endless age.
Therefore for the last time, O Balder, hail!'

He spake; and Balder answer'd him and said:—
'Hail and farewell, for here thou com'st no more.
Yet mourn not for me, Hermod, when thou sitt'st
In Heaven, nor let the other Gods lament,
As wholly to be pitied, quite forlorn:
For Nanna hath rejoin'd me, who, of old,
In Heaven, was seldom parted from my side;
And still the acceptance follows me, which crowned
My former life, and cheers me even here.
The iron frown of Hela is relax'd
When I draw nigh, and the wan tribes of dead
Trust me, and gladly bring for my award
Their ineffectual feuds and feeble hates,
Shadows of hates, but they distress them still.'

And the fleet-footed Hermod made reply:—
'Thou hast then all the solace death allows,
Esteem and function: and so far is well.

Yet here thou liest, Balder, underground,
Rusting for ever: and the years roll on,
The generations pass, the ages grow,
And bring us nearer to the final day
When from the south shall march the Fiery Band
And cross the Bridge of Heaven, with Lok for guide,
And Fenris at his heel with broken chain:
While from the east the Giant Rymer steers
His ship, and the great Serpent makes to land;
And all are marshall'd in one flaming square
Against the Gods, upon the plains of Heaven.
I mourn thee, that thou canst not help us then.'

He spake; but Balder answer'd him and said:—
'Mourn not for me: Mourn, Hermod, for the Gods:
Mourn for the men on Earth, the Gods in Heaven,
Who live, and with their eyes shall see that day.
The day will come, when Asgard's towers shall fall,
And Odin, and his Sons, the seed of Heaven:
But what were I, to save them in that hour?
If strength could save them, could not Odin save,
My Father, and his pride, the Warrior Thor,
Vidar the Silent, the Impetuous Tyr?
I, what were I, when these can naught avail?
Yet, doubtless. when the day of battle comes,
And the two Hosts are marshall'd, and in Heaven
The golden-crested Cock shall sound alarm,
And his black Brother-Bird from hence reply,
And bucklers clash, and spears begin to pour—
Longing will stir within my breast, though vain.
But not to me so grievous, as, I know,
To other Gods it were, is my enforc'd
Absence from fields where I could nothing aid:
For I am long since weary of your storm

Of carnage, and find, Hermod, in your life
Something too much of war and broils, which make
Life one perpetual fight, a bath of blood.
Mine eyes are dizzy with the arrowy hail;
Mine ears are stunn'd with blows, and sick for calm.
Inactive therefore let me lie, in gloom,
Unarm'd, inglorious: I attend the course
Of ages, and my late return to light,
In times less alien to a spirit mild,
In new-recover'd seats, the happier day.'

He spake; and the fleet Hermod thus replied:—
'Brother, what seats are these, what happier day?
Tell me, that I may ponder it when gone.'

And the ray-crowned Balder answer'd him:—
'Far to the south, beyond The Blue, there spreads
Another Heaven, The Boundless: no one yet
Hath reach'd it: there hereafter shall arise
The second Asgard, with another name.
Thither, when o'er this present Earth and Heavens
The tempest of the latter days hath swept,
And they from sight have disappear'd, and sunk,
Shall a small remnant of the Gods repair:
Hoder and I shall join them from the grave.
There re-assembling we shall see emerge
From the bright Ocean at our feet an Earth
More fresh, more verdant than the last, with fruits
Self-springing, and a seed of man preserv'd,
Who then shall live in peace, as now in war.
But we in Heaven shall find again with joy
The ruin'd palaces of Odin, seats
Familiar, halls where we have supp'd of old;
Re-enter them with wonder, never fill

Our eyes with gazing, and rebuild with tears.
And we shall tread once more the well-known plain
Of Ida, and among the grass shall find
The golden dice with which we play'd of yore;
And that will bring to mind the former life
And pastime of the Gods, the wise discourse
Of Odin, the delights of other days.
O Hermod, pray that thou mayst join us then!
Such for the future is my hope: meanwhile,
I rest the thrall of Hela, and endure
Death, and the gloom which round me even now
Thickens, and to its inner gulph recalls.
Farewell, for longer speech is not allow'd.'

He spoke, and wav'd farewell, and gave his hand
To Nanna; and she gave their brother blind
Her hand, in turn, for guidance; and The Three
Departed o'er the cloudy plain, and soon
Faded from sight into the interior gloom.
But Hermod stood beside his drooping horse,
Mute, gazing after them in tears: and fain,
Fain had he follow'd their receding steps,
Though they to Death were bound, and he to Heaven,
Then; but a Power he could not break withheld.
And as a stork which idle boys have trapp'd,
And tied him in a yard, at autumn sees
Flocks of his kind pass flying o'er his head
To warmer lands, and coasts that keep the sun;
He strains to join their flight, and, from his shed,
Follows them with a long complaining cry—
So Hermod gaz'd, and yearn'd to join his kin.

At last he sigh'd, and set forth back to Heaven.

The Death of Baldur, George John Cayley (1826-1878) (?)
Trinity College, Cambridge

"Woe in high Asgard! wailing, and the moan
Of anguish, and deep agony, awaken
Echoes in the Aesir's blessed abodes unknown:
Ah ! blessed no longer now, but joy-forsaken!
Baldur! heart-cherished Baldur! thou art slain,
By treachery before the time o'ertaken;
Not in the glorious fight of Vigrid's plain
Battling with Surtur's hosts; when, carnage-rife,
Muspel's empyrean to that dread campaign
Vomits her daemon hordes; and the ancient strife
Of elemental discord shall attain
Its issue in a nobler, holier life:

When from the quivering boughs of Yggdrasil
Shattered Creation falls; in ruined state
Impregnate with new birth; where seeds of ill,
By the ordeal of Fire annihilate,
No more through Nature shall their taint distil;
And from the whelming Ocean-depths of Fate
Shall rise a realm of Light for evermore.
That hour in Hela's hall thou must await
(Since Nature's tears avail not to restore)
In the dim regions of inglorious death;
Whose clammy caverns echo with the roar
Of spray-clothed storms, and the heart-chilling breath
Of Nifelhel. Ah weary — weary days !

Weep, Aesir's children! weep, albeit your tears
May not recal the lost one — Him, whose praise
Exceeds all utterance. Brighter than the spheres

Around the Zones of Space celestial rays
Diffusing, Mundilfari's charioteers—
Lovely, beyond all power of love to speak
Its wondering intensity, was he!
The melody of Bragi's lyre were weak
In echo of his spirit-melody;
Though Heaven-toned harmony may most express
The soul's emotion, whose high ecstasy
Of unrevealed ineffable tenderness
Yearns flickering tow'rd perfection's holy blaze;
And he was essence of all perfectness,
Beaming sublime — unshadowed — without haze !

Weep Aesir's children! Ye have seen him borne
To the sand-strewn margin of old Niord's domain,
With steps woe-laden; silent, pale, forlorn,
Sweet Nanna following in the mournful train.
Such unison of hearts, so roughly torn,
Left her soul weltering deep in mortal pain:
But when on Ringhorn's bale-pyre she beheld
Her loved one stretched all lifeless, then again
Her agony, bursting from its swoon, rebelled
Against the slender prison of her breast;
And so she perished: but her spirit, impelled
On passion's pinion, winged itself to rest.
So Nana's corse beside her lord's was lain:
And both were lost to Asgard; yet both blest—
Lost to all else, each other to regain.

Then sacred Mölnir flashed upon the pyre—
From spar to spar the nimble lightnings leapt:
Veiled in one vast white fluttering sheet of fire,
O'er Aegir's plain afar the vessel swept:
The wild winds wailed— With sad and solemn roar

The wild waves burst in showery spray and wept,
Sobbed down the keel, and toward the echoing shore
Rolled their hoarse dirge. Slow on the horizon set
That waning beacon dear— At last no more
Glimmered in eyes divine with weeping wet.

"Who is there a reft mother's heart will earn?
Who will approach grim Hela, to reclaim
Our lost delight, and ransom his return?"
Thus weeping spake Fensalir's queenly dame:
But Hermod answered— " Gladly for thy sake,
Sweet mother, as for his, and in the name
Of brotherhood, will I that journey make."

Now, while lit Ringhorn speeds before the blast
Which huge Hraesvelgur, from the topmost peak
Of Ymir's brow, wafts eagle-wing'd, he passed
The tremulous bridge's triple-woven streak.
In Himinbiorg's high portal arch, the clang
Of Sleipnir's tramp resounded; through the bleak
And desolate chasms its clattering cadence rang
From crag to crag; as, leaving far behind
The holy fountain whose weird sisters rule
By runic spells the destiny of mankind,
He galloped by the venom-welling pool,
Where Nidhogg and her serpent kindred wind
Their slimy coils, and gnaw the Eternal Tree.

Nine days he rode through darkness dense and deep,
Where Niorvi's children hold no rivalry;
Where reigns unbroken the primordial sleep
Of nothingness; as, ere the birth of Time,
When Elivagar first began to creep
In turbid streams; and from the drifting rime,

By Muspel's fire impregnate, Ymir sprung;—
Great Ymir— first-born of creation's prime.
Him slew the sons of Bor: his carcase, flung
Into Ginnunga-gap, was Earth. The gore
Flowed round— a purple eea. His bones they strung
In mountain-chains; and fenced the outward shore
With his high beetling brows 'gainst Utgard; home
Of his sons the huge Hrimthursar: arching o'er
The Heavens his hollowed scull;— a wondrous dome!

But Hermod galloped on along the tracts
Of melancholy gloom with stedfast soul ;
Until he heard the booming cataracts
That roar adown the rocky rush of Gioll;
Until he saw the golden arches bend.

"Whence are thy steps, rash rider! and what goal
Tempts thee upon our desert way to wend?
Thou wearest not the livid hues of death,
For in thy cheek the rose and lily blend:
The golden bridge beneath thee quivereth—
What brings thee hither?"— "I to Hela ride.
Oh dark-haired maiden, to demand the breath
Of Baldur slain, the flower of Aesir's pride."
"Baldur, with many horsemen, yestere'en
Rode o'er the golden arches;" she replied:
"There dips the way down yonder dark ravine."

On! on!— Lo! rise the ebon walls that gird
The dismal city of the dead. Its gate
Frowns high with iron bars:— but on he spurred;
Nor deigned for doubtful access to debate:
A rush— a pause— upreared, on haunches bent—

A bound, thew-strained— and horse and horseman's weight,
As bolt from arbalist, o'er the barrier went,—
And far beyond: with cumb'rous staggering shock
Lighting, the iron hoofs, deep-planted, rent
The adamantine bosom of the rock.

"Now shall be proved the love which, as ye say,
Is Baldur's birthright! Now let all things weep,
His fate lamenting; and to the realms of day
He shall return from this my dungeon deep!
But if, in his behoof, the boon denay
Living or lifeless thing in Heaven or Earth,—
Mid joyless gloom he unredeemed shall stay,
Till Hela perish in Time's second birth."

And Aesir, by their messengers, entreat
All nature's mournful tribute far and near:
Those ravens who each day, on pinions fleet,
Borne through all space, bring to the monarch's ear
All tidings, swoop from off their sacred seat:
And the swift maiden, on her wingèd steed,
Bears the great mother's prayer from sphere to sphere:
Glisten with tears the forest and the mead,
The rock-piled mountain and the sandy plain:—
As when at dawn, from nightly trammels freed,
Hrimfaxi shakes the dew-drops from his mane.

All wept save one. The unrelenting hag,
Fit incarnation of most hideous hate,
Squatted like toad beneath the caverned crag,
Spat forth her poisonous spite, and sealed the fate
Predestined. But that loathsome frame contained
The traitor-heart malignly obdurate,

Now with its two-fold murder doubly stained:
Him everlasting agonies await!
Close iron-clenched on Nästrond's dismal shore,
Shall keen-edged flint-jags gall his festering weight;
And from the fell snake's fangs for evermore
Sharp scorching venom on his brow distil:
There, howling, shall he bitterly deplore,
In abject anguish, these his deeds of ill.

Baldur is gone! but mild Forseti sways
With even hand the balance and the sword:
Justice to Love succeeds, in evil days
When hearts no longer are of one accord;
And from his righteous lip the sentence spoken
Dispenses retribution and reward.
For now, alas ! the reign of love is broken:
Mute is the golden-stringèd harmony
Of soul with soul, in sweetest union yoken,
Mingling melodious diversity:
Yet faintly linger in our bosoms still
The echoes of its music memory;
And ever and anon some fitful thrill
Startles the spirit from its world of sense;
A holier sunshine piercing through the chill
And misty scope of Earth's intelligence."

Thus sang the Scald who, in bedarkened days,
(Ere yet, upon his Zone of arctic gloom,
Had dawned the orient dayspring) hymnèd praise
To names long sunken in oblivion's tomb—
Who born in outer darkness, yet could win
From his wild natural heart a spirit-bloom
Of love, weed-tangled truly— but akin
To the pure growth that rays of grace illume.

Our being is for love, and not for thought!
To love alone should thought and action tend:
For, reft of love, all power availeth nought :
While perfect love must all perfections blend.
Science, Earth's deepest mysteries to the light
Unveiling, may her lofty claims extend
To track the starry mazes of the night;
And from its manifold undulation, rend
Day's blinding secret.— Yet if in her height
Of proud discovery she forget to own
The guerdon of her toil, a glimpse more bright
Of the vast scheme of Heavenly Love, alone;
Then is the infant's wondering awe more wise
By far, who, to the star-bespangled throne
Of his Creator, lifting innocent eyes,
Pours forth his simple little orison:
Yea— deeper in the learning of the skies!

The Dwarves, Henry Wadsworth Longfellow

Loke sat and thought, till his dark eyes gleam
With joy at the deed he'd done;
When Sif looked into the crystal stream,
Her courage was wellnigh gone.

For never again her soft amber hair
Shall she braid with her hands of snow;
From the hateful image she turned in despair,
And hot tears began to flow.

In a cavern's mouth, like a crafty fox,
Loke sat 'neath the tall pine's shade,
When sudden a thundering was heard in the rocks,
And fearfully trembled the glade.

Then he knew that the noise good boded him naught,
He knew that 't was Thor who was coming;
He changed himself straight to a salmon trout,
And leaped in a fright in the Glommen.

But Thor changed too, to a huge seagull,
And the salmon trout seized in his beak;
He cried: Thou, traitor, I know thee well,
And dear shalt thou pay thy freak!

Thy caitiff's bones to a meal I'll pound,
As a millstone crusheth the grain.
When Loke that naught booted his magic found,
He took straight his own form again.

And what if thou scatter'st my limbs in air?

He spake, will it mend thy case?
Will it gain back for Sif a single hair?
Thou 'lt still a bald spouse embrace.

But if now thou 'lt pardon my heedless joke,--
For malice sure meant I none,--
I swear to thee here, by root, billow and rock,
By the moss on the Beata-stone,
By Mimer's well, and by Odin's eye,
And by Mjolmer, greatest of all,
That straight to the secret caves I'll hie,
To the dwarfs, my kinsmen small;

And thence for Sif new tresses I'll bring
Of gold ere the daylight's gone,
So that she will liken a field in spring,
With its yellow-flowered garment on.

Loke promised so well with his glozing tongue
That the Asas at length let him go,
And he sank in the earth, the dark rocks among,
Near the cold-fountain, far below.

He crept on his belly, as supple as eel,
The cracks in the hard granite through,
Till he came where the dwarfs stood hammering steel,
By the light of a furnace blue.

I trow 't was a goodly sight to see
The dwarfs, with their aprons on,
A-hammering and smelting so busily
Pure gold from the rough brown stone.

Rock crystals from sand and hard flint they made,

Which, tinged with the rosebud's dye,
They cast into rubies and carbuncles red,
And hid them in cracks hard by.

They took them fresh violets all dripping with dew,
Dwarf women had plucked them, the morn,--
And stained with their juice the clear sapphires blue,
King Dan in his crown since hath worn.

Then for emeralds they searched out the brightest green
Which the young spring meadow wears,
And dropped round pearls, without flaw or stain,
From widows' and maidens' tears.

When Loke to the dwarfs had his errand made known,
In a trice for the work they were ready;
Quoth Dvalin: O Lopter, it now shall be shown
That dwarfs in their friendship are steady.

We both trace our line from the selfsame stock;
What you ask shall be furnished with speed,
For it ne'er shall be said that the sons of the rock
Turned their backs on a kinsman in need.

They took them the skin of a large wild-boar,
The largest that they could find,
And the bellows they blew till the furnace 'gan roar,
And the fire flamed on high for the wind.

And they struck with their sledge-hammers stroke on stroke,
That the sparks from the skin flew on high,
But never a word good or bad spoke Loke,
Though foul malice lurked in his eye.

The thunderer far distant, with sorrow he thought
On all he'd engaged to obtain,
And, as summer-breeze fickle, now anxiously sought
To render the dwarf's labour vain.

Whilst the bellows plied Brok, and Sindre the hammer,
And Thor, that the sparks flew on high,
And the slides of the vaulted cave rang with the clamour,
Loke changed to a huge forest-fly.

And he sat him all swelling with venom and spite,
On Brok, the wrist just below;
But the dwarf's skin was thick, and he recked not the bite,
Nor once ceased the bellows to blow.

And now, strange to say, from the roaring fire
Came the golden-haired Gullinburste,
To serve as a charger the sun-god Frey,
Sure, of all wild-boars this the first.

They took them pure gold from their secret store.
The piece 't was but small in size,
But ere 't had been long n the furnace roar,
'T was a jewel beyond all prize.

A broad red ring all of wroughten gold,
As a snake with its tail in its head,
And a garland of gems did the rim enfold,
Together with rare art laid.

'T was solid and heavy, and wrought with care,
Thrice it passed through the white flames' glow;
A ring to produce, fit for Odin to wear,

No labour they spared, I trow.

They worked it and turned it with wondrous skill,
Till they gave it the virtue rare,
That each thrice third night from its rim there fell
Eight rings, as their parent fair.

Next they laid on the anvil a steel-bar cold,
They needed nor fire nor file;
But their sledge-hammers, following, like thunder rolled,
And Sindre sang runes the while.

When Loke now marked how the steel gat power,
And how warily out 't was beat
--'T was to make a new hammer for Ake-Thor,--
He'd recourse once more to deceit.

In a trice, of a hornet the semblance he took,
Whilst in cadence fell blow on blow,
In the leading dwarf's forehead his barbed sting he stuck,
That the blood in a stream down did flow.

Then the dwarf raised his hand to his brow for the smart,
Ere the iron well out was beat,
And they found that the haft by an inch was too short,
But to alter it then 't was too late.

His object attained, Loke no longer remained
'Neath the earth, but straight hied him to Thor,
Who owned than the hair ne'er, sure, aught more fair
His eyes had e'er looked on before.

The boar Frey bestrode, and away proudly rode,
And Thor took the ringlets and hammer;

To Valhal they hied, where the Asas reside,
'Mid of tilting and wassail the clamour.

At a full solemn ting, Thor gave Odin the ring,
And Loke his foul treachery pardoned;
But the pardon was vain, for his crimes soon again
Must do penance the arch-sinner hardened.

Death of Odin. Robert Southey (1774-1843

Has Odin's life bedew'd the land:
I rush to meet thee by a self-will'd doom.
No more my clattering iron car
Shall rush amid the throng of war;
No more, obedient to my heavenly cause.
Shall crimson conquest stamp his Odin's laws.

I go--I go;
Yet shall the nations own my sway
Far as yon orb shall dart his all-enlivening ray :
Big is the death-fraught cloud of woe
That hangs, proud Rome, impending o'er thy wall, For
Odin shall avenge his Asgard's fall.
Thus burst from Odin's lips the fated sound,
As high in air he rear'd the gleaming blade;
His faithful friends around In silent wonder saw the scene,
affray'd:: He, unappall'd, towards the skies Uplifts his
death-denouncing eyes;

" Ope wide Valhalla's shield-roof 'd hall,
" Virgins of bliss ! obey your master's call;
" From these injurious realms below
" The sire of nations hastes to go."

Say, faulters now your chieftain's breath ?
Or chills pale terror now his death-like face ?
Then weep not, Thor, thy friend's approaching death, Let
no unmanly tears disgrace
The first of mortal's valiant race:
Dauntless Heimdal, mourn not now,
Balder ! clear thy cloudy brow;

I go to happier realms above,
To realms of friendship and of love.
This unmanly grief dispelling,
List to glory's rapturous call;
So with Odin ever dwelling,
Meet him in the shield-roof 'd hall:
Still shall Odin's fateful lance
Before his daring friends advance;

When the bloody fight beginning.
Helms and shields, and hauberks ringing,
Streaming life each fatal wound
Pours its current on the groundj
Still in clouds portentous riding
O'er his comrade host presiding.
Odin, from the stormy air,
O'er your affrighted foes shall scatter wild despair.

'Mid the mighty din of battle,
Whilst conflicting chariots rattle.
Floods of purple slaughter streaming.
Fate-fraught falchions widely gleaming;
When MISTA marks her destin'd prey.
When dread and death deform the day;
Happy he amid the strife.
Who pours the current of his life ;
Every toil and trouble ending,
Odin from his hall descending.
Shall bear him to his blest retreat,
Shall place him in the warrior's seat.

Not such the destin'd joys that wait
The wretched dastard's future fate:
Wild shrieks shall yell in every breath, —

The agonizing shrieks of death.
Adown his wan and livid face
Big drops their painful way shall trace;
Each limb in that tremendous hour
Shall quiver in disease's power.
Grim Hela o'er his couch shall hang,
Scoff at his groans, and point each pang;
No Virgin Goddess him shall call
To join you in the shield-roof 'd hall;
No Valkery for him prepare
The smiling mead with lovely care :
Sad and scorn'd the wretch shall lie,
Despairing shriek — despairing die !
No Scald in never-dying lays
Shall rear the temple of his praise ;
No Virgin in her vernal bloom
Bedew with tears his high-rear'd tomb;
No Soldier sound his honor'd name;
No song shall hand him down to fame;

But rank weeds o'er the inglorious grave
Shall to the blast their high heads wave;
And swept by time's strong stream away,
He soon shall sink — oblivion's prey;
And deep in Niflehim — dreary cell,
Aye shall his sprite tormented dwell,
Where grim Remorse for ever wakes,
Where Anguish feeds her torturing snakes,
Where Disappointment and Delay
For ever guard the doleful way ;
Amid the joyless land of woe
Keen and bleak the chill blasts blow ;
Drives the tempest, pours the rain,
Showers the hail with force amain j

Yell the night-birds as they fly
Flitting in the misty sky;
Glows the adder, swells the toad,
For sad is Hela's cold abode.

Spread then the Gothic banners to the sky,
Lift your sable banners high;
Yoke your coursers to the car,
Strike the sounding shield of war;
Go, my lov'd companions, go
Trample on the opposing foe;
Be like the raging torrent's force.
That, rushing from the hills, speds on its foaming course.

Haste, my sons, to war's alarms,
Triumph in the clang of arms ;
Joy amid the warlike toil.
Feed the raven with your spoil;
Go, prepare the eagle's food.
Go, and drench the wolf with blood,
'Till ye shall hear dark Hela's call,
And virgins waft ye to my hall;
There, wrapt in clouds, the shadowy throng
To airy combat glide along;
Till wearied with the friendly fight, _
Serimner's flesh recruits their might;
There, whilst I grasp the Roman skull,
With hydromel sweet-smiling full,
The festive song shall echo round,
The Scald repeat the deathless sound:

Then, Thor, when thou from fight shall cease,
When death shall lay that arm in peace.
Still shall the nations fear thy nod.

The first of warriors now, and then their god;
But be each heart with rage possest.
Let vengeance glow in every breast j
Let conquest fell the Roman wall.
Revenge on Rome my Asgard's fall.
The Druid throng shall fall away,
And sink beneath your victor sway ;
No more shall nations bow the knee,
Vanquish'd Taranis, to thee;
No more upon the sacred stone,
Tentates, shall thy victims groan;
The vanquish'd Odin, Rome, shall cause thy fall,
And his destruction shake thy proud imperial wall.

Yet, my faithful friends, beware
Luxury's enerving snare; 'Twas this that shook our Asgard's dome, That drove us from our native home; 'Twas this that smooth'd the way for victor Rome: Gaul's fruitful plains invite your sway. Conquest points the destin'd way ; Conquest shall attend your call. And your success shall gild still more Valhalla's hall.

So spake the dauntless chief, and pierc'd his breast, Then rush'd to seize the seat of endless rest.

From: "Poems: containing The retrospect, odes, elegies, sonnets, &c (1795)"

CPSIA information can be obtained
at www.ICGtesting.com
Printed in the USA
LVHW020722220620
658650LV00001B/68